D0105283

GREAT COMMANDERS OF THE MEDIEVAL WORLD

GREAT COMMANDERS OF THE MEDIEVAL WORLD

Edited by

Andrew Roberts

Quercus

Dedicated to Johnnie Heffer and Matthew Sadler

First published in Great Britain in 2008 by Quercus

This paperback edition published in 2011 by

2

Quercus
55 Baker Street
7th Floor, South Block
London
W1U 8EW

Text designed and typeset by Ellipsis Digital Ltd
Printed and bound in Great Britain by Clays Ltd, St Ives plc

CONTENTS

GREAT COMMANDERS OF THE MEDIEVAL WORLD

INTRODUCTION TO THE HISTORY OF
MEDIEVAL MILITARY COMMAND

This second volume of the *Great Commanders* covers that long period of world history from the fall of the Roman Empire in the West in the early fifth century AD right up to the late sixteenth century, when battlefields started to be changed for ever by the scourge of gunpowder. There is an active debate among historians as to whether the 'Dark Ages', roughly the post-Roman period from AD 410 to the Renaissance, deserves the soubriquet. Was it a vicious, Hobbesian nightmare of nothing but rampaging barbarians and ignorant peasantries kept in feudal bondage for a millennium, or was it – as a new generation of historians argue – a period when Christianity informed the flowering of a Western civilization that had finally escaped the stultifying power of the Roman Empire?

*

One of the most interesting aspects of this volume is that it provides compelling arguments for both sides of the great debate. Of course there were the rampaging conquerors whose names spread terror throughout the lands unfortunate to stand between them and their dreams of unlimited territorial acquisition. The Great Khans of the Mongols, Genghis and his grandson Kublai, were two such, Tamerlane and Hernán Cortés another two. In this volume, which largely covers the period before the printing press and mass literacy, civilization was in daily face-to-face, raw contention with barbarism, and often on the losing side. Mass terror was frequently the easiest and most efficacious way to hold subject peoples in awe and obeisance; if leaders couldn't be loved, they reasoned, they could at least be feared. The practices of Tamerlane of building pyramids of human skulls, or of Genghis Khan of slaughtering entire cities and then demanding the ears of the dead to prove that his orders had been effectively carried out, were all too often the natural ways of war.

Yet also featured in this volume are Charlemagne, whose empire based at Aachen brought peace to large parts of Europe; Alfred the Great, whom many see as the father of the English nation; William the Conqueror, whose Domesday Book is our best insight into that nation's society in the late eleventh century; Joan of Arc, who breathed life into a moribund France; and Akbar the Great, who in many ways can be seen as the founder of Indian national consciousness. The dichotomy between destruction and creation is very evident in these pages. By choosing the Age of Gunpowder as the natural cut-off point, I hope to underline a fundamental shift that overcame the art of war in the late sixteenth and early seventeenth centuries. Before gunpowder, it took subtly different qualities to lead men into battle than those required after muskets, cannonballs and the wide-spread use of explosives began to dominate battlefields. Many of the phenomena of military leadership are genuinely timeless, and include charisma, heroism, judgement, loyalty and often ruthlessness, but in the age before gunpowder – when death was dealt face to face and often with cold steel – such qualities were at a premium.

As with the elephant, it's hard to define a great military leader from first principles, but you certainly know one when you see one. Thus when Alexander Nevsky crossed the frozen waters at the Battle of Lake Chud, or Henry V chose the narrow front line for his defensive position at Agincourt, or William the Conqueror feigned retreat before the Saxons at Hastings, they each showed that exceptional gift of insight that justifies selection for a book such as this. Military genius needs the right time and place to shine, and one common aspect of the leaders in this volume was their preternatural ability to grasp the hem of the cloak of history as it swept past, and to hang on tightly. Sultan Mehmet II hauled his ships overland to enter the Golden Horn at precisely the right moment in 1453, for example.

These leaders tended to share a keen intelligence – Muhammad, Charlemagne, Süleyman the Magnificent and Akbar the Great might each qualify for the soubriquet 'intellectual' – and Tamerlane used to spare chess-players and historians from the general massacres he ordered – but there was a calculating worldliness to almost all of them, too. The devastating combination of a commander's fast-thinking brain and his sturdy, earthbound practicality was often enough to defeat forces many times his opponents' size, as Henry V, Cortés and Gonzalo de Córdoba were each to find. Similarly, emphasis on maintaining high morale through the exhibition of unavailing self-confidence was common to many of the greatest warriors over the three millennia covered in this volume. Victory seems to have gone to the leader who willed it the more, a phenomenon also regularly seen in the medieval era, however illogical that might seem. Because warfare is so raw, so elemental and played for the highest stakes possible, outcomes can rarely be taken for granted.

The last attribute displayed by a surprisingly large number of these great commanders was resilience in defeat. However talented the general, setbacks will be experienced sometimes; virtually none of the people featured in this book or its sister volume went undefeated throughout their entire military careers. Yet they came back from adversity undaunted, having learnt the lesson of what had gone wrong and resolved not to allow it to happen again. Above all, their self-belief communicated itself to the outside world, and saw them through to ultimate victory. In that sense, this book perhaps contains lessons of value beyond the sphere of military history.

While we can admire many of the commanders featured in this volume, others are among the most vicious genocidal killers ever to stain the pages of human history. In several of these superbly written biographies both builder and barbarian contend for the upper hand in the same individual. I hope you will enjoy them.

Andrew Roberts, May 2011
www.andrew-roberts.net

CONTRIBUTORS

NICCOLÒ CAPPONI

Born and raised in Florence in an Anglo-Italian environment, Niccolò Capponi developed a passion for history in his youth. The holder of a doctoral degree from the University of Padua, he is a former fellow of the Medici Archive Project. His well-received *Victory of the West: The Story of the Battle of Lepanto* was published by Macmillan in 2006.

ANNE CURRY

Anne Curry is a graduate of the University of Manchester and began her academic career at Teesside and Reading Universities before becoming Professor of Medieval History at the University of Southampton in 2004. She is well known for her researches on the fifteenth-century phase of the Hundred Years War and especially for her detailed work on the armies of the period, which prompted her major re-evaluation of the Battle of Agincourt and the creation of an online database, www.medievalsoldier.org, listing all known English soldiers serving between 1369 and 1453. She is now developing a new project on women and warfare. Her main publications include *Agincourt: A New History* (Tempus Publishing, 2005); *The Hundred Years War* (Macmillan Press, 1993, 2nd edn Palgrave, 2003) and *The Battle of Agincourt: Sources and Interpretations* (Boydell Press, 2000). She also edited the Rolls of the English Parliament between 1422 and 1454. She is currently President of the Historical Association and a Vice-President of the Royal Historical Society.

FELIPE FERNÁNDEZ-ARMESTO

Felipe Fernández-Armesto is Prince of Asturias Professor at Tufts University in Massachusetts and a Professorial Fellow of Queen Mary, University of London. His awards include Spain's Premio Nacional de Investigación, the John Carter Brown Medal, the Caird Medal, and the World History Association Book Prize. His journalism appears widely in Spain, Britain and the USA. Among his many broadcasting credits, he is the longest-serving presenter of *Analysis* on BBC Radio 4, and co-wrote the ten-part CNN series *Millennium*, which was based on his book *Millennium: A History of Our Last Thousand Years* (Bantam Press, 1995).

His recent books include *Amerigo: The Man Who Gave His Name to America* (Weidenfeld & Nicolson, 2006); *Pathfinders: A Global History of Exploration* (Oxford University Press, 2006); *Humankind: A Brief History* (Oxford University

Press, 2004); *The Americas: A History of Two Continents* (Weidenfeld & Nicolson, 2003) and *Food: A History* (Macmillan, 2001), which won the International Association of Culinary Professionals' Prize for the best food-writing.

JOHN GILLINGHAM

John Gillingham studied history at Oxford and Munich Universities. He is a Fellow of the British Academy and Emeritus Professor of History at the London School of Economics and Political Science, where he taught for more than thirty years. He was awarded the Prix Guillaume le Conquérant in 1997 and for five years (2000 to 2004) was Director of the Battle Conference on Anglo-Norman Studies which meets annually on the field of the Battle of Hastings. Three of his essays on war are reprinted in *Anglo-Norman Warfare*, edited by Matthew Strickland (Boydell Press, 1992); and he contributed to *Medieval Warfare: A History*, edited by Maurice Keen (Oxford University Press, 1999). His most recent books are *The Wars of the Roses: Peace and Conflict in Fifteenth Century England* (Phoenix Press, 2001); *The Angevin Empire* (Hodder, 2001); *The English in the Twelfth Century: Imperialism, National Identity and Political Values* (Boydell Press, 2000) and *Richard I* (Yale University Press, 1999).

ROBERT HARDY

Robert Hardy, CBE, is an internationally acclaimed actor

with an extensive career in theatre, film and television. He is, in addition, a medieval military historian. During the Second World War he spent a year at Magdalen College, Oxford, where his tutors were C. S. Lewis and J. R. R. Tolkien, before joining up and training as a fighter pilot with the Royal Air Force, finishing his degree after demobilization. His acting career has taken him to London, New York, California, Paris and Stratford-upon-Avon, and his many roles have included Henry V, Hamlet, Siegfried Farnon and Cornelius Fudge. He has played Winston Churchill several times on film, television and stage – including a performance in French in Robert Hossein's spectacular Paris production of *Celui qui a dit Non* (1999–2000).

An acknowledged expert on the military longbow in the late Middle Ages, his published works include *Longbow: A Social and Military History* (Patrick Stephens Ltd, 2006) and *The Great War Bow* (The History Press, 2005) with Professor Matthew Strickland, as well as various chapters in collections of medieval studies. He also lectures, speaking in Paris at the Musée de L'Armée in 2001. He is a Fellow of the Society of Antiquaries, an honorary Doctor of Literature of Reading, Durham and Portsmouth Universities, and a Consultant and Trustee of the Mary Rose Trust. He served for several years as Trustee of the Royal Armouries at Her Majesty's Tower of London.

JOHN HAYWOOD

John Haywood studied medieval history at the universities of Lancaster, Cambridge and Copenhagen. His doctoral
research was on early medieval naval warfare. He is now
a full-time historical writer with more than a dozen titles
to his credit, including *The Penguin Historical Atlas of the
Vikings* (1995) and *The Penguin Atlas of British and Irish History*
(2001). His most recent books are *The Dark Ages: Building
Europe* (Thalamus, 2008) and *The Great Migrations* (Quercus,
2008).

EFRAIM KARSH

Professor Efraim Karsh is head of Mediterranean and Middle
Eastern Studies at King's College London. He has held
various academic posts – at Harvard and Columbia
Universities, the Sorbonne, the London School of
Economics, Helsinki University, the International Institute
for Strategic Studies in London, the Kennan Institute for
Advanced Russian Studies in Washington, D.C., and the
Jaffee Center for Strategic Studies at Tel-Aviv University.
Professor Karsh is a regular commentator for the media:
he has appeared on all the main radio and television
networks in Britain and the USA, and has contributed art-
icles to leading newspapers including *The Times*, *The Sunday
Times*, *The New York Times*, *The Wall Street Journal* and *The
International Herald Tribune*.

He is the author of over a hundred academic publications, and his books include *Islamic Imperialism: A History* (Yale, 2006); *Rethinking the Middle East* (Frank Cass, 2003); *Empires of the Sand: The Struggle for Mastery in the Middle East, 1789–1922* (Harvard University Press, 1999); *Fabricating Israeli History: The 'New Historians'* (Frank Cass, 1997) and *Saddam Hussein: A Political Biography* (Free Press, 1991).

ISABEL DE MADARIAGA

Isabel de Madariaga was born in Scotland and educated in Switzerland, Spain, France and England. She studied Russian Language and Literature at the School of Slavonic and East European Studies in the University of London, where she completed her Ph.D. in History, published as *Britain, Russia, and the Armed Neutrality of 1780* (Yale University Press and Hollis and Carter, 1963). After several years as Assistant to the Editor of the *Slavonic and East European Review*, she was appointed Lecturer in History at the University of Sussex, then Senior Lecturer in History at Lancaster University in 1970 and Reader in Russian Studies in SSEES, then Professor, and now Emeritus Professor in the University of London. She is a Fellow of the British Academy, of the Royal Historical Society, and a Corresponding Member of the Royal Spanish Academy of History. She has written mainly about Catherine II and eighteenth-century Russia. Her *Ivan the Terrible* (Yale University Press) was published in 1985.

JUSTIN MAROZZI

Justin Marozzi is a travel writer, historian and a political risk and security consultant in post-conflict environments. A former *Financial Times* foreign correspondent, he is a Fellow of the Royal Geographical Society and has written widely about travel, exploration and the history of the Muslim world. His first book, *South from Barbary* (Harper-Collins, 2001), told the story of a 1,200-mile expedition by camel across Libya. More recently he has written an acclaimed history of the fourteenth-century Central Asian conqueror Tamerlane. His latest book, *The Man Who Invented History: Travels with Herodotus* (John Murray, 2008), is based on expeditions in Turkey, Iraq, Egypt and Greece. He is married and lives in Norfolk and London.

JOHN JULIUS NORWICH

John Julius Norwich is the author of histories of Norman Sicily, Venice, Byzantium and the Mediterranean; he has also written on Mount Athos, the Sahara, English architecture, Shakespeare's histories and nineteenth-century Venice. His most recent book was *The Popes: A History* (Chatto & Windus, 2011). Since 1970 he has compiled an annual pamphlet anthology, *A Christmas Cracker*.

He has made some thirty historical documentaries for television, and was for four years chairman of the BBC panel game *My Word*. For three years he presented the Evening Concert, six nights a week, on Classic FM.

Formerly Chairman of Colnaghi, the oldest fine art dealers in London, he is Honorary Chairman of the Venice in Peril Fund and Chairman of the World Monuments Fund in Britain. He is a regular lecturer on art-historical, architectural and musical subjects. In 2006 and 2007 he gave one-man shows nightly for a week at two London theatres, reading from his *Christmas Crackers* and singing to the piano.

JONATHAN PHILLIPS

Jonathan Phillips is Professor of Crusading History at Royal Holloway, University of London. He is the author of *The Second Crusade: Extending the Frontiers of Christendom* (Yale, 2007); *The Fourth Crusade and the Sack of Constantinople* (Jonathan Cape, 2004); *The Crusades, 1095–1197* (Longman, 2002) and *Defenders of the Holy Land: Relations between the Latin East and the West, 1119–1187* (Oxford University Press, 1996). He is a frequent contributor to *BBC History* and *History Today* magazines and an editor of the academic journal *Crusades*. He has acted as consultant for the television programmes *The Cross and the Crescent* (History Channel, 2005) and *Holy Warriors – Richard and Saladin* (BBC2, 2004).

JUSTIN POLLARD

Justin Pollard specialized in Anglo-Saxon archaeology at Cambridge University. A historical writer and consultant in print, film and TV, he is the author of *The Rise and Fall of Alexandria* (Viking Books, 2006); *Alfred the Great, the Man Who Made England* (John Murray, 2005) and *The Seven Ages of Britain* (Hodder & Stoughton, 2003). He was also a contributor to the *The QI Book of General Ignorance* (Faber and Faber, 2006). His film credits include *Elizabeth* and its sequel *Elizabeth – The Golden Age*, as well as *Atonement*, *The Four Feathers* and *The Boy in the Striped Pyjamas*. In television he has made over twenty-five documentary series, including *Time Team* for Channel Four, and has written for Tony Robinson, Terry Jones, Stephen Fry, Vic Reeves, Bettany Hughes and Bob Geldof. He also writes for the BBC quiz show *QI* and is the script consultant on Showtime's hit US drama *The Tudors*.

FRANCIS ROBINSON

Francis Robinson has been Professor of the History of South Asia, Royal Holloway, University of London, since 1990, and from September 2008 will also be Visiting Professor, Faculty of History, University of Oxford. He was President of the Royal Asiatic Society, 1997–2000 and 2003–06. He was made CBE in 2006 for contributions to Higher Education and to the History of Islam. His books include: *Separatism*

Among Indian Muslims: The Politics of the United Provinces' Muslims 1860–1923 (1974); *Atlas of the Islamic World since 1500* (1982); *Varieties of South Asian Islam* (1988); *The Cambridge Illustrated History of the Islamic World* (1996); *Islam and Muslim History in South Asia* (2000); *The 'Ulama of Farangi Mahall and Islamic Culture in South Asia* (2001); *The Mughals and the Islamic Dynasties of India, Iran and Central Asia, 1206–1925* and *Islam, South Asia and the West* (2007). His edited volume of the *New Cambridge History of Islam, Islam in the Age of Western Domination*, was published in 2009.

JONATHAN SUMPTION

Jonathan Sumption was a History Fellow of Magdalen College, Oxford, until 1975. He is a QC practising at the commercial bar, and is the author of *The Hundred Years War*, a multi-volume history which includes, *Trial by Battle* (Faber and Faber, 1990), *Trial by Fire* (Faber and Faber, 1999), and *Divided Houses* (Faber and Faber, 2009).

STEPHEN TURNBULL

Stephen Turnbull took his first degree at Cambridge University, then received from Leeds University an MA and Ph.D. in Japanese Religious Studies and an MA in Military History. He is currently Lecturer in Japanese Religious and Military History at Leeds, and was until recently Visiting Professor of Japanese Religious and Military History at Akita

International University in Japan. He is the author of sixty published books on religious and military topics, including *The Kakure Kirishitan of Japan* (Folkestone, 1998); *The Samurai Sourcebook* (London, 1998); *The Samurai and the Sacred* (Oxford University Press, 2006); *The Great Wall of China* (Oxford University Press, 2007) and several other illustrated monographs on the military history of Japan, China, Korea and the Mongol Empire. His other research interests include comparative military studies of Early Modern Europe and East Asia and the development of fortifications; the history of Christianity in Japan and the evolution of Shintō in the modern age.

THEODORIC

c. 454–526

JOHN HAYWOOD

KING OF THE OSTROGOTHS FROM 471 TO 526, Theodoric conquered Italy in 489–493 and founded the most sophisticated of the barbarian kingdoms. Throughout his reign he fought to protect and preserve his people and win for them a prosperous and secure homeland. In achieving this he showed great military and diplomatic abilities, as well as inspiring leadership, personal bravery and ruthlessness.

Born in 454, Theodoric was the son of Thiudemir, who, with his brothers Valamir and Videmir, was king of the Ostrogoths. He belonged to the Amal family which claimed to be descended from a long line of illustrious, semi-legendary kings. Later tradition had it that he was born, auspiciously, on the same day that his uncle Valamir won a great victory over the Huns. The Ostrogoths ('Eastern Goths') were descendants of the Greuthungi, a branch of the Goths who had been conquered by the Huns around 374 (the other main branch of the Goths, the Tervingi, had escaped into the Roman Empire, where they became known as the Visigoths or 'Western Goths'). The Ostrogoths kept their own kings under the Huns and played an important role in Attila's campaigns in the 450s. Following the death of Attila in 453, the Hun empire disintegrated and the Ostrogoths became independent. Shortly after this, the Romans allowed them to settle as semi-autonomous *foederati* ('allies') in the province of Pannonia on the middle Danube.

In 461 Theodoric was sent as a hostage to Constantinople where he remained for ten years. As a high-ranking hostage Theodoric was well treated and became a favourite of the emperor Leo I (r. 457–474). His upbringing in what was then the world's largest and most splendid city made a great impression on Theodoric, but if Leo thought that this would make him into a compliant puppet of the empire he was to be disappointed. Throughout the time that Theodoric was in Constantinople, the Ostrogoths were fighting their German neighbours and wandering remnants of the Huns. During these wars Valamir had been killed, leaving Theodoric's father Thiudemir as the senior Ostrogothic king. On his return to his people in 471, Theodoric set out to prove himself a war leader. The Sarmatians had recently captured the Roman city of Singidunum (Belgrade) and Theodoric, still aged only 18, raised an army on his own initiative and drove them out. Instead of returning the city to the Romans, he kept it for the Ostrogoths. For this Theodoric was acclaimed king, alongside his father and uncle Videmir.

In 473, Thiudemir and Videmir decided that war-ravaged Pannonia was no longer a suitable homeland for their people. To pressure the Romans into relocating them, they decided that Videmir would invade Italy while Thiudemir would attack the Eastern Empire. Videmir's campaign failed: he died in Italy and the survivors went to Gaul and joined the Visigoths. Thiudemir launched his campaign from Singidunum and advanced as far as Nish. From there he sent Theodoric, with a couple of grizzled veterans as advisers, to lead a raid through the Balkans and into Greece. Thiudemir followed up his son's success by laying siege to Thessalonica. Negotiations followed and the Romans allowed the Ostrogoths to settle in Macedonia. Shortly after, probably in 474, Thiudemir died and Theodoric succeeded to sole kingship of the Ostrogoths. The settlement in Macedonia proved to be unsatisfactory, however, and a few years later the Ostrogoths were moved by the Romans to Thrace.

Rival leaders

The next few years of Theodoric's reign were dominated by his rivalry with Theodoric Triarius, the leader of a separate band of Goths that the Romans had settled in the Balkans as *foederati* some years previously. The eastern emperor, Zeno (r. 474–491), was only willing to support one Gothic leader, so the two Theodorics had to compete for imperial recognition. When Triarius rebelled in 478, Zeno allied with Theodoric to mount a joint attack on him. In the event, Zeno failed to supply the troops he had promised and Theodoric found himself facing his rival alone. However, the Goths refused to fight one another and the two leaders were reconciled. Zeno broke up this alliance by offering Triarius a generous settlement, including a generalship, and abandoning Theodoric and the Ostrogoths. Angry at his betrayal, and with his people facing starvation, Theodoric led his men on a campaign of plundering and indiscriminate killing through the Balkans until Triarius rebelled again, forcing Zeno to open negotiations. As the price of his support, Theodoric demanded that he be given Triarius' command and Roman citizenship. Wary of replacing one troublesome barbarian general with another, Zeno refused. Zeno's hand was strengthened when the Roman general Sabinianus ambushed an Ostrogothic baggage train in 479, taking five thousand prisoners and two thousand wagons. Sabinianus then blockaded Theodoric in Epirus until 482, when Zeno ordered his execution on suspicion of treason. Sabinianus' less able replacements failed to prevent Theodoric escaping.

Theodoric's position was simplified in 481 when Triarius, once again in rebellion, was fatally injured in a riding accident. His son Recitach took over but was murdered by Theodoric when they met for a banquet in 484. Recitach's following of around thirty thousand joined the Ostrogoths, raising their strength to around one hundred thousand men, women and children. In these years Theodoric swung between loyalty to the empire – in 484 he was made consul – and rebellion. This reflects the difficulty of his position. Although the Romans were not strong enough to expel the Ostrogoths, the Ostrogoths were not strong enough to dictate terms to the Romans. Theodoric's rebellions were even becoming counterproductive: the Balkans was now so war-ravaged that the land could hardly support his people.

Zeno's commission

Zeno provided the solution to Theodoric's problem: in 488 he gave him a commission to invade Italy, overthrow its ruler Odovacer and govern it until 'the emperor should come to claim his supremacy'. Odovacer was a German general who in 476 had overthrown Romulus Augustulus, the last, powerless, Roman emperor of the west, and been proclaimed king by the German (mainly Herul and Rugian) mercenaries he commanded. Zeno accepted Odovacer's face-saving offer to rule Italy as viceroy, which at least maintained the legal position that it remained part of the Roman Empire. From Zeno's point of view, sending Theodoric west was a win-win situation. If Theodoric lost, that would be the end of the Ostrogoths, and if he won, at least they would be a long way from Constantinople. The offer was attractive to Theodoric, too. He was well aware that the Ostrogoths were in a very insecure position in the Eastern Roman Empire and Zeno's commission gave him the opportunity to win legitimate control of a rich kingdom. The question of what would happen if Zeno actually did 'come to claim his supremacy' was left hanging.

Invasion of Italy

The Ostrogoths gathered at Novae (Cezava) and set off for Italy in the autumn of 488, perhaps an unpromising time of year to begin what was not so much a military campaign as a migration of a whole people, but it would have been easier to find (buy or plunder) food supplies so soon after the harvest. The early stages of the route, up the lower reaches of the Sava river valley, lay across territory occupied by the Gepids, old enemies of the Ostrogoths, who refused them passage. The Gepids held a strong position on the opposite bank of the River Ulca, somewhere near

Sirmium, and they repulsed all attacks until Theodoric led a charge across the river in person and broke the Gepid line. Part of the plunder from the battle was a Gepid wagon train loaded with grain.

Once out of Gepid territory Theodoric followed the same route through the Julian Alps that Alaric the Visigoth had taken when he had invaded Italy eighty years before. The Ostrogoths moved slowly, encumbered as they were by thousands of wagons, pack animals, herds of cattle, flocks of sheep, and non-combatants. Of the one hundred thousand or so Ostrogoths, only around one third would have been able-bodied men capable of bearing arms; the rest would have been women, children and old people. It is unlikely that the migrating horde could have made much more than about 4½ miles a day, so it was not until summer 489 that they began to descend to the plains around Aquileia. Odovacer had prepared his defences and was waiting for the Ostrogoths in a strongly fortified camp over-looking a ford crossing the Isonzo river. On 28 August Theodoric forded the river, stormed the camp and put Odovacer to flight. Nothing is known about the conduct of this crucial battle: most of the descriptions of Theodoric's battles come from the work of his court poet Ennodius and, though strong on heroic imagery, they are almost totally lacking in tactical detail.

Odovacer retreated to Verona and built another fortified camp outside the city, on the east bank of the Adige river. By placing their backs to the river, and by breaking the bridge that linked his camp to Verona, Odovacer hoped to force his men to fight more stubbornly than they had at the Isonzo. Once again leading from the front, on 30 September Theodoric stormed the camp. Odovacer and some of his followers managed to break out of the self-made trap and fled south to Ravenna, his capital. Theodoric continued west and in October occupied Milan. There, Odovacer's chief of staff Tufa, together with a large body of German troops, surrendered to Theodoric. In a rare error of judgement, Theodoric took Tufa and his men into his own service, sending them to besiege Odovacer in Ravenna. Once there, Tufa reverted to his old allegiance and the Ostrogoths Theodoric had sent with him were handed over to Odovacer and murdered.

On hearing of Tufa's betrayal, Theodoric immediately moved to Pavia, a more easily defended position than Milan, being protected on two sides by rivers. The Ostrogothic non-combatants would remain there, in crowded and uncomfortable conditions, for the remainder of the war. Both kings spent the winter of 489–490 in diplomatic activity. Theodoric won support from the Visigoths, while Odovacer persuaded the Burgundians to invade Italy by playing on their fears of encirclement by Goths. While Theodoric was distracted with the Burgundians – he was eventually able to negotiate their withdrawal – Odovacer began to reassert control in northern Italy. By the summer he was in Milan, which he treated roughly for having been too welcoming to the Ostrogoths. With an army of Ostrogoths and Visigoths, Theodoric left Pavia, and on 11 August he inflicted another heavy defeat on Odovacer at the River Adda, 10 miles east of Milan. Odovacer fled back to Ravenna and prepared for a siege.

Laying siege to Ravenna was a daunting prospect. The city was a natural stronghold, being surrounded by malarial marshes that were not only difficult to cross, but would make life uncomfortable and unhealthy for any besieging army. As capital of the Western Roman Empire from 402, and Odovacer's capital from 476, Ravenna had been heavily fortified, and it was also a port, so it could be supplied and reinforced from the sea. Moreover, Theodoric did not have enough troops to seal off Ravenna completely from the outside. His main siege camp was in the Pineta, a strip of sandy pine forest lying between Ravenna and the open sea, a healthier environment in which to camp than the marshes.

In September 490, Theodoric began to send out regular mounted patrols to stop any traffic going to the city by road but, lacking a fleet, Theodoric was unable to stop ships delivering supplies. Odovacer sent out raiding parties to harass the Ostrogoths at every opportunity. To protect his rear, Theodoric sent death squads throughout Italy to eliminate as many of Odovacer's supporters as they could find, but Odovacer's general, Tufa, remained at large with an army in Lombardy.

In mid July 491 Odovacer received reinforcements from the Heruls, who lived beyond the Danube, and tried to win back the initiative with a surprise night attack on Theodoric's camp. After hard fighting, and heavy casualties on both sides, Theodoric again prevailed and again, as he had throughout the war, showed his ability to rally his soldiers in difficult situations. The leadership of his opponent, on the other hand, was consistently lacklustre. Still the siege dragged on. In August 492 Theodoric captured Rimini, which was still held for Odovacer, and with it a fleet of dromons, a type of light and fast war galley. He did what perhaps he should have done earlier – began to blockade Ravenna from the sea, cutting off all supplies. By January 493 the population of Ravenna was beginning to starve, and on 27 February, with no hope of relief, Odovacer surrendered. Theodoric entered Ravenna, to the welcoming cheers of its people, just six days later.

Theodoric agreed not only that Odovacer's life should be spared but that the two of them would share the kingship of Italy. On 15 March Theodoric invited Odovacer to a feast to celebrate the peace. When he had been separated from his guards, Theodoric drew his sword and with a single blow cut Odovacer in half, from the collarbone to the groin.

Surprised by his own strength, Theodoric is said to have commented that he always knew that Odovacer was a spineless wretch.

The outstanding problem of Fredericus and Tufa solved itself in 494 when the two fell out over a division of plunder. Fredericus killed Tufa and then vanished from history. At no time throughout the long war had the Roman population of Italy taken sides; what was it to them which barbarian ruled them?

A system of military apartheid?

Like Odovacer, Theodoric continued to rule Italy as if it were still part of the Roman Empire. Theodoric never described himself as king of Italy (because of its implication of territorial sovereignty), only as king of the Ostrogoths in Italy. He respected the right of the emperor in Constantinople to appoint the consuls of Rome and even his right to make laws. Though he always ruled from Ravenna, Theodoric consulted the Roman Senate, continued the dole of free grain to the Roman poor and sponsored games in the circus. Whatever his failings, Odovacer had ruled Italy competently through the existing Roman institutions, and Theodoric continued this policy, his government being run entirely by Roman bureaucrats. The military, on the other hand, was the exclusive preserve of the Ostrogoths: under the veneer of civilian government,

Theodoric remained a barbarian warlord. Goths were even forbidden to have a Roman education lest it sap their martial vigour. Romans were forbidden to carry any weapon larger than a penknife. The separation of Roman and Ostrogoth extended into all aspects of life, amounting to a system of apartheid that was intended to maintain the dominance of the Ostrogoths and to prevent their assimilation into the far more numerous Roman population. Romans and Ostrogoths could not legally marry and they were judged in different courts. Religion was a major obstacle to assimilation. The Ostrogoths were Arian Christians and were regarded by their Catholic subjects as heretics. To maintain their cohesion as a people, Ostrogothic settlement was concentrated in the Po valley and in smaller military settlements at strategic locations. The Ostrogoths lived on the revenues from estates allocated to them and on annual donatives. To preserve the link between the king and his warriors, the donatives had to be collected in person from Theodoric himself.

After the fall of Ravenna, Theodoric never personally led an army in the field again, but he continued to direct campaigns run by able subordinates. By the year 500 he had extended his frontier as far north as the Danube and as far east as the Rhône, establishing a common frontier with the Visigoths. Theodoric regarded the Visigoths as kin and he intervened to help them preserve their kingdom after their king Alaric II was killed by the Frankish king Clovis (r. 481–511) at the Battle of Vouillé in 507. In 508 Theodoric fought a short war with the Eastern Roman Empire, as a result of which the emperor Anastasius (r. 491–518) recognized his control over Illyricum. When, shortly afterwards, the Visigoths recognized his sovereignty, Theodoric had gone a considerable way towards reuniting the Western Roman Empire under his rule. The edifice of Romanitas survived more intact in Italy than in any other barbarian kingdom and this undoubtedly lent a quasi-imperial majesty to Theodoric's rule. Indeed, Theodoric saw himself, and was widely accepted, as the elder statesman of the barbarian kingdoms.

Under Theodoric, Italy enjoyed thirty years of peace and prosperity but, in his later years, he began increasingly to question the loyalty of his Roman subjects and his rule became more oppressive. This may have been because he feared for the future of his kingdom, having failed to father a son. When he died of dysentery in 526 he was succeeded by his 8-year-old grandson, Athalaric, under the regency of his daughter Amalasuntha. She was never able to assert her authority over the Ostrogoths, who could not accept being ruled by a woman. Her murder in 535 gave the emperor Justinian (r. 527–565) the pretext to initiate the reconquest of Italy by his general Belisarius.

It is difficult to assess Theodoric's achievements. Was

his separation of Goth and Roman doomed to failure, as many historians argue? Or did he lay the foundations of a sustainable state on which a more able successor might have built? Theodoric was certainly the most powerful of the barbarian kings of his day and a great military leader. Even the Frankish king Clovis, whose reign saw an unbroken succession of conquests, would back down rather than risk outright war with Theodoric. However, unlike Clovis' achievements, which continued to have a seminal impact on European history, Theodoric's, perhaps through no fault of his own, died with him.

CLOVIS
465–511

JOHN HAYWOOD

THE FIRST GREAT KING OF THE FRANKS, Clovis (r. 481–511) was arguably the most successful of the Germanic conquerors of the fifth century. Energetic and ruthless, Clovis led the Franks on successful military campaigns that transformed them from a minor people into a great power that, more than any other, shaped the future of medieval Europe.

The son of Childeric (r. 460–481), king of the Franks of Tournai in modern Belgium, Clovis was born in 466 and brought up as a traditional Germanic pagan. He belonged to the Merovingian dynasty, named for his grandfather Merovech (d. 456), an obscure chieftain who, legend claimed, was the son of a sea monster.

Clovis was only 16 when he inherited the throne, but

very soon displayed outstanding abilities. The situation that Clovis inherited was a complex one. The Franks were not a united people and Clovis was only one of several kings, each with a small kingdom based usually on a former Roman town. Most of the kings seem to have been related to one another either by blood or marriage.

Frankish kings were set apart from their subjects by their long hair, which embodied the mystique of kingship. To cut a king's hair was to depose him. Childeric, Clovis' father, was probably the most powerful of the Frankish kings of his day but he was still little more than a local warlord whose power was based on his personal retinue of household warriors. These men expected to be rewarded for their service with a share of plunder, so a king who was not a good leader in war would not keep his army for long. Clovis would have been well aware that the advantage he inherited from his father would not last unless he proved himself as a war leader too.

Salians and Ripuarians

Though older tribal identities still survived, the Franks were gradually coalescing into two main groups, the Ripuarians and the Salians. The Ripuarians inhabited the traditional Frankish homeland on the lower Rhine, from Cologne northwards almost to the sea. The Salians were descended from Franks who had migrated west into Toxandria (roughly northern Flanders) in northeast Gaul in the middle of the fourth century. The Romans, who were distracted with campaigns elsewhere, allowed the Franks to settle as *foederati* ('allies') as a temporary expedient until they got the chance to expel them. This never happened and, as the Franks were mostly loyal to their alliance, the Romans left them alone. This may seem an unspectacular migration compared with those of the Vandals and Goths, but the Franks were able to put down deep roots in Toxandria, which remains part of the Germanic-speaking world today, and it made a secure base from which to expand into Gaul when Roman power entered its final decline in the middle of the fifth century. By the time Clovis became king, Frankish territory extended as far west as the River Somme and south over the Moselle valley.

The Visigoths also exploited Rome's decline and seized most of Gaul southwest of the Loire, and the Burgundians built a kingdom centred on Lyons and the Rhône valley. Britons had crossed the Channel to settle in Armorica (soon to become known as Brittany, after them) and were pushing east under their king, Riothamus. Seafaring Saxons had founded colonies on the Channel coast of Gaul and around the mouth of the Loire. The last vestiges of Roman authority in Gaul were to be found between the Loire and the Somme. After the deposition in 476 of the last Roman emperor of the west, the Gallo-Roman cities in this area became, in effect, independent under the leadership of their bishops and local magnates who could afford to maintain armed retinues recruited from redundant Roman soldiers.

The defeat of Syagrius

It was against the Gallo-Romans that Clovis enjoyed his first major military success. In 486 he allied with Ragnachar, the king of the Franks of Cambrai, against Syagrius 'king of the Romans' who was based at Soissons. Syagrius was the son of a Roman general, Aegidius, who had fought to maintain Roman authority in Gaul in the dying days of the Western Empire and, left to his own devices after 476, had created some sort of kingdom for himself. Clovis won an annihilating victory over Syagrius' army, after which he was able to conquer the whole area between the Somme and the Loire. Syagrius fled to the Visigoths but their king, Alaric II (r. 484–507), handed him over to Clovis, who imprisoned him and later had him secretly murdered. Clovis was still very much the leader of a war band at this point in his career. (After the defeat of Syagrius, a bishop came to Clovis to ask for the return of a sacred vessel looted by the pagan Franks. Clovis was agreeable but had to ask his warriors if they would give him the vessel above his agreed share of the loot.)

In 491 Clovis conquered a small group of Thuringians who had settled between the Franks and the territories of the Alamanns and the Burgundians. The Alamanns responded to this move by invading Frankish territory in 496. In an important first step towards establishing his authority over all the Franks, Clovis united the armies of all the Salian and Ripuarian kings under his leadership to repel the invaders. Clovis also enjoyed the support of at least one Gallo-Roman magnate, Aurelianus, who brought his own warriors to join the Frankish army. The two armies met at Tolbiac (Zülpich), about 30 miles south of Cologne, and the Alamanns were defeated. Clovis proceeded to take over the bulk of the Alamannic kingdom but was warned against attacking any Alamanns who lived south of the Danube by Theodoric, the Ostrogoth king of Italy, who regarded the river as the border between the Frankish and Ostrogothic spheres of influence.

The conversion of Clovis

By the time of his victory over the Alamanns, Clovis had married Chlothild, a Catholic Christian princess of the Burgundian royal house. Chlothild tried unsuccessfully to persuade Clovis to convert to Christianity but he refused, partly because of a lack of conviction, but also because he feared it would alienate many of his warriors, most of whom were still pagans. He finally made his decision to convert after supposedly calling on the Christian God for help at a difficult moment during the battle of Tolbiac and he was subsequently baptized into the Catholic church by Bishop (later Saint) Remigius at Reims. This was a turning point in Clovis' reign but its immediate impact was much as he had predicted: thousands of the warriors he had led against the Alamanns defected to Ragnachar of Cambrai.

Such a serious loss of manpower begs the question, why did Clovis convert? He may indeed have had some profound religious experience but he was such a ruthless and cynical man that this can hardly be the whole story. His conversion may have been a deliberate overture to his Catholic Gallo-Roman subjects, who, since his defeat of Syagrius, now outnumbered his Frankish subjects. Winning their active collaboration would have more than made up for the loss of a few thousand warriors.

Other barbarian peoples, such as the Goths and Vandals, had long since converted to Christianity but they belonged to the Arian sect, which Catholics regarded as heretical because it denied the true divinity of Christ (the Burgundians were divided on the issue; some, such as Clovis' wife Chlothild, were Catholic, others Arian). This created an unbridgeable gulf in the other barbarian kingdoms between the German minority and the 'Roman' majority and prevented them forming any sense of loyalty to their rulers. This proved to be a fatal weakness, and those barbarian rulers that clung to Arianism did not survive long. Even those Arians, like the Visigoths, who eventually adopted Catholicism, remained tainted in their subjects' eyes by their association with heresy. This was not a problem for the Franks because they converted to Catholicism directly from paganism. The Gallo-Roman bishops gladly ignored the unsavoury side of Clovis' character and lent him their support and administrative expertise in return for his protection and patronage. In addition, Clovis gained diplomatic support from the papacy and the eastern Roman emperor Anastasius, who awarded him the rank of consul, so legitimizing his rule in the eyes of his Gallo-Roman subjects. This made possible, over the next century or so, the complete assimilation of the Gallo-Romans to Frankish identity. By the seventh century, Gaul had become known as Francia.

A family affair

Clovis' marriage to Chlothild drew him into the complex politics of the Burgundian royal family. Kingship of the Burgundians was shared between two brothers, Godigisel and Gundobad. In 500 or 501 relations between the two brothers broke down and Godigisel secretly appealed to Clovis for help against Gundobad in return for an annual subsidy and some territorial concessions. As Gundobad had murdered Chlothild's parents, Clovis had a ready-made justification for intervention. When Clovis invaded the Burgundian kingdom, Godigisel appealed to Gundobad, who knew nothing of his brother's plotting, to take the field with him to repel the Franks. When the three armies met near Dijon, Gundobad was taken completely by surprise when his troops were attacked by both his brother and by Clovis. Though his army was crushed, Gundobad escaped and took refuge in the fortified city of Avignon. Clovis pursued and laid siege to the city, whereupon Gundobad negotiated a peace settlement, agreeing to pay Clovis an annual subsidy if he withdrew. Once free of Clovis, Gundobad settled scores with Godigisel, capturing and killing him and his family. A few years later Gundobad refused to pay any more tribute to the Franks, only escaping retribution because Clovis needed his support against the Visigoths.

Clovis' next campaign was against the Bretons, although the exact date is uncertain. He was again victorious and the Bretons became in some way tributary to the Franks because they supplied troops for his armies. Some of these troops were the descendants of Roman soldiers and, when they went to war, still marched under the old legionary standards of their fathers and grandfathers.

War against the Visigoths

Clovis' greatest military campaigns were against the Visigoths who ruled a kingdom comprising Aquitaine and most of Spain from their capital at Toulouse. According to the Gallo-Roman church-man Gregory of Tours, whose *History of the Franks* is the main source of information about his reign, Clovis was motivated by Catholic zeal to overthrow the heretical Arian Visigoths. However, it is clear that Clovis had already captured Visigothic territory as far south of the Loire as Saintes in the early 490s, some years before he converted to Christianity. In 496 the Visigoths recaptured Saintes, perhaps taking advantage of Clovis' war with the Alamanns. In 498 the Franks returned and captured Bordeaux but seem not to have held it for long. In 502 a temporary peace was agreed when Clovis and Alaric II met on neutral territory, an island in the Loire, the river that marked the border between their two kingdoms. It is likely that Alaric agreed to pay tribute to Clovis and also that he tried to do so using debased coin. If this was true, then it is no surprise that the peace treaty did not last.

After putting down a resurgence of Alamannic resistance in 506, Clovis went back to war with Alaric in 507. Clovis was mindful of the propaganda value of his Catholicism and he ordered his men to respect church property when passing through Visigothic territory and to take nothing but water and grass for horses. He is said to have killed one of his own soldiers who robbed an old man. His advance was slowed by bad weather, but his army reached the vicinity of Poitiers and brought the Visigoths to battle at Vouillé, about 10 miles northwest of the city. The outcome was a crushing defeat for the Visigoths. Clovis deployed archers and spear-throwers to the rear of his formation to shower the Visigoths with missiles over the front ranks of his army, who engaged the enemy in hand-to-hand combat. Clovis fought and killed Alaric in single combat but came close to being killed himself when he was attacked by two Visigothic spearmen. He was saved by the strength of his leather cuirass and the speed of his horse. Many Gallo-Romans took part in the battle, commanded by 'men of senatorial rank', though it is not clear whose side they fought on. King Gundobad of the Burgundians had helped divide the Visigothic forces by invading from the east at the same time as Clovis invaded from the north.

In the aftermath of the battle Clovis captured Bordeaux, this time permanently, and spent the winter there. He sent his eldest son Theuderic to mop up Visigothic resistance in Auvergne. The following year Clovis seized the royal treasury at Toulouse and ousted an isolated Visigothic garrison from Angoulême. Obviously intending that his readers should see Clovis as a latterday Joshua, Gregory informs us that God made the walls of Angoulême fall down of their own accord. In the same year, Clovis laid siege to Carcassonne while another Frankish-Burgundian force laid siege to Arles. This attempt to seize a foothold on the Mediterranean coast was challenged by Theodoric, who sent Ostrogothic troops to support the Visigoths, and Clovis was forced to withdraw. Despite this failure, Clovis had added a prosperous and very Romanized region to his kingdom, nearly doubling its size.

The unification of the Franks

This succession of conquests had established Clovis as by far the most eminent of the Frankish kings and he now felt strong enough to unite the Franks under his sole rule, managing during this period to achieve the codification of the law of the Salian Franks. But it was during these years of his reign that his cynicism is most clearly revealed, as he used bribery, deceit and murder to eliminate his rivals one by one and take over their kingdoms. The last to die was Ragnachar, after which his pagan warriors joined Clovis and submitted to baptism. Gregory of Tours tells the story that in his last years Clovis would tearfully express his regret at having murdered all his relatives so that he was condemned to lonely isolation. But, Gregory says, 'he said this not because he grieved for their deaths, but because in his cunning way he hoped to find some relative still in the land of the living whom he could kill'.

Clovis died in 511, aged 45, at his favourite residence at Paris and his kingdom, according to the Frankish custom of partible inheritance, was divided between his four sons. Murderous family politics resulted in the kingdom being reunited under Clovis' last surviving son Chlothar in 558.

On his death in 561, the kingdom was divided between his four sons and the whole bloody process began again. Division in no way inhibited the expansion of the Frankish kingdom, however, and by 536 Clovis' sons had conquered the Burgundian kingdom, Bavaria, Thuringia and Provence, at last gaining a foothold on the coast of the Mediterranean Sea.

The reign of Clovis was one of the most significant in early medieval Europe. His military campaigns turned the Franks from a minor, disunited people of the North Sea region into the major power of western Europe, and his political abilities ensured that they would retain this position long after his death. He is often presented as being the first king of France but this is anachronistic. France as a political entity was born of the break-up of the Carolingian empire in the late ninth century. Nevertheless, his reign was critical for the formation of France as it was from the assimilation of the Gallo-Romans and the Franks, which began in his reign, that the French national identity would eventually develop. As a war leader, Clovis was brave, leading from the front, but there is simply too little evidence to assess other aspects of his military leadership. But he was undoubtedly one of the great commanders of his age, as the far-reaching results of his campaigns testify.

Frankish armies in the age of Clovis

As with other aspects of Clovis' military activities, there is little evidence to explain the organization of his armies. His army was built around his retinue or *trustis*. The *trustis* included the *pueri* ('lads') or household warriors that Clovis kept with him at all times, and the *leudes* or sworn military followers. The *leudes* were men of high social rank, many of whom brought warrior retinues of their own to the army. The loyalty of the *leudes* was essential; Clovis was able to overthrow his rival Ragnachar by bribing his *leudes* to desert him. After the defeat of Syagrius in 486, Gallo-Roman magnates were admitted to the ranks of the *leudes* and they added their own armed retinues to the Frankish army. Though they did not fight in person, the Gallo-Roman bishops also kept armed retinues to defend their sees in the turbulent conditions of post-Roman Gaul and no doubt these too served in Clovis' armies. Clovis probably also inherited some remnants of Roman military institutions as the sources mention *laeti*, a term used to describe barbarian settlers who were given farms in return for military service. In Roman times the Franks had been pirates and in the sixth century they still maintained a fleet somewhere near the mouth of the Rhine.

Frankish armies were not large: for Clovis' war with the Alamanns the Salian and Ripuarian Franks could raise only around six thousand warriors between them. Though their leaders might fight on horseback, most Franks were foot soldiers. The most distinctive Frankish weapons were a barbed spear called an *ango*, a throwing axe, known after them as the *francisca*, and the *scramasax*, a long single-edged fighting knife also popular with the Anglo-Saxons. For protection most warriors relied on a large round shield and probably a hardened leather cap and cuirass. Swords, iron helmets and body armour were the preserve of high-ranking warriors only. There is little evidence of the battlefield formations used in Clovis' time. The Franks probably fought like other Germans, forming up behind a wall of overlapping shields for both offence and defence. Siege warfare was not something in which the Germans had great expertise but in his later campaigns Clovis had engineers who could build siege engines.

BELISARIUS

c. 505–565

JOHN JULIUS NORWICH

'BY THE UNION OF LIBERALITY AND JUSTICE he acquired the love of the soldiers, without alienating the affections of the people. The sick and wounded were relieved with medicine and money, and still more efficaciously by the healing visits and smiles of their commander . . . In the licence of a military life, none could boast that they had seen him intoxicated with wine; the most beautiful captives of Gothic or Vandal race were offered to his embraces, but he turned aside from their charms, and the husband of Antonina was never suspected of violating the laws of conjugal fidelity . . . The spectator and historian of his exploits has observed that amidst the perils of war he was daring without rashness, prudent without fear, slow or rapid according to the exigencies of the moment; that in deepest distress he was animated by real or apparent hope, but that he was modest and humble in the most prosperous fortune.'

It is not often that Edward Gibbon allows himself such an unqualified paean of praise. Admittedly its subject lived in the sixth century, and early medieval sources are always inadequate; even those few that have come down to us are seldom entirely reliable. (We are lucky indeed to have the highly educated Syrian-Greek Procopius of Caesarea, who was an eyewitness to much of what he records and is thus a good deal more trustworthy than most of his fellow chroniclers.) Such evidence as we possess, however, suggests that although the emperor Justinian's most brilliant and celebrated general – like every other military leader of his time – could be capable on occasion of considerable brutality, he may otherwise have been something approaching the paragon described by this normally least charitable of our historians.

The *Nika* riots

Belisarius was, like his master, a Romanized Thracian. His early career was meteoric. His military gifts were unquestioned; his personal courage was proved again and again, and he was a natural leader of men. In 529, while still in his twenties, he had inflicted an overwhelming defeat on a far superior Persian army at Dara, a few miles northwest of Nisibis. He achieved still greater prominence, however, in Constantinople itself at the time of the most serious political crisis of Justinian's reign, the so-called

Nika riots. There were several reasons for these distur-
bances, the most important of which was the division of
the populace into two rival factions, the Blues and the
Greens. Their names had originally referred to the colours
worn by the two principal teams of charioteers in the
Games, but the factions themselves had long since left
the narrow confines of the arena. By now they existed
as two independent semi-political parties, both of which
wielded a dangerous amount of power. Once secure on
the throne, Justinian had therefore embarked on a policy
of firm repression, depriving them of their privileges and
curbing their excesses with harsh, sometimes even savage,
punishments.

Thus it was that when, on 13 January 532, Justinian
took his seat in the Hippodrome, his appearance caused
uproar. Now, suddenly and for the first time, the Blues
and the Greens were united; and their cries of *'Nika!
Nika!'* – 'Win! Win!' – were no longer addressed to their
favoured teams. The word had now become a menacing
chant, directed against the person of the emperor. The
races began, but were soon abandoned. The mob poured
out of the circus, hell-bent on destruction, and for five
days smoke lay thick over the city as nearly all its principal public buildings went up in flames. A panic-stricken
Justinian was preparing to flee in disguise and was
restrained only with difficulty by the empress Theodora,

who preferred death to flight. If she had to die, she said, the imperial purple would be the noblest winding-sheet.

Fortunately, Belisarius was present in the palace. He rallied his soldiers – principally Scandinavian mercenaries – and marched on the Hippodrome, bursting in and taking the mob by surprise. Meanwhile the commander of the imperial bodyguard, an elderly and deceptively frail-looking Armenian eunuch named Narses, had stationed his men at the exits with orders to cut down all who tried to escape. What followed was a massacre. The number of dead is said by Procopius to have been thirty thousand. It was a heavy price to have paid, but Belisarius had almost certainly saved the lives of the imperial couple. He may well have saved the Byzantine Empire. His reputation was made.

In the period of relative domestic tranquillity that followed the riots, Justinian was at last able to concentrate on the primary objective of his reign: the recovery of the Roman Empire of the west from the Vandals and the Goths. And Belisarius was, he knew, the one man to whom this task could confidently be entrusted. He sailed first to Carthage, then capital of the North African Vandal kingdom occupying roughly the site of modern Tunis, where a nobleman named Gelimer had recently seized the throne. On the flagship, together with Belisarius himself, were

Procopius – serving as his military secretary – and, as usual, his wife Antonina.

Antonina nearly always accompanied Belisarius on his campaigns – perhaps so that he could keep an eye on her. Her background had been not unlike that of the empress, of whom she was a close friend. The relationship was valuable to them both. Theodora knew that she could always control Belisarius – who by now, after Justinian himself, was the most powerful man in the empire – through his wife, while Antonina could rely on the empress to protect her from the consequences of her countless adulteries. Like Theodora, Antonina had also been brought up in the theatre and circus. Both women had a lurid past; but, unlike the empress, Antonina had made no attempt to reform her character after her prestigious marriage. At least twelve years older than her husband – Procopius claims twenty-two – she had already had several children, in and out of wedlock, and in the coming years was to cause her husband much embarrassment and, occasionally, anguish; but his love for her remained, none the less, deep and enduring.

The conquest of Carthage

On Midsummer Day 533 the great expedition set sail from the Golden Horn. It consisted of five thousand cavalry and twice as many infantry – at least half of them barbarian mercenaries, mostly Huns but with a strong contingent of Scandinavians. They travelled in a fleet of five hundred transports, escorted by ninety-two *dromons*. (The *dromon* was the smallest type of Byzantine warship, carrying a crew of only twenty rowers at a single bank of oars.)

After brief stops in Sicily and Malta, the expedition landed at the easternmost point of the Tunisian coast and headed north towards Carthage. The army of the Vandal king was waiting near the tenth milestone, where the road from the south entered a narrow valley. His plan of attack was threefold: his brother Ammatas would attack the vanguard, his nephew Gibamund would sweep down on the centre and he himself would deal with the rear. Unfortunately for Gelimer, his communications let him down. Ammatas moved too soon; Belisarius was ready for him, and in the ensuing battle Ammatas was killed. The soldiers around him lost heart and fled. The flanking attack was no more successful; the Byzantine cavalry was composed of Huns, hideous and implacable. The Vandals took one look and ran for their lives. All now depended on Gelimer. At first he seemed to have the advantage – but then he came upon his brother's body. He refused to move until he had seen the corpse carried from the field. Belisarius seized his chance, bore down upon the Vandal host and scattered it. Carthage lay open.

On Sunday 15 September the victorious general made

his formal entry into the city. Gelimer, however, was still at large, regrouping his army and rallying support from the local Punic and Berber tribes; one more battle was necessary before Belisarius' task was done. It was fought in mid December. This time it was Belisarius who took the initiative, charging three times into the thick of the Vandal ranks. Once again Gelimer hesitated; his soldiers, seeing his indecision, began to draw back – and once again the Huns charged, quickly turning the Vandal retreat into a rout. Gelimer fled back into the wilds of Numidia, his army pell-mell after him. The imperial army lost fifty men, the Vandals eight hundred. This time it was the end. Belsarius advanced to the city of Hippo – which opened its gates at once – and took possession of the royal treasure. Then, with a train of Vandal prisoners behind him and his wagons loaded with plunder, he returned to Carthage.

It was typical of him that on the occupation of that city he should have given his men strict orders to respect the local people who, despite a century of occupation, technically remained Roman citizens like themselves. There was no swagger, no insolence or arrogance; everything bought in the shops was properly paid for. On his return to Constantinople Belisarius was awarded a triumph – the first non-imperial recipient to be granted such an honour for five and a half centuries, and the last ever to receive one.

The conquest of Italy

Belisarius was now ready to take command on the second stage of the emperor's master plan: the reconquest of Italy. It was to prove a good deal harder than the first. He sailed for Sicily in the summer of 535 with seven thousand five hundred men, and took the island almost without a struggle; the only show of resistance was made by the Gothic garrison in Panormus (Palermo). Belisarius is reported to have massed his fleet so close inshore that its masts rose above the town walls. He then filled the ships' boats with men and hoisted them up to the yard-arms, whence they could fire their arrows down on the defenders and, we are told, leap directly down on to the battlements. Before he could cross the straits, however, he was called urgently to Africa to deal with a serious mutiny in the imperial army of occupation; not until the late spring of 536 did he land on the Italian mainland.

Belisarius' advance was once again unchallenged until he reached Naples, the citizens of which defended their city stoutly for three weeks. He had warned them that if they resisted he would be unable to restrain his semi-savage barbarians from the murder, rapine and pillage that they would consider their just reward, and the Neapolitans now paid a heavy price for their heroism. The Huns, pagan to a man, had no compunction in burning down the churches in which their intended victims had sought asylum.

The next objective was Rome. King Vitiges – an elderly

general whom the Gothic leaders had recently appointed
to the throne – had announced that he would not be
defending the city, and Pope Silverius had accordingly opened
the gates to the imperial army; but if the Pope and his flock
imagined that by so doing they had avoided the miseries
of a siege they were to be disappointed; Belisarius enter-
tained no such delusion. He suspected, with good reason,
that Vitiges was merely giving himself an opportunity to
consolidate – and he was right. The siege that followed
lasted for a year and nine days, during which time the
besiegers cut all the aqueducts, dealing Rome a blow from
which it would not recover for a millennium. But the walls
of Rome held. Not until March 538 did the Goths finally
withdraw; as they retreated northwards along the Via
Flaminia, Belisarius pursued them and fell on them at the
Milvian Bridge – the same spot where Constantine the Great
had routed the forces of his rival Maxentius 226 years before
– leaving several hundred drowned in the Tiber.

A few days later the general himself headed north;
but trouble awaited him. While he was at Ancona, reinforcements arrived from Constantinople under the
command of the most powerful member of the imperial
court – the eunuch Narses. Narses was no soldier. His life
had been spent in the palace, and even his command of
the bodyguard had been more of a domestic appointment
than a military one. His presence can thus have had but

one explanation: Justinian was beginning to have doubts about Belisarius. He was too brilliant, too successful, too rich – and, being still only in his early thirties, too young. He was, in short, the stuff of which emperors were made; more disturbing still, he was the stuff of men who made themselves emperors. The eunuch's instructions confirmed the fact. He was to obey Belisarius in all things, *so far as seemed consistent with the public weal*. In other words, he could overrule him in all major decisions of state policy. His arrival effectively split the army down the middle. Some generals remained loyal to Belisarius, whereas others would obey only Narses. It was as a direct result of this division that the imperial garrison in Milan was starved into surrender, all the male citizens massacred by the Goths and not a house left standing.

The catastrophe had one useful consequence. Justinian immediately summoned Narses back to the capital leaving Belisarius, meanwhile, to move on to Ravenna. The city was already surrounded – on the landward side by his army; on the seaward by the imperial fleet, which had set up a virtually impenetrable blockade. One night a secret emissary arrived in the imperial camp with an extraordinary proposal: Vitiges would resign his throne to Belisarius, on the understanding that the latter should then proclaim himself Emperor of the West. Many an imperial general would have leapt at the chance. The bulk of the army would probably have supported him, and with the Goths at his back he would have been more than capable of dealing with any punitive expedition from Constantinople. But Belisarius was nothing if not loyal; in the words of Procopius, 'he hated the name of usurper with a perfect hatred', and it is unlikely that he gave the Goths' proposal a moment's consideration. Here, however, was an ideal means of bringing the war to a quick and victorious end. He accepted. The gates were duly opened, and the army marched in.

But there was no proclamation. The Goths soon realized that they had been deceived. Vitiges and his court were led into captivity, but there is no indication that Belisarius suffered any qualms of conscience. The proposal itself had been perfidious, and he had saved untold bloodshed on both sides. His triumph after the capture of Carthage had been magnificent; how much more so might be his reward for returning the whole Italian peninsula, including Ravenna and even Rome itself, to the empire?

The emperor's jealousy

Alas, he was disappointed. Every victory he won now increased the emperor's jealousy. There was certainly no feeling of victory in the air when in June 540 he returned home to learn that the Persian king Chosroes had captured Antioch. His presence would be required, not in the Hippodrome, but on the eastern front. And another shock, too, awaited him. Antonina, who had not accompanied him to Italy, had embarked on a passionate liaison with her godson, actively abetted by the empress herself. This delayed him for some time in Constantinople; but the Persian campaign was anyway to prove indecisive, owing to an outbreak in both camps of bubonic plague. In 542 Chosroes was forced to retire; but Belisarius returned to more trouble. Justinian had succumbed to the epidemic, and Theodora had taken control. Accused of having enriched himself unduly with barbarian treasure, Belisarius found his household disbanded; anything of any value that he possessed had been transferred to the imperial palace. Not until the emperor's recovery the following year was he partially restored to favour.

And just in time: under their young king Totila, the Goths in Italy had retaliated and had already recaptured Naples. Belisarius was despatched back to the peninsula – but with a lesser rank, little authority, less money and only a handful of inexperienced troops. He did his best, but by now it was no longer just the Goths who were hostile; it was virtually the whole population. Justinian reluctantly sent reinforcements, but Belisarius was unable to prevent Totila from capturing Rome. Although fighting continued up and down the peninsula, it was soon clear that a stalemate had been reached. After the glory of his first Italian campaign, the second had brought only frustration and disappointment. But he had saved Italy, at least temporarily, for the empire. He had laid the foundations for re-conquest, making it easy for his old rival Narses – possessed of all the resources for which he himself had appealed in vain – to win the victories that should rightfully have been his own. In 549 Belisarius returned disconsolately to Constantinople.

Last years

Justinian gave him a warm welcome. The two had been kept apart by Theodora, who had continually poisoned her husband's mind against Belisarius; but Theodora had died in 548, and with her death his trust had quickly revived. The general's career, however, was drawing to its close. He was to fight two more minor campaigns, regaining Corsica from the Visigoths in Spain and successfully dealing with a Hunnish tribe known as the Kotrigurs, who had suddenly swarmed into imperial territory, advancing eastward through Thrace to within 20 miles of the capital. By this time he was in his middle fifties, but although it was ten years since he had seen serious action in the field, he had lost none of his energy or his tactical imagination. With only a few hundred men at his disposal he organized a brilliant guerrilla campaign, drawing the Kotrigurs into a carefully planned ambush and leaving four hundred dead where they had fallen. It must have been a considerable surprise to him when Justinian awarded himself a triumph, suggesting a great and glorious victory for which Belisarius alone had been responsible. That old jealousy that had always smouldered in his heart had suddenly flared up again, for the first time since Theodora's day.

Belisarius doubtless took note, and retreated once more into the background. Even then, probably no one was more surprised than he when, in the autumn of 562, several distinguished citizens were accused of plotting against the emperor's life, and one of them named him as being among those implicated. Nothing, of course, was ever proved; but he was shorn of all his dignities and privileges, and lived for eight months in a state of disgrace until Justinian, finally persuaded of his innocence, reinstated him. (It was presumably this incident that gave rise to the legend of his being blinded and thrown out into the streets with a begging-bowl. The earliest authority for this story dates from more than five centuries later, however, and can safely be rejected.) After his final return to favour it is pleasant to record that Belisarius lived out his life in tranquillity and comfort, dying in March 565 aged about 60. Antonina, now possibly well into her eighties, survived him.

After fifteen centuries, the name of Belisarius is still remembered as one of the great generals in world history. Was his reputation deserved? It is not easy to judge – we simply do not know enough about him, either as a strategist or as a tactician. The only real evidence we have is the evidence of his success in almost every military expedition that he ever undertook. The exception is, of course, his second Italian campaign; but here the blame can be laid squarely on the emperor himself. Had Justinian conquered his instinctive – but wholly unjustified – mistrust of his greatest general, had he given him not only the authority and the troops he needed but also his fullest trust, there can be little doubt that the second campaign would have been as victorious as the first, and that of Narses would have been unnecessary. On the other hand, the story – which Robert Graves turned into the superb novel, *Count Belisarius* – would have been far less interesting. Military history provides few examples of a career in which human frailty plays so significant a part.

MUHAMMAD

570–632

EFRAIM KARSH

'I WAS ORDERED TO FIGHT ALL MEN until they say "There is no god but Allah".' With these final words, the Prophet Muhammad summed up not only the international vision of the faith he brought to the world but also his own life story and political career.

Born in AD 570 in the merchant town of Mecca in the Hijaz, the northwestern part of the Arabian peninsula, Muhammad ibn Abdullah is believed to have experienced his first divine revelation at the age of 40. Initially the Meccans viewed his claim to prophetic powers with indifference, but this turned to outright hostility as Muhammad launched a frontal assault on their most cherished beliefs and values, deriding their gods, emphasizing the perdition of their ancestors who had died in disbelief, and demanding an unequivocal profession of belief in Allah, as Muhammad called his god, and total submission (the meaning of 'Islam' in Arabic) to His will.

For a while Muhammad managed to hold his ground, but as his position became increasingly untenable he began to look for an alternative home from which to spread his divine message. As early as 615 he sent a group of his followers to Ethiopia to escape persecution and to explore the possibility of cooperation with its Christian king. But Ethiopia was too remote and isolated to serve as a permanent base of operations, so Muhammad began to look closer to home. After a humiliating rebuff by the notables of Ta'if, a hilly town some 60 miles southeast of Mecca, and a string of abortive overtures to neighbouring Bedouin tribes, Muhammad eventually reached an agreement with a group of Muslim converts from the town of Yathrib, some 275 miles north of Mecca, who gave him their oath of allegiance and undertook to fight with him against his enemies. In the early summer of 622, about seventy of his followers quietly left Mecca in small groups for Yathrib. A few months later, on 24 September, Muhammad himself arrived in the town.

From preacher to leader

The *Hijra* – the migration of Muhammad and his followers from Mecca to Medina ('the city'), as Yathrib would hitherto

be called, was a watershed in Islamic history, aptly designated after the Prophet's death as the official starting point
of the Muslim era. Almost immediately, Muhammad was
transformed from a private preacher into a political and military leader and the head of a rapidly expanding community,
while Islam graduated from being a persecuted cult into a
major religious and political force in the Arabian peninsula.

Muhammad created this inextricable link between religious authority and political power in the 'Constitution of
Medina', set up shortly after the *Hijra*, which organized
his local followers (*Ansar*) and those who had migrated
with him from Mecca (*Muhajirun*) into 'one community
(*umma*) to the exclusion of all [individual] men', designed
to act as a unified whole against external enemies and
internal dissenters. The document wisely refrained from
specifically abolishing existing tribal structures and practices, yet it broke with past tradition by substituting religion for blood as the source of social and political
organization, and by making Allah, through the aegis of
His chosen apostle, the supreme and exclusive sovereign:
'If any dispute or controversy likely to cause trouble should
arise it must be referred to God and to Muhammad, the
apostle of God. God accepts what is nearest to piety and
goodness in this document.'

Having established himself as the *umma*'s absolute
leader, Muhammad spent most of his Medina years fighting

external enemies and domestic opponents. During the first eighteen months after the *Hijra* he carried out seven raids on merchant caravans as they were making their way to Mecca. This was an attempt to build up the wealth and prestige of his followers, who had lost their livelihood as a result of their move to Medina, and to weaken Mecca's economic lifeline. It was also the logical thing to do. The caravans from Syria to Mecca passed between Medina and the Red Sea coast and were militarily unprotected, which made them easy prey for potential raiders who could intercept them at a substantial distance from their base and then disappear before the arrival of a rescue party. Yet as the Muslims lacked military experience, having themselves been merchants rather than fighters, they normally returned home empty-handed. It was only in January 624 that Muhammad scored his first real success. A small raiding party of eight to ten Muslims, disguised as pilgrims, ambushed a convoy at Nakhla, southeast of Mecca, killed one of its attendants, captured another two (the fourth attendant managed to escape), and led the caravan to Medina. Yet as the raid occurred during the holy month of Rajab, when bloodshed was forbidden according to pagan convention, it was met with a wave of indignation in Medina. The embarrassed Muhammad claimed that his orders had been misunderstood and waited for a while before distributing the booty. Eventually a new Qur'anic revelation appeared to justify the raid, and two months later the incident was all but forgotten as a Muslim contingent headed by Muhammad himself routed a numerically superior Meccan force near the oasis of Badr, southwest of Medina, carrying home substantial booty and a few dozen prisoners.

Eliminating potential rivals

The Battle of Badr boosted Muhammad's position in Medina and allowed him to move against his local opponents. The first to find themselves in the firing line were Medina's three Jewish tribes (the town had originally been established by Jewish refugees fleeing Roman persecution and their local Arab proselytes), whose refusal to acknowledge the validity of Muhammad's revelations weakened the appeal of the nascent faith, and whose affluence made them a natural target for plunder. Using a trivial incident as a pretext, he expelled the weakest of these tribes, the Qainuqa, from the town and divided its properties among the Muhajirun. (Muhammad had originally meant to kill the Qainuqa men but was dissuaded from doing so by a local sheikh.) In March 625, after a Muslim defeat in the Battle of Mount Uhud, near Medina, had dented Muhammad's prestige in the eyes of the neighbouring Bedouin tribes, it was the turn of the second tribe, the Nadir, to pay the price of the Prophet's setback: after a few weeks' siege they were driven from the city and their lands were taken over by the Muslims. The last and most powerful Jewish tribe – the Quraiza – suffered more profusely following the abortive Meccan siege of Medina in the spring of 627. Charged with collaboration with the enemy, the tribe's six to eight hundred men were brought in small groups to trenches dug the previous day, made to sit on the edge, then beheaded one by one and their bodies thrown in. The women and children were sold into slavery and the money they fetched, together with the proceeds from the tribe's possessions, was divided among the Muslims.

On to the offensive

By now Muhammad had consolidated his power to a considerable extent. The Uhud defeat, where over seventy Muslims were killed (including some of Muhammad's oldest and most trusted followers and his formidable uncle Hamza), was a humbling experience for the Prophet. Yet the Meccans failed to achieve their strategic goal of destroying the *umma* and were increasingly forced to rely on a network of alliances with Bedouin tribes in their fight against the Muslims. Muhammad, however, was not to be easily overcome. He managed to maintain the loyalty of the tribes around Medina, conducted a string of successful raids throughout the peninsula, and even resorted to the assassination of political rivals. These efforts did not prevent the Meccans from forming a grand alliance against Muhammad, yet they kept many potential participants out of this grouping, thus ensuring a more equal balance of forces in the final encounter.

This came at the end of March 627, when a 10,000-strong Meccan–Bedouin force advanced northward and laid siege to Medina, only to be confronted with a number of tactical surprises. To begin with, the Muslims had dug a trench around the city wherever it lay open to cavalry attack, a defence method hitherto unknown in Arabia. This caused considerable operational confusion among the Meccans, whose hopes of victory largely rested on their superior cavalry. This was further compounded by Muhammad's negotiations with the main Bedouin group in the coalition, the Ghatafan, aimed at bribing them out of the war. While the talks came to naught, since the Medinese considered such a deal to be beneath their dignity, the Ghatafans had been sufficiently compromised in the eyes of their Meccan allies to preclude a cohesive military effort. After two weeks of abortive attempts to break the resistance of the far more committed and disciplined Muslims, the coalition disintegrated and its members went their separate ways.

The Hudaibiya agreement

With the failure of the siege of Medina, Mecca ceased to pose a threat to Muhammad, and in the spring of 628 he felt confident enough to attempt to make the 'little pilgrimage' (*umra*) to his native town. As the Meccans vowed to prevent him from doing so, Muhammad stopped in the small nature spot of Hudaibiya, some 10 miles northwest of the town, where the two sides negotiated a ten-year truce. The Muslims were given the right to carry out the pilgrimage the following year and the Meccans agreed to vacate the town for three days in order to allow them to perform their religious duties unhindered. Muhammad agreed to send back anyone who came to him from Mecca without the explicit permission of his guardian, while the Meccans were not obliged to reciprocate this move.

Many Muslims viewed these conditions as an unnecessary and humiliating surrender. They were particularly resentful of Muhammad waiving any reference to himself in the treaty as Allah's Messenger, and were indignant at the loss of booty attending the stoppage of raids on the caravans to Mecca that was implicit in the agreement. To deflect this simmering discontent, Muhammad found a handy scapegoat that had served him well in the past: the Arabian Jews. Having eliminated the Jewish presence in Medina, he now turned to the affluent Jewish community in the oasis of Khaibar, some 90 miles north of the town. After a month of siege the Jews surrendered. They were then stripped of their possessions before being granted free passage with their women and children. Yet when Muhammad was unable to find the necessary manpower for tilling the site, he relented and allowed the Jews to stay on their land in return for an annual tribute of half of their produce. A number of neighbouring Jewish communities surrendered shortly afterwards under the same terms, thus laying the ground for what would become the common arrangement between the *umma* and its non-Muslim subjects (or *Dhimmis*).

In the end, Muhammad proved more far-sighted than his critics. Far from diverting him from the ultimate goal of occupying his native town, the Hudaibiya agreement actually turned out to be a Trojan horse, facilitating the attainment of his objective. Besides putting the *umma* on a par with Mecca, the treaty gave both signatories a free hand in their dealings with the nomadic tribes. On the face of it, this provision was of a reciprocal nature. In fact it worked in Muhammad's favour, as increasing numbers of tribes, including some that had previously been aligned with Mecca, sought to associate themselves with the *umma*.

The Battle of Mecca

When, in 629, Muhammad performed the deferred 'little pilgrimage', it made a great impression. A fresh influx of converts flocked to the Prophet's camp, and Muhammad took immediate advantage of the opportunity. Using the killing of a Muslim by a Meccan in the course of a private dispute as a pretext for reneging on the Hudaibiya agreement, on 1

January 630 he set out from Medina at the head of a formidable force. Ten days later, without offering any serious resistance, Mecca surrendered.

The capture of Mecca was the ultimate prize for Muhammad. Less than eight years after his undignified departure, the ridiculed and despised preacher had returned as the city's undisputed master and Arabia's most powerful leader. In the course of the following year a steady stream of tribal dignitaries from all corners of the peninsula would flock to the warrior-prophet to profess their subservience. For many of them, this was more a pragmatic response to the newly established balance of power than a true conversion to Islam. Yet being the astute politician and statesman that he was, Muhammad was prepared initially to content himself with a merely verbal profession of faith and payment of tribute. Paganism, as a social and political phenomenon, was virtually a spent force, so there was no need to bring about an instantaneous transformation of these independent-minded tribes. As long as they gave him their political obeisance and financial tribute, he could afford to wait and allow the socioeconomic dynamics, which now favoured Islam, to run their natural course. Even in Mecca Muhammad refrained from following up his victory with mass conversions, leaving the population very much to its own devices, and incorporating many of the local leaders into his administration. Some of them were given handsome rewards, including his arch-enemy and the town's grand old man Abu Sufian ibn Harb and his two sons, Yazid and Mu'awiya, the future founder of the Umayyad dynasty.

Preparing for Allah's empire

As we have seen, the formation of the *umma* created a sharp dichotomy between Muslims and 'infidels' and presupposed a permanent state of war that would only end with the establishment of a global political order in which all humankind would live under Muslim rule as either believers or subject communities. In order to achieve this goal it is incumbent on all free, male, adult Muslims to carry out an uncompromising struggle 'in the path of Allah', or jihad. As the fourteenth-century historian and philosopher Abdel Rahman ibn Khaldun wrote: 'In the Muslim community, the jihad is a religious duty because of the universalism of the Islamic mission and the obligation [to convert] everybody to Islam either by persuasion or by force.'

Muhammad devised the concept of jihad shortly after his migration to Medina as a means of enticing his local followers to raid Meccan caravans, and he developed and amplified this concept with the expansion of his political ambitions until it became a rallying call for world domination. The Qur'anic revelations during this period abound with verses extolling the virtues of jihad, as do the countless sayings and traditions (*hadith*) attributed to the Prophet.

Those who participate in this holy pursuit are to be gener-
ously rewarded, both in this life and in the afterworld,
where they will reside in shaded and ever-green gardens,
indulged by pure and virtuous women. Accordingly, those
killed while waging jihad should not be mourned: 'Allah
has bought from the believers their soul and their possessions against the gift of Paradise; they fight in the path of
Allah; they kill and are killed . . . So rejoice in the bargain
you have made with Him; that is the mighty triumph.'

But the doctrine's appeal was not just otherworldly.
By forbidding fighting and raiding within the *umma*,
Muhammad deprived the Arabian tribes of a traditional
source of livelihood. For a time, the Prophet could rely on
booty from non-Muslims as a substitute for the lost war
spoils, which is why he never went out of his way to
convert all of the tribes seeking a place in his Pax Islamica.
Yet given his belief in the supremacy of Islam and his relentless commitment to its widest possible dissemination, he
could hardly deny conversion to those wishing to undertake it. Once the whole of Arabia had become Muslim, a
new source of wealth and an alternative outlet would have
to be found for the aggressive energies of the Arabian tribes:
it was, in the Fertile Crescent and the Levant.

As early as the summer of 626, Muhammad sent a
small force to fight some hostile tribes in the area of Dumat
al-Jandal, some 500 miles northeast of Medina. The ease

and rapidity of the operation seemed to have whetted Muhammad's appetite, and in the following year he sent his freedman and adopted son Zaid to Syria on a trading mission. This failed to produce concrete results, but another mission in the same year resulted in a treaty of alliance with the Dumat prince.

At this stage, Muhammad was apparently not interested in occupying these territories on a permanent basis, or converting their largely Christian populations to Islam. Yet during the last three years of his life he attempted to incorporate the tribes on the road to Syria into his Islamic order and even made overtures to tribes in the direction of Iraq. Muhammad was also reported to have sent emissaries to a number of prominent Arab and non-Arab rulers, including the Byzantine, Iranian, and Ethiopian emperors, with the demand that they embrace Islam. In October 630 he ventured toward the Byzantine frontier at the head of a 30,000-strong army. Advancing as far as the oasis of Tabuq, some 500 miles north of Medina, Muhammad camped there for twenty days, during which time he negotiated a peace treaty with the Christian prince of Aylah (the biblical Eilat), at the northern tip of the Gulf of Aqaba. In return for an oath of allegiance and an annual tribute, the Christians were placed under the protection of the *umma* and granted freedom of worship. At ⋯ point Muhammad decided to return to Medina, having ⋯ly realized the impracticability of his Byzantine ambitions. Yet this did not imply the disappearance of his interest in northern expansion. No sooner had he returned from his pilgrimage than he began preparations for a campaign in Transjordan and southern Palestine, which were only brought to an abrupt end by his sudden death on 8 June 632. And while it is unlikely that Muhammad had imagined the full scope of Islam's future expansion, let alone planned it in detail, he left behind a new universal religion and a community of believers organized on its basis – an unprecedented phenomenon in Arabian history that not only accounted for the prophet's military exploits but also made Islam's worldwide expansion inevitable.

CHARLEMAGNE

742–814

JOHN HAYWOOD

NO RULER OF THE EARLY MIDDLE AGES has made a greater impression on posterity than the emperor Charlemagne (r. 768–814). Even within his own lifetime he was called Charles the Great, or in Latin Carolus Magnus, *from which the Old French name Charlemagne derives. In a lifetime of constant campaigning, Charlemagne united a larger area of western Europe into a single state than any ruler since of the demise of the Western Roman Empire. After his death he attained legendary stature and is claimed as a national hero by both the French and the Germans.*

Charlemagne was born in 742, the eldest son of Pippin III, then mayor of the Franks. He was given the usual educa-
~~f~~ an aristocratic Frank, being taught to ride, hunt and
~~as~~ also a man of considerable intellect who spoke

Latin fluently and had a keen interest in astronomy and theology. Pippin's elevation to kingship in 751, however, dramatically changed Charlemagne's prospects. On Pippin's death in 768, the Frankish kingdom was divided equally between Charlemagne and his younger brother Carloman. The two brothers did not get on well, and when, soon after his accession, Charlemagne faced a serious rebellion in Aquitaine and asked for Carloman's help, this was refused. Charlemagne gathered what forces he could and moved swiftly and decisively to crush the rebellion. When Duke Lupus of Gascony gave sanctuary to the fugitive leader of the Aquitainians, Charlemagne invaded and forced him to submit to Frankish rule. Charlemagne had made his first conquest. Two years later, Carloman died and the Frankish kingdom was reunited under Charlemagne's sole rule: he was now indisputably the most powerful ruler in western Europe.

The conquest of Italy

Charlemagne's first conquest after he became sole king of the Franks was the Lombard kingdom of Italy. Early in 773 envoys arrived from Pope Hadrian I (r. 772–795) asking for Charlemagne's help against King Desiderius of the Lombards, who had seized papal lands. Charlemagne's father had only become king with the support of the papacy, so this was a summons he could not ignore. Hoping to force Desiderius to divide his forces, Charlemagne led one army into Italy over the Mont Cenis Pass, while sending another through the Great St Bernard Pass. Charlemagne's weight of numbers counted for little in the narrow Alpine valleys, however, and both his armies found their way blocked by Lombard defences. After a brief stand-off, Charlemagne's scouts found an alternative route through the mountains; in order to prevent himself being outflanked, Desiderius withdrew his forces to his heavily fortified capital at Pavia, being followed there by Charlemagne, who laid siege to the city.

The Lombards had faced Frankish invasions before and knew from experience that they always withdrew in the autumn to avoid getting cut off in Italy when winter snows closed the Alpine passes. As it was already September when Desiderius retreated to Pavia, he was probably confident that the siege would be short. It was a fatal miscalculation: Charlemagne had no intention of withdrawing. With Desiderius and his army bottled up in Pavia, he was free to spend the winter taking over the rest of the Lombard kingdom. Pavia finally surrendered in June 774. The Lombards submitted to Charlemagne, and Desiderius was deposed and imprisoned in a monastery. Though Charlemagne returned the lands seized by Desiderius to the papacy, he took the title 'Patrician of the Romans' and left Hadrian in no doubt as to who was the ruler of Rome. This was an important moment in Charlemagne's reign, paving the way as it did for his assumption of the imperial title in 800.

The Saxon wars

In the opinion of Charlemagne's friend and biographer Einhard, 'no war ever fought by the Franks was more prolonged, more full of atrocities and more demanding of effort than the conquest of Saxony'. It took dozens of campaigns spread over thirty-three years before Saxon resistance was completely extinguished. In the eighth century, the Saxons were still a decentralized tribal people, divided into four main groups: the Westphalians, the Angrarians, the Eastphalians and the Nordliudi. Despite the efforts of Anglo-Saxon missionaries, who felt duty bound to bring the benefits of Christianity to their continental cousins, the Saxons were still committed pagans, and there was a long history of conflict between them and the Franks. The Saxons frequently raided across the border and the Franks retaliated by invading and imposing tribute, which the Saxons stopped paying at the earliest opportunity. From the beginning of his reign, Charlemagne was convinced that the only way to reach a lasting settlement with the Saxons was to conquer them and to convert them to Christianity by whatever means necessary.

Charlemagne began the conquest of the Saxons in 772 by capturing the most important of their pagan shrines. He plundered the shrine of its treasure and provocatively destroyed its great idol, the Irminsul, to demonstrate the superior power of the Christian god. The need to intervene against the Lombards in Italy prevented him from following up this campaign until 775, and by 777, when the Saxon war leader Widukind fled to Denmark, Charlemagne felt his control of Saxony was secure enough to hold the annual general assembly of the kingdom there (at Paderborn). Charlemagne's declaration of victory was premature. When in 778 the Saxons heard that Charlemagne had suffered a defeat in Spain, they rebelled, massacred the Frankish garrisons, burned churches and ravaged the Rhineland. More Frankish campaigns followed. Pitched battles were rare; the Saxons generally avoided battle with the better equipped Franks, preferring to fight a guerrilla war. Charlemagne's strategy was usually to establish a camp deep in Saxon territory and send out fast-moving cavalry units, called *scaras*, to ravage the surrounding countryside and wear down Saxon resistance.

By 780 the Saxons again seemed to be pacified. Charlemagne divided Saxony up into counties, the normal unit of local government in the Frankish kingdoms, and punitive laws were introduced to suppress paganism. But once again Charlemagne was premature. In 782 a new rebellion broke out under Widukind, who had returned from exile, and the Saxons inflicted a serious defeat on a

Frankish army in the Süntel mountains, which had rushed into battle without adequate scouting. As the Frankish royal annalist commented, 'since the approach had gone badly, badly also went the battle'. The Franks were surrounded and few escaped: the dead included twenty-six high-ranking members of the nobility. Charlemagne's revenge was swift and brutal: he ordered the execution of 4,500 Saxon prisoners at Verden. Widukind escaped capture and continued to lead resistance until 785, when he finally submitted and accepted baptism. Saxony enjoyed seven years of peace, but in 792 another widespread revolt broke out while Charlemagne was campaigning in the east. Once again churches and the clergy were attacked, but this was the Saxons' last effort. By 797 Charlemagne had broken Saxon resistance south of the Elbe. Resistance continued north of the Elbe until 805, however, when Charlemagne finally deported and dispersed most of the population.

It may seem surprising that Charlemagne took so long to subdue the tribal Saxons when he was able to conquer the wealthy and centralized Lombard kingdom in less than ten months. However, in the early Middle Ages, political centralization was not always the advantage it seems. In a centralized kingdom, where power and leadership were concentrated in few hands, an invader could simply remove the political elite and then use the institutions of the state to control the rest of the population. This is what happened to the Lombards (and also to the English in 1066). After deposing Desiderius, Charlemagne simply took his place, adopting the title king of the Lombards, while the Lombard kingdom kept its separate identity, laws and institutions. In Saxony, this approach was impossible. The Saxons had many different chiefs, so there was little chance of eliminating the elite in a single campaign, there was no-one with whom to negotiate a lasting peace, nor were there any institutions of government to be taken over. Charlemagne probably did not appreciate this, apparently believing, wrongly, that the submission of one Saxon tribe could be binding on the others.

Disaster at Roncesvalles

As well as conquering the Lombards and Saxons, Charlemagne campaigned against the Avars, Spanish Moors, Bretons, Bavarians and Slavs, Venetians and Byzantines, approximately doubling the size of the Frankish kingdom. Other than towards the end of his long reign, when his health was failing, there were few years in which he did not lead a military campaign in person, and only one when a Frankish army was not campaigning somewhere on the empire's borders. The year in question was 790, when the royal annalist remarked simply that 'this year, the Franks were quiet'.

Charlemagne was undoubtedly a great military leader but, ironically, his most celebrated campaign was also his greatest failure. In 777 Ibn al-Arabi, the Moorish governor of Zaragoza in northern Spain, rebelled against his overlord, the emir of Córdoba, and offered to hand over his territory to Charlemagne in return for his protection. The following year, Charlemagne invaded Spain in massive strength. He himself led one army across the western Pyrenees from Aquitaine and advanced on Zaragoza to enforce Ibn al-Arabi's offer of submission. A second Frankish army crossed the Pyrenees from Provence and approached Zaragoza from the east. After receiving hostages from Zaragoza, Charlemagne returned to Aquitaine over the pass of Roncesvalles, where his rearguard was ambushed and massacred by the Basques. It was a major disaster, with several important nobles among the dead, including Roland, the count of the Breton March. After the battle the Basques melted away into the mountains, frustrating Charlemagne's attempts to exact reprisals against them. The battle was later immortalized in the Old French epic *The Song of Roland*, though a generous amount of poetic licence has transmuted the Spanish campaign into a prototype crusade. The expedition produced no lasting results to compensate for this defeat – Ibn al-Arabi soon went back on his word and Charlemagne never again led an expedition to Spain. However, through the efforts of the margraves (border lords who were given considerable freedom of military action) and, later, his son Louis the Pious, the frontier was pushed slowly south. The capture of

Barcelona in 801, after a two-year siege, firmly established Frankish power south of the Pyrenees.

Military service

All freemen were expected to attend the annual general assembly of the kingdom and all were liable for military service and expected to provide their own equipment. For infantry this usually comprised a spear, bow, shield, mail coat and helmet. In addition to these arms, horsemen were also expected to own two swords. These duties were beyond the means of poorer freemen and various measures were used to ease the burden on them. However, even in Charlemagne's time unscrupulous lords deliberately made repeated demands for military service to impoverish freemen and force them into serfdom. For administrative purposes, Charlemagne's empire was divided into around six hundred counties, each governed by a count, whose responsibility it was to raise the levy in his county, lead the men to the assembly and command them in battle. The core of Charlemagne's armies was made up of his military vassals. These were men who had commended themselves, and become sworn dependants of the king in return for which they received a benefice, usually an estate, so that they could devote themselves to military service. Such agreements were the basis of what has become known as feudalism (from *foedus*: 'agreement').

The Avar campaign

Pitched battles were relatively rare events in early medieval warfare. Charlemagne is known to have led an army in battle in person on only two occasions, both in 783 and, though he won both, nothing is known about the tactics he used. His general strategic approach to campaigning is much clearer. As ruler of the largest kingdom in western Europe, Charlemagne had considerable manpower at his disposal. This enabled him to deploy two or more separate armies on major campaigns, so forcing opponents to divide their forces. Meticulous planning was a characteristic of Charlemagne's campaigns and armies set out with three months' supplies in waterproofed wagons, siege engines and entrenching tools. Where possible, fleets were deployed on inland waterways to transport troops and supplies.

The most meticulously planned of Charlemagne's campaigns were those he fought against the Avars, a pagan nomad people who had settled in Pannonia (roughly modern Hungary) in the sixth century. Charlemagne's first Avar campaign in 791 involved a total of three armies. Two of these armies were gathered at Regensburg on the Danube. One army was ordered to march along the north bank of the river; the other, under Charlemagne's personal command, along the south bank. A fleet accompanied the armies, to carry supplies and to ferry troops across the river if either army needed reinforcements, and to bypass the fortifications that the Avars had built on the riverbanks. At the Avar border the armies halted for three days of fasting and prayer to ensure that the campaign had divine support. A cavalry *scara* was sent to invade the Avar kingdom from Italy. Seeing the massive forces arrayed against them, the Avars simply abandoned their positions and for several weeks the Franks ravaged their territory at will.

Charlemagne's preparations for a follow-up campaign were even more ambitious and imaginative. These included the construction of a portable pontoon bridge and an unsuccessful attempt to link the Rhine and Danube with a canal to speed movement of troops and supplies to the front. In the event, no further major campaigns were needed. A civil war broke out among the demoralized Avars, and a Frankish army led from Italy by Duke Eric of Friuli met little opposition when it captured the Avar capital, a fortress at an unidentified location known as the Ring, in 795. A vast hoard of treasure, looted by the Avars during centuries of raiding, was carted back to Francia. The conquest of the Avar kingdom was completed in 796 by Charlemagne's son Pippin, who led another army from Italy to destroy the Ring and carry off the Avars' remaining treasure.

Imperial coronation

As Charlemagne's realm expanded, his rule became increasingly imperial in character. Much of his legislation and relations with the church were clearly modelled on the practice of the Christian Roman and Byzantine emperors. The culmination of this development came on Christmas Day 800, when Charlemagne was crowned emperor by Pope Leo III at Rome. The exact meaning of the imperial coronation has been debated by generations of historians, but it is likely that Charlemagne believed that he was restoring the Roman Empire, which, to medieval Europeans, represented the ideal of Christian unity.

A sincerely pious Christian, Charlemagne believed that he had a responsibility to defend Christendom against unbelievers and to support the church in creating an orderly and just Christian society. To this end, he was an active legislator and promoter of monasticism and learning. Today, these are seen as non-military aspects of his reign, but Charlemagne would not have recognized the distinction. Medieval Christians believed that success in all human enterprises ultimately depended on the will of God. Good laws and a well-educated clergy would encourage Charlemagne's subjects to live more Christian lives, and so win God's favour for his kingdom and his armies.

The Viking threat

By the time of Charlemagne's imperial coronation, the Frankish empire was reaching the practical limits of expansion and there were few significant territorial gains after the capture of Barcelona in 801. New threats to the empire emerged in the shape of raids by Muslim pirates in the Mediterranean and by Vikings on the North Sea and Channel coasts. Charlemagne delegated the defence of the Mediterranean coast to subordinate commanders, but he personally oversaw the preparation of defences against the Vikings. Fleets were stationed on all the major navigable rivers, and coastguard garrisons were stationed in forts at harbours and vulnerable river mouths. His decision to concentrate defences in these places shows clearly his mastery of the strategic and tactical situation.

Charlemagne understood that rivers, in particular the Rhine, Scheldt, Seine, Loire and Garonne, were the key to an effective defence against the Vikings. If raiders penetrated these river systems they could roam at will in the empire, as they were to do later in the century. Fleets and fortifications at these points could, with luck, prevent the Vikings from getting into the heartlands in the first place or, if this failed, the raiders' escape to the sea could be blocked and they could be brought to battle. Charlemagne showed similar tactical sense in stationing a fleet at Boulogne to control the bottleneck of the Straits of Dover. There was, however, little that could be done to protect the open coastline from attack. In 810 the Danish king Godfred launched a major raid on the exposed Frisian islands. Charlemagne mobilized the fleet and immediately set off for Frisia with an army, but the Danes had already set off home before all his forces had gathered. This was to be the last time that Charlemagne, now nearing 70 years old, led his troops in person.

Despite this kind of occasional failure, Charlemagne's coastal defences prevented any Viking incursions inland for over twenty years after his death. Similar success was enjoyed by Frankish naval forces in the Mediterranean against the Muslims. However, the effectiveness of Charlemagne's military system depended on the maintenance of strong royal government that ensured that subjects performed their military duties. During the years of expansion, men served willingly enough because of opportunities to plunder enemy territory. They were less enthusiastic about serving on defensive campaigns, however, when they incurred the same costs and ran the same risks but, being on friendly territory, had no opportunity for plunder. This was already a problem in Charlemagne's later years. When, under his less able successors, royal authority collapsed, so too did the defences against the Vikings and Muslim pirates and, as a result, the Frankish lands suffered years of devastating raids.

ALFRED THE GREAT

c. 849–899

JUSTIN POLLARD

WHEN ALFRED THE GREAT ASCENDED to the throne of Wessex in 871, the old kingdoms of Anglo-Saxon England stood on the brink of collapse. What had driven them to this point was a new threat that had emerged in the late eighth century and which today we call the Vikings. During the ninth century Viking raiding parties on the English coast had rapidly expanded into full-scale invasion armies, and one by one the crowns of Northumbria, East Anglia and Mercia had fallen, leaving only Alfred's Wessex. Even that came briefly under Viking control, but after months hiding on the Isle of Athelney in the Somerset Levels, Alfred managed – in a brilliant counter-attack – not only to defeat his enemy, but also to create an in-depth system of defence that would protect his people from future attacks and lay the foundations of the English nation.

Alfred was an unlikely king. As the youngest of the four sons of King Aethelwulf he is not even mentioned in the chronicles during the reigns of his two eldest brothers, and only when his closest brother Aethelred succeeded to the throne did he emerge into the somewhat dim political spotlight of the ninth century. Aethelred's Wessex was a country fighting for its life. The threat posed by the Vikings was new in both its type and its scale. Even amongst the martial Anglo-Saxon states, warfare had developed particular rules. Armies attacked other armies; soldiers fought other soldiers and fighting was reserved for the summer when food supplies were plentiful and the fyrd (the peasant levy that made up much of the army) was not required on the land. Truces and treaties were backed by religious sanctions, the swearing of Christian oaths usually being enough to ensure compliance in what was then an overwhelmingly Christian society. The Vikings neither understood nor cared for any of these rules of engagement. They operated guerrilla armies, and were happy to attack rich undefended sites such as monasteries and slaughter the occupants who, to them, simply seemed ludicrously unprepared. Caught in a tight corner they would swear Christian or pagan oaths (and even convert to Christianity, sometimes repeatedly) but just as easily break that oath as soon as their situation improved, unbothered by the threats of supernatural retribution.

Yet the Vikings were not simply the demons portrayed

in the Anglo-Saxon chronicle. Their form of warfare was not only new but also brilliantly effective in three key areas against the old Christian states of Europe. First, they moved quickly, thanks to ocean- and river-going ships, which could carry invasion forces across the open sea and could both infiltrate and exfiltrate raiding parties deep inland without being noticed. For them the rivers of England were not boundaries between states (as Anglo-Saxons tended to see them), but highways. Second, they fought practically, hitting hard but seeing no dishonour in then rapidly retreating before a response could be mounted. Third, and perhaps most important of all, they had an acute understanding of the power politics behind the fault lines in Anglo-Saxon society, playing rival aristocratic families off against each other and allowing internecine warfare to cripple their targets before simply stepping into the bloody void left behind.

The early campaigns

The history of Alfred's campaigns against the Vikings follows his slow and painful realization of their tactics and tells of how, at his lowest moment, he created a series of brilliant and innovative strategies for countering them. Alfred's first experience of the Vikings was in 865, with the arrival in England of what the chroniclers call 'The Great Heathen Army'. Unusually large for its day, this Viking warband certainly numbered in the thousands (although no accur-ate figures are available). Led by two of the most feared names in ninth-century Europe – Halfdan and Ivarr the Boneless – the Vikings landed in East Anglia where the king, Edmund, agreed to let them overwinter and prob-ably paid them tribute in return for a promise to leave. The following year, as good as their word, they left East Anglia and marched to the kingdom of Northumbria; here their real intentions became only too apparent. Dividing the rival aristocratic families, the Vikings seized control and installed their own puppet ruler, before striking back south into the once great nation of Mercia.

With a Viking army camped in Nottingham, the Mercian king Burgred decided to take the diplomatic option and paid them off. But this proved to be a major tactical mistake. The following spring the Great Heathen Army did leave Mercia, to put down a revolt in Northumbria, but they then marched straight back to where they had been paid off before – East Anglia. Here they slaughtered King Edmund (later Saint Edmund), destroyed his army and took over his kingdom. For Wessex and Mercia it was only a matter of time before Halfdan and Ivarr applied the same tactics to them.

The first assault on Wessex

In fact Aethelred's Wessex became the target the very next year. Towards the end of 870 the Great Heathen Army moved to Reading and began a series of probing raids into the Wessex heartlands. Here Alfred finally met them in a series of battles which taught both sides important lessons for the future conflict. Of these, the most notable was Ashdown, where Alfred was said to have entered battle raging like a wild boar whilst his brother Aethelred remained at his prayers. The battle was a shock for the Vikings, who had expected a weaker and less organized defence; instead they found themselves driven from the field. The West Saxons failed to follow up on this, however, perhaps due to the failing health of King Aethelred who died in the spring of 871, possibly from battle wounds. Just a month after Alfred's accession, and reinforced by another army which had arrived at Reading from the continent, the Vikings attacked Alfred at Wilton. Rather optimistically, the chroniclers give Alfred the credit for another victory, but the outcome seems to have been far less certain; his decision following the engagement to pay Halfdan to leave Wessex would suggest that, if it was a victory, it was certainly a Pyrrhic one.

In paying off the Vikings, Alfred must have been aware that he was only postponing the next battle. The following year they would want more money and, crucially, it was clear that they were intent not simply on extortion, but on invasion. Money might buy them off temporarily, but only long enough to give them time to regroup, plan and execute the inevitable attempted conquest of the country.

Yet fortune smiled on Alfred after Wilton. The Vikings did not return for the following five years, which they spent annexing Mercia. Alfred failed to use the time wisely, however, and no records survive from this period to indicate that any attempt was made to reorganize or fortify his kingdom. Perhaps blinded by his success in the Battle of Ashdown, he seems to have still been unaware that the old-fashioned forms of Saxon warfare would ultimately prove inadequate against this enemy.

The Vikings' return

The second invasion of Wessex began in 875, with the Viking army making an impressive dash from Cambridge, right through the Wessex heartland to Wareham on the Dorset coast. Having outrun their supplies, the Vikings now agreed to terms, which this time included giving hostages as well as oaths. Alfred was about to learn another important lesson. Believing he had again protected his kingdom, he stood back and watched as his enemy flouted their oaths, abandoned their hostages and simply moved their base to Exeter. Here though, the Vikings' luck failed them. Their breaking of the terms of the Wareham treaty was predicated on their knowledge that a reinforcing fleet was at that time heading along the south coast. When the army arrived at Exeter, however, they learnt that the fleet had been wrecked off Swanage and that they would not be relieved. Further oaths and hostages followed and this time the Heathen Army did retire back into Mercia.

Alfred's tactic at this stage seems to have been to buy time, in the hope that Halfdan's men would tire of years in the field and eventually settle down to divide up the kingdoms they had already conquered. If this was the case, he was mistaken. The Vikings had no intention of abandoning their dream of seizing the richest prize – Wessex – and even if this army did disband, there were many more Vikings in Scandinavia. So it was, and in 878 a third invasion of Wessex was mounted, led by a new warlord, Guthrum.

Guthrum's invasion

This time Alfred was caught entirely unawares. It was mid winter, a Christian holiday, and a truce was in place. But on Twelfth Night the Viking army, probably in collusion with elements of Alfred's own court, crept up on Chippenham, where the king was spending the holiday, and attempted to seize him. A last-minute warning saved Alfred's life and he escaped into the mazy marshes of the Somerset Levels, but Wessex was now, to all intents and purposes, a Viking state.

Alfred was deposed but safe and entering into the period of his life most associated with myth and legend.

This is the period in which the famous story of Alfred burning the cakes is set, when a despondent king, left to watch some cakes in the oven of a peasant's house, fell to dreaming and let them burn, only to be scolded by the housewife who was unaware of her noble guest's identity. In the light of his military campaigns up to this point, this can clearly be seen as an allegory. Alfred is the man who took his eye off the ball, who wasted the time he had bought and now saw his kingdom fall to ruin. In return he had been scolded by his people. Now he had to take that reproach and recover.

In fact, having failed to capture Alfred or drive him overseas (like Burgred of Mercia) it was Guthrum who found himself in a difficult position. He was now the static ruler trying to organize a large state and Alfred was the guerrilla, moving quickly and silently through difficult terrain that he knew better than his enemy. During that winter and early spring, Alfred seems to have been able to re-establish contact with key members of his court who did not support the new regime, and news that he had survived and was still in Wessex prevented the collapse in resistance that had been witnessed in East Anglia and Mercia. So it was that in early May 878 Alfred emerged from Athelney and rode to the unidentified site of 'Egbert's Stone' (possibly Kingston Deverill in Wiltshire) where the fyrds (or partial fyrds) of Somerset, Wiltshire and Hampshire awaited him. He was ready to retake his kingdom.

The recovery

News that a large Saxon army was in the field must have reached Guthrum at Chippenham very quickly, presenting him with a choice – to play the king and meet this army in open battle, as Alfred wanted, or continue to play the Viking, sue for peace or slip away in the night. Significantly, Guthrum chose to play the king, and on the ramparts of the old Iron Age fortress of Bratton Camp, on the escarpment above Eddington in Wiltshire, the two sides met in battle. As with all battles of this date we have no detailed accounts of tactics, troop movements or even the order of events. What the chronicles make clear is that the Viking army was routed, and fled back to Chippenham where they were besieged until, starving and exhausted, they surrendered.

Alfred's terms were lenient by Viking standards. Guthrum gave hostages, Alfred gave none (a first, as the chroniclers proudly state), the Vikings would retreat into their territory to the east of Watling Street and Guthrum himself would be baptized, Alfred becoming his godfather. This treaty was a magnificent piece of realpolitik on the part of Alfred. He could have slaughtered the Viking garrison – indeed they probably expected that – but that would simply have left a vacuum for another younger and more hungry warband to fill. Alfred chose instead to make Guthrum the Saxon-style king he had shown he wanted to be. He would have his land in East Anglia but on Saxon terms, under rules of kinship that both sides could understand, with Alfred as the overlord restraining and protecting his protégé. It was a good deal for Guthrum too. Viking warlords who survived their enemies were often deposed by their own men. Alfred was offering him the position of an anointed king with all the protection offered by that role; in return Guthrum would be a restraining hand on any future Viking army intent on invading England, as he was now a part of that land.

A new England

Freed from the imminent threat of invasion, Alfred finally put the lessons of the war to use by completely reorganizing his country and the means it adopted to deal with this new form of threat. This was perhaps a greater victory than Eddington. First, he reorganized his court and defences, putting his administration and army on a shift basis; in the case of the army, this meant that half were on duty at any one time, allowing the other half – who were largely, of course, a peasant levy – to work their fields. He also built a coastal patrol force, the first tentative step towards a royal navy, allowing him to exploit the same rivers and coastal waters which had given the Vikings their great mobility.

But defence has to be funded and it was here that Alfred really changed the whole structure of the kingdom.

He created a system of burhs – small towns about 20 miles apart from each other. When invading, Vikings traditionally headed for the capital of a state and decapitated the regime there to seize control, but with all these towns there was no one place to strike, as they formed a distributed defence network. Wessex was neither wealthy nor organized enough to build and permanently man forts, however. Alfred's solution, uniquely, was therefore to invest in his people. He granted land to inhabitants in each burh so that they could set up in business. The same roads that helped armies to march between towns also encouraged trade, so these people profited. The burhs were defended market towns, not forts, and their inhabitants provided the means and the manpower to defend them because the financial success of the towns gave them the wealth and the desire to do so. The success of the scheme is indicated by the fact that these towns founded by Alfred – which include Winchester, Chichester, Hastings, Southampton, Shaftesbury and Oxford – are still the backbone of the south of England's economy today.

Finally, Alfred instituted a programme of education, and most importantly literacy. He understood that ruling this new country with its new network of towns required a new level of communication. Few men in his administration before this time were literate, and orders had to be given by word of mouth. With a literate administration,

government orders, military orders, intelligence and information could all be carried and distributed quickly and
widely in written form – another crucial advantage over
the largely illiterate Viking enemy.

The last battle

Alfred was right to prepare. The Vikings did return in 892
under the leadership of the near legendary warlord Hastein
(or Haesten, to use the Anglo-Saxon spelling of his name).
This Viking war proved very different from the first one,
however, illustrated by the fact that Hastein's army arrived
in 330 ships but left in just five. Alfred had learnt the
lessons of this new form of war. He had watched the old
states of Anglo-Saxon England collapse, and had seen his
own crown nearly fall from his grasp. But intelligent,
educated Alfred had studied his opponent and learnt.

The Vikings that returned to Alfred's coast in 892 found
a very different country from the one Guthrum had invaded.
Wessex no longer yielded easy pickings, and during their
initial raids they were confronted at Farnham not by a fyrd
exhausted after months chasing an elusive enemy, but by
a highly mobile force supported by local burh garrisons.
The result was a Viking rout in which they were forced to
flee across the Thames to an island then known as 'Thorney'.

Before these raiders could be fully contained, however,
news reached Alfred of other attacks at Exeter and on the

north Devon coast and, having detached a small force to march to London, he had no choice but to head back west.

This probably co-ordinated attack gave the Viking leader Hastein the chance to regroup at Shoebury, where he was joined by new East Anglian and Northumbrian contingents. Realizing now that attacking the heart of the shires and their well-organized fyrds was simply too costly, he decided to try his luck in the wilder territories of the Welsh marches and, skirting the Wessex burhs, he cut along the Thames and then up the Severn to Buttington.

The fyrd followed in hot pursuit and, thanks to improved communications, found when they arrived that the men of Somerset, Wiltshire and Wales were waiting for them. This cosmopolitan army then besieged the Vikings until they faced starvation, and a desperate attempt to break out led to a comprehensive defeat.

For Hastein there followed another dash back across England to Essex, then north, further from the burhs of Wessex, skirting the lands where Alfred held sway, until they came to the deserted Roman city of Chester. The fyrd pursued them all the way, seizing the crops and animals in the immediate vicinity before leaving the bitter winter to do their work for them.

By the early spring of 894, hunger forced Hastein to leave, but he did not dare set foot in Mercia. Instead, he picked his way back south through Viking-held territory to the island of Mersea, in Essex. With Alfred bearing down on them, the Vikings escaped up the Thames and the Lea to the vicinity of Hertford, where they dug in to overwinter.

Alfred reacted quickly. Surveying the river environs south of the enemy camp, he found a suitable bottleneck where the surrounding landscape constricted, and set about building a fortress there on each side of the river. As soon as his enemy became aware that he was preparing to choke off their escape route, they ran. Eventually they reached Bridgnorth, which is the last place we hear of them. The following summer they left Alfred's lands for good.

He knew this was an enemy too flexible and too driven to ever simply 'go away', so he used his victory not to crush them but to remould them into something that he could live with. He then proceeded to remodel his entire country and administration to prevent such attacks ever happening again. When he died in 899, Wessex was secure, and his scheme of burhs, his organization of the military and his style of government spread, until his descendants could call themselves not kings of Wessex but kings of England.

HASTEIN

fl. c. 856–895

JOHN HAYWOOD

HASTEIN WAS ONE OF THE MOST SUCCESSFUL, and notorious, Viking leaders. In a career that lasted forty years, Hastein (who is called 'Haesten' in English sources) left a trail of destruction behind him in France, the Low Countries, the Mediterranean and in England, yet probably survived to old age. The early eleventh-century Norman writer Dudo of St Quentin (d. c. 1043) described Hastein in lurid terms as a 'cruel and harsh, destructive, troublesome, wild, ferocious, infamous and inconstant, brash, conceited and lawless, death-dealing, rude, ever alert, rebellious traitor and kindler of evil' and, as if this were not enough, a 'double-faced hypocrite and an ungodly, arrogant, deceiving, lewd, unbridled, contentious rascal' to boot. Sources as hostile as this need to be treated with caution, but other writers are agreed that Hastein was exceptionally ruthless and cunning, very much the archetypal Viking freebooter of popular imagination.

Though he was certainly a Dane (as, in fact, were the majority of Vikings), Hastein's origins are obscure. One tradition has it that he was the son of a peasant farmer, but it is more likely that he came from the chieftain class. The driving force of the Viking age was the beginning of state formation and political centralization in Scandinavia. Scandinavian society had a large class of men who, by possession of royal blood, were eligible for kingship. However, the progressive centralization of power meant that opportunities to rule were severely reduced. Competition for power was intense and civil wars were common. For the losers in these struggles, the best option was to become a Viking and go on plundering raids, to win wealth and a military reputation, either to support a renewed bid for power at home or for the chance to carve out a new kingdom abroad. Possessing the charisma of royal blood made it easy to raise an army, and it was not actually necessary to possess a kingdom to be recognized as a king. Scandinavian kings were still essentially rulers of men rather than territory. Such landless kings were known as 'sea kings'. According to the Norman writer William of Jumièges, Hastein began his career as the councillor of one such sea king, Björn Ironside, who is said to have been exiled by his father, the semi-legendary Viking Ragnar Lodbrok. Hastein is never described as a king, and his lack of royal blood may be why, for all his success, he seems never to have attempted to set up a kingdom of his own, but continued to live by plunder throughout his long career. In this, he was probably unusual. Most 'rank-and-file' Vikings were not full-time professional pirates: raiding was considered to be a short-term option to raise funds to buy a farm or win a share of land conquered abroad.

Viking armies

The Viking armies of the ninth century had a loose segmentary organization. The basic military unit was the *lid* (pronounced 'lith'), a king's or chieftain's personal retinue of warriors, the size of which depended on the wealth and status of its leader. The warriors of a *lid* formed a sworn fellowship or *félag*, which was bonded together solely by mutual loyalty. Discipline was maintained mainly by the individual warrior's fear of dishonour if he abandoned his companions in the thick of battle. Warriors expected to be rewarded for their loyalty with a share of plunder, and could transfer their allegiance to another leader if their own was unsuccessful in battle. A Viking army was essentially a group of *lidr* which had come together for a common purpose, and when a campaign was over the army simply broke up into its respective fellowships to settle, return home or join another army somewhere else. Because of their segmentary nature, Viking armies often had joint leadership, but a leader with an established reputation, like Hastein, could sometimes exercise unchallenged command. Because contemporary annalists usually described the size of Viking armies in terms of the number of ships in which they arrived, it is uncertain how large they really were. The ninth-century Viking ship from Gokstad in Norway had a crew of at least thirty-three men. If this was typical, the fleet of eighty ships that Hastein took to England in 892 would have carried a force of over two thousand, six hundred men, a substantial army for the time.

When on campaign, Viking armies built forts to use as raiding bases and to protect their ships, loot, and the women and children who sometimes accompanied them. Though women did not fight, they cooked and tended the wounded. The favoured battle tactic of Vikings was to form a defensive shield wall or *skjaldborg* ('shield-fort') to meet the enemy attack. In attack, a wedge-shaped formation called a *svinfylkja* ('swine-wedge') was often adopted to try to break the enemy shield wall. The Vikings' main military advantage was not superior weapons, tactics or organization – most northern Europeans waged war in a similar way at the time – but mobility, which kept them one step ahead of the defenders. Their fast longships drew only about 18 inches of water and were ideal for hit-and-run raids on coastal settlements or transporting armies along rivers. On land the Vikings campaigned as mounted infantry, covering long distances quickly on commandeered horses but dismounting for battle. Usually, by the time local forces had gathered in sufficient strength, the Vikings were long gone with their loot. Once their opponents found ways to curtail their freedom of movement, even experienced Viking commanders like Hastein could achieve little.

The early raids

Hastein's earliest exploits were in the Frankish empire in 856–859. With Björn Ironside, he sailed up the River Seine sacking the monasteries of St Quentin, St Médard, St Eloi, the royal abbey of St Denis, and finally St Geneviève in Paris. This was meat and drink to the Vikings: the first securely dated Viking raid was an attack on the famous monastery of Lindisfarne on the coast of northeast England in 793. Early medieval monasteries were wealthy and unguarded because no Christian would dare risk the wrath of the saints by attacking them. This, of course, was of no concern to the pagan Vikings. Because they often doubled as trade and craft centres, monasteries were also commonly sited on the coast or navigable rivers and so they were highly vulnerable to Viking hit-and-run raids.

Hastein first came to prominence when, with Björn Ironside, he led a fleet of sixty-two ships on a plundering expedition around the western Mediterranean in 859–862. Algeciras and Pamplona in Spain, Mazimma in Morocco, Narbonne, Nîmes, Valence (nearly 125 miles inland on the

River Rhône) and Arles in France, and Pisa, Fiesole and Luna in Italy were among the many places attacked. Dublin's slave market was reported to have been flooded with Moors captured during the expedition.

According to Dudo's colourful but surely legendary account, Hastein mistook the Italian city of Luna for Rome and was determined to capture it. Judging the city's defences to be too strong to storm, he tried to gain entry by a ruse. Viking emissaries approached the townspeople, telling them that they were exiles seeking provisions and shelter for their sick chieftain. On a return visit the emissaries told the townspeople their chieftain had died and asked permission to enter the city to give him a Christian burial. The townspeople agreed and a procession of Vikings followed their chief's coffin to the grave, at which point Hastein, very much alive and fully armed, leapt out of the coffin and slew the city's bishop. In the resulting confusion, the Vikings sacked the city. When he was told that he had not, after all, sacked Rome, such was Hastein's disappointment that he had Luna's entire male population massacred.

This story was repeated by many Norman writers and the same ruse was attributed to later Norman leaders such as Robert Guiscard, Bohemond of Taranto and Roger I of Sicily – evidence that medieval warriors admired cunning as much as bravery and skill at arms. Although the daring nature of this raid established Hastein's reputation as a great commander, in fact the Vikings had faced fierce resistance everywhere. Only twenty of Hastein's ships made it home, and the Vikings never returned to the Mediterranean. After the expedition Björn and Hastein split up. Björn headed back to Denmark, perhaps to launch a bid for the throne, but he never made it and died in Frisia. Hastein went to the Loire where he became a thorn in the flesh of both the Bretons and the Franks.

Raiding on the Loire

Soon after his arrival on the Loire, Hastein hired himself out as a mercenary to fight for Duke Salomon of Brittany. In 866 he helped Salomon defeat the Franks at the Battle of Brissarthe (near Le Mans), where he killed two Frankish counts, and he was probably also the leader of raids on Bourges in 867 and Orléans in 868. In 869 he turned on his former ally, Duke Salomon, and forced him to pay 500 cattle for peace during the grape harvest season. In the same year, King Charles the Bald (r. 843–877) ordered the fortification of Tours and Le Mans, so that they could act as refuges from Viking raids, and Hastein had to move quickly in order to extort protection money from the two cities while he still had the chance. When in 872 he seized Angers on the River Marne, a tributary of the Loire, King Charles allied with Duke Salomon and laid siege against him, surrounding the town with earthworks, then diverting the course of the river to leave his ships high and dry. This persuaded Hastein to agree to withdraw from Angers, but he soon re-established himself in a base on an island near the mouth of the Loire and continued raiding. Finally, faced with the prospect of a crushing attack by King Louis III of the West Franks, Hastein agreed to leave the Loire in 882, but he went no further than the Channel coast. Vikings were not military supermen and when forced to battle they lost as often as they won. They committed atrocities to sap their victims' will to resist, but generally avoided battle if they could and were more than happy to be bought off by payments of Danegeld. Hastein's success may be due, in large part, to his skill (and duplicity) as a negotiator of such deals.

Hastein's movements for the next ten years are uncertain. A late, and unreliable, source says that he was with the large Viking army that unsuccessfully besieged Paris in 885–886. However, no contemporary source mentions Hastein as one of that army's leaders and he may, instead, have been in England. By 890 he had moved to Flanders and built a fort at Argoeuves-sur-Sommes near Amiens. In a rather unprincipled attempt to save his abbey from destruction, the abbot of St Vaast, near Arras, reached an agreement which gave Hastein free rein to plunder the surrounding countryside so long as he spared the monastery. Hastein had no intention of keeping his word. After plundering the monastery's lands, he allied with another Viking band to launch a surprise attack on the abbey. However, the Franks were getting used to his treacherous ways, and Hastein was repulsed by the troops that the abbot had ready.

Returning to England

In 892 an unusually hot and dry summer caused crop failure and famine across northern Francia. Because they had to live off the land, the Vikings were forced to leave. Most made for England, which had seen little Viking activity since Alfred the Great's victory over the Danes at Eddington in 878. A major Danish army had landed in England in 865 and had quickly conquered East Anglia, Northumbria and eastern Mercia. Alfred had saved his own kingdom of Wessex only by the narrowest of margins. However, England in 892 was much better prepared for a Viking attack than it had been in 865. During the years of peace, Alfred had reorganized his army, created a navy, and founded a network of fortified garrisoned towns across his kingdom, which were intended to deny the Vikings their greatest advantage – their freedom of movement.

The main Viking army in northern Francia gathered at Boulogne and sailed to Appledore in southern Kent in 250 ships supplied by the Franks. Presumably they thought the ships a small price to pay to be rid of their unwanted guests. Shortly after, Hastein arrived with a fleet of eighty ships in the Thames estuary and built a fort at Milton Regis opposite the Isle of Sheppey in north Kent. His fort was well sited across the main road from London to Canterbury, and with easy escape to the open sea if things went wrong. Alfred responded by placing his army in mid Kent between the two Viking armies. A long stand-off followed. Alfred could not concentrate his forces against one Viking army without leaving the other free to plunder as it wished, but with a large English army in the field, the Vikings were also reluctant to stray far from their camps. At some point Alfred entered negotiations with Hastein. These resulted in the baptism of Hastein and his family and a payment of Danegeld in return for his promise to withdraw. Christian rulers commonly demanded that Viking leaders accept baptism as a way of sealing a peace treaty, as had Alfred himself when negotiating the Treaty of Wedmore with the Danish king Guthrum in 878. Many conversions secured in this way were certainly insincere – some Vikings are known to have been 'converted' more than once – and, in the event, Hastein did not keep his side of the bargain.

The arrival in spring 893 of a third Viking army in Devon broke the stalemate by forcing Alfred to split his forces. It had proved too easy for Alfred to contain the Vikings in Kent, so both armies decided to move across the

Thames estuary to East Anglia, where they could count on support from local Danish settlers. Hastein built a new fort at Benfleet in Essex, while the Vikings at Appledore sent their ships to Mersea Island, also in Essex, and then set out to join them by marching overland through English territory, plundering as they went. Weighed down by their booty, the Vikings moved slowly and were intercepted by Alfred's son Edward at Farnham in Surrey and badly mauled. The survivors withdrew to Mersea, but their king had been so badly injured that he could not provide effective leadership. Many of the Vikings defected to Hastein at Benfleet, reflecting the fluid nature of Viking armies.

Encouraged by this reinforcement to his army, Hastein set out on a plundering expedition in the east Midlands. In his absence, the ealdorman Aethelred raised an army from London and stormed Hastein's camp at Benfleet, capturing all his ships, booty and his wife and two sons. Many of the ships were broken up and burned, the rest taken to London and Rochester. Hastein built a new fort at Shoebury, 10 miles east of Benfleet, where he received new reinforcements from the East Anglian Danes.

Undeterred by the defeat at Benfleet, Hastein launched a raid into the west Midlands. Harried by English and Welsh forces, he was besieged on an island in the River Severn. Hastein fought his way out, but suffered heavy casualties and retreated back to Shoebury. Reinforced by more East

Anglian Danes, Hastein set out for the Midlands again in the autumn. This time he captured Chester, but the English cleared the surrounding countryside of food. With winter coming on, he again retreated, this time to Mersea. Alfred now returned Hastein's family to him as one son was his godson, the other was ealdorman Aethelred's. Alfred's generosity was not reciprocated.

In 894 Hastein sailed up the Thames and built a new fort on the River Lea, north of London, but was forced to abandon his ships in 895 when Alfred built a stockade to block the river. Another Danish raid into the west Midlands that summer also failed. Though the Danes had not suffered a decisive defeat, the English had denied them the freedom to plunder. Frustrated, the Danish army broke up, some to settle in the Danelaw – that part of England under Danish law – others to return to Francia.

Hastein's last years

A twelfth-century English source says that Hastein returned to Francia in 895. According to a story recorded by Dudo, Hastein acted as a negotiator on behalf of King Charles the Simple (r. 893–922) with another, more politically astute, Viking leader, Rollo, who became the founder of Normandy. The negotiations collapsed, fighting broke out and the Franks were put to flight. There is some suggestion that Hastein was playing a double game and had used the offer of talks to lure the Franks into a trap. However, Hastein's star was now fading. Before the talks, without revealing his identity, he asked some of Rollo's men, 'Did you ever hear anything of Hastein, who was born in your country and sailed here with a great army?' They answered, 'We've heard of him. A good fortune was foretold of him, and he began well; but a bad outcome in the end is his lot.' Hastein's ultimate fate is unknown. By the mid 890s, he must have been in his sixties, which in those days was a good age. A later tradition claimed that Hastein died in 931, fighting against Raoul, the count of Burgundy, but this is improbable as he would have been getting on for 100 years old by then. The death in battle of so notorious a Viking would surely have been trumpeted by contemporary chroniclers, so it is, perhaps, more realistic to imagine that he finally settled down in Normandy or the Danelaw, his raiding days behind him, and died in relative obscurity of natural causes – not such a bad outcome after all.

WILLIAM THE CONQUEROR

c. 1027/8–87

JOHN GILLINGHAM

WILLIAM THE CONQUEROR'S REPUTATION as a great commander rests securely on that most familiar of dates – 1066 – and on his victory in one of the most decisive conflicts in military history, the Battle of Hastings. The Norman Conquest meant that England received not just a new royal family, but also a new ruling class, a new culture and a new language. Some of the castles William built, at Colchester and at London (the Tower, for example), were the largest buildings of their kind to be erected in northern Europe since the fall of Rome, and they stand to this day as monuments to a duke who conquered a kingdom that was much larger and richer than his duchy.

The Norman Conquest was one of the most astonishing military achievements in European history. Yet in any serious assessment of William as a commander, the almost mythical fame of this one year should not be allowed to block out the fact that he spent his whole adult life, some forty years, in making or preparing for war.

The risks of battle: Val-ès-Dunes, 1047

When William, as his father's only son, inherited the Duchy of Normandy in 1035, he was at most 8 years old, and ambitious Norman nobles seized the opportunity to build castles and make themselves more independent. On coming of age, William's first important lesson in war came when he began the fight to restore ducal authority. He was fortunate in being able to call upon the aid of his own lord, King Henry I of France, whose rank and long experience of war meant that he was the one in command when king and duke overwhelmed Norman rebels in the Battle of Val-ès-Dunes in 1047. Even though their leader, Guy of Brionne, did not surrender until Brionne fell after a long siege, it is clear that the battle had broken the back of resistance, and William had learned that a pitched battle could be decisive. In the fiercely competitive world of eleventh-century France, small-scale wars were the normal continuation of local politics by other means.

By 1066 William had become a highly experienced commander, with at least twenty campaigning seasons behind him. Yet in not one of these campaigns did he himself take command in a pitched battle. A moment of confusion or panic in battle and the work of months or years might be undone, with catastrophic consequences for the losing side. This does not mean that William was unusually cautious. In that age political morality required that rulers who sent men to war must themselves share in its perils – rather than, as today, lurk many miles behind the danger zone. If the imminent prospect of battle brought to all soldiers the terrible fear of injury or death or shame, how much worse must this have been for the commander himself. It was widely acknowledged that the surest way to win was to kill or capture the opposing leader; the flight of the English when they learned that King Harold was dead is only the most famous example of the outcome of a battle being decided by the fate of the commander. Harold's own victory two weeks earlier, when he defeated the Norwegians at Stamford Bridge, had been sealed by the killing of the Norwegian commanders, Harold Haardrada and Tostig. At Hastings, the duke's chaplain, William of Poitiers, reported that William had three horses killed under him. If so, it may have been merely a matter of luck as to which of the two leaders was killed first.

A commander who sought battle was thus putting himself in great personal jeopardy. Not surprisingly, battles were rare events. Only the over-confident ignored the advice given by the 'soldier's Bible', the *De re militari* composed by

Vegetius, one of the most influential of all handbooks on the conduct of war. His advice on giving battle was simple: Don't. Just possibly you might, if you heavily outnumbered the enemy, if their morale was low and they were tired and poorly led, but otherwise, no. 'Battle', he wrote, 'is the last resort. Everything else should be tried first.'

The capture of Domfront

In the years after 1047, William proved himself a master of 'everything else'. In the struggles for power and territory between the princes of northern France, among them the King of France (who ruled over little more than the region around Paris), castles were both the main bones of contention and the focal points around which campaigns revolved. In 1051 William established his reputation as a brilliant soldier by capturing the fortress-town of Domfront (on the border between Normandy and Maine) from the most formidable warrior of his generation, Count Geoffrey Martel of Anjou. After an initial attempt to take it by surprise, he settled down to the only possible alternative: an attack on Domfront's economic base. He mounted a blockade by building four siege castles. To keep his own garrisons supplied, William of Poitiers reports, 'he rode out on patrol by day and night, both to defend his foragers against attack and to ambush those trying to bring provisions or messages into Domfront'. Geoffrey Martel responded by bringing up an army, not so close as to risk battle, but close enough to inhibit William's foraging and threaten his supply lines.

At this point Geoffrey had the upper hand. But William's scouts reported that the defences of Alençon, 30 miles away, were in a poor state. William rode through the night and attacked at dawn, calling upon the defenders of a small fort across the river to yield. They refused, and made insulting jokes about his mother's status. He responded by taking the fort by assault and then cutting off the defenders' hands and feet, an act of such ferocity that it persuaded the people of Alençon to surrender rather than risk the same fate. Leaving a garrison there, William rapidly returned to Domfront, which, on hearing the news, also decided to yield. In what turned out to be a closely supervised strategy of attrition, William succeeded not only because he moved with great speed and was prepared to be brutal, but also – frequently riding on patrol for the purpose – because he made sure he was well-informed.

The 1050s: the defence of Normandy

Alarmed by his success, neighbouring princes sought to cut William down to size. In 1053, 1054 and 1057 the King of France and his allies invaded Normandy. In 1054 Henry launched a two-pronged attack, one army under his own command and another under his brother's. According to

William of Poitiers, 'burning and looting, the invaders were intent on reducing the whole land to a miserable desert'. In other words, like all armies of the time, they sent out foraging parties and whatever they could not take with them by way of provisions or plunder, they destroyed. This was the gospel according to Vegetius: 'The main and principal point in war is to secure plenty of provisions for one's self and to destroy the enemy by famine.' Simultaneously foraging and looting while ravaging suited both the commander's overall campaign strategy and the individual soldiering for private profit. A method that worked on so many levels at once was a supremely efficient way of conducting war. How was it to be countered without running the risk of battle? Certainly not by the defender shutting himself up in his castle and allowing the invaders a free hand. William put forces into the field to shadow both armies. By moving close enough to deter them from spreading out to ravage and forage, while at the same time taking care not to risk being forced into a battle, his troops harassed the invaders. William himself shadowed the king's army; the outcome was stalemate. But the commanders of the other French army failed to discipline soldiers who, naturally enough, saw looting as the main point of going to war. As soon as William was informed of this he dispatched an elite force, which rode through the night, and at dawn caught the enemy off guard. The Battle of Mortemer, as it is conventionally called, was essentially an attack on troops who were enjoying ravaging too much to be prepared for battle; its effect, however, was to persuade King Henry, on hearing the news, to call off the invasion.

Three years later, in 1057, William defeated another invasion of Normandy when, at Varaville, King Henry and Count Geoffrey Martel allowed the rear of their army to get separated from the rest. William, shadowing them with a small rapid reaction force, at once seized the chance, cutting to pieces those who had been left behind.

The conquest of Maine

By coincidence, both King Henry and Count Geoffrey Martel died in 1060, and this transformed the situation. Throughout the 1060s, the second phase of his military career, William could take the strategic offensive. His first target was the city of Le Mans and the county of Maine. He adopted precisely the same methods as had Henry and Geoffrey in their attacks on Normandy. The first step was to ravage the whole region, 'sowing terror in the land by frequent and sustained invasion', in the words of William of Poitiers. Deprived of its economic base, Le Mans capitulated in 1063.

Crossing the Channel

The death of Edward the Confessor in January 1066 gave

William an excuse to challenge Harold's right to the English throne. His ship-building preparations for the invasion of England, on a scale unprecedented in Norman history – and extraordinary enough to warrant illustration in the Bayeux Tapestry – spurred Harold to take defensive action. From May onwards an English army and navy was stationed along the south coast. By August, the large army which William assembled at Dives-sur-Mer was probably seven to eight thousand strong, with one in four being mounted. Throughout that month he sat at Dives, despite the logistical problems caused by immobility. Possibly the winds in the Channel were against him, but it seems more likely that William was unwilling to take the huge gamble of disembarking an army in the presence of hostile forces. But Harold too faced logistical problems, and on 8 September, after keeping his forces together for well over three months, he was forced to disband them. Now at last William had his chance to strike. Despite bad weather, his fleet put to sea on 11 September. But the wind was unquestionably against him now. Some of his ships sank and the rest were forced to seek shelter in the Somme estuary. Harbour-bound for two weeks at St Valéry-sur-Somme, William prayed for a south wind. What he got was something even more fortunate; the arrival in the Humber estuary of the invasion fleet of Harald Haardrada, king of Norway.

Harold raised an emergency army and marched north.

By the time he reached Tadcaster on 24 September, Haardrada had already defeated the northern levies at Fulford Gate. But Haardrada had underestimated the speed of Harold's response and, presumably made over-confident by recent victory, had failed to send out reconnaissance patrols. Encamped at Stamford Bridge just outside York, the Norse king and his allies, believing themselves secure, were overwhelmed on 25 September. Just three days later the wind in the Channel changed direction. On the evening of 28 September, while King Harald's men were still celebrating their victory and recovering from their exertions, the Norman fleet set sail. The next morning William, after managing to keep most of his several hundred ships together during the night crossing, made an unopposed landing in Pevensey Bay. This news brought Harold south as fast as he had gone north. By the time he reached London, William had established a fortified bridgehead, exploiting and strengthening the ancient forts at both Pevensey and Hastings.

Bringing Harold to battle

In October 1066, for all his twenty years' experience of war, William faced a challenge unlike any he had dealt with hitherto. Enormous odds were against his being able to continue governing Normandy and hold his cross-Channel bridgehead during the coming winter months. He would not be able to keep what was, by the standards of the age, an unusually large army together for much longer. Only if he defeated Harold in battle could he make gains in any way commensurate with the scale and cost of his preparations. All this must have been obvious from the start, however. For the first time in his military career he had launched a campaign with the intention of forcing a battle. So great was the potential prize that for once it was a risk worth taking. But it takes two to make a battle. Almost always the commander with most to lose could avoid it. The problem for William was how to lure Harold into a position in which the Englishman had no choice but to stand and fight.

Ever since they disembarked, the Normans had ravaged the region around Hastings. All kings felt under some pressure to protect their subjects, but for Harold there was an extra dimension: this was East Sussex, an area in which many of his family estates lay; the landholders here were his tenants, many of them people he would have known personally. The ravaging of East Sussex was in part intended as a provocation to draw Harold into striking range. But it may also be that, elated by his great victory at Stamford Bridge, Harold aimed at repeating the trick, choosing to take risks in the hope of once again taking invaders by surprise.

But any miscalculation Harold may have made was punished only because William, as he did throughout his career, moved fast and took great care to be well informed before so doing. William of Poitiers noted that although all leaders were accustomed to send out scouts, Duke William often went on reconnaissance himself, as he did again after landing in England.

On the evening of 13 October William's scouts informed him that Harold was approaching. He hurriedly recalled those of his troops who were out foraging; fearing a night attack, he made those in the camp stand to arms till dawn. In this anxious moment, William put his hauberk on the wrong way round. But the feared attack never came, the English having decided to rest for the night. At first light the whole Norman army advanced rapidly, giving Harold no chance of withdrawing in good order. The moment for which William had long been preparing had come. Battle was now unavoidable. Achieving this in what was, for him, an unprecedented strategic situation, was William's masterstroke.

The great battle: 14 October 1066

But Harold still had time to draw up his army in a strong defensive position on the ridge at what is now called Battle. All he needed to do was to hold his ground. William had no choice but to gamble on an all-out attack. The surviving sources are not remotely good enough to allow us to reconstruct the events of that autumn day (which has not stopped many historians from trying), but it is possible that William's army possessed a decisive advantage in its missile-delivery systems – either a technological edge in the shape of the crossbow, a weapon with which the English were unfamiliar, or perhaps just an advantage in the numbers of archers present. Courageous warrior though Harold was, he lacked William's many years experience of command. For the last fifty years, except on the Scottish and Welsh borders, the English had had little direct experience of war. The stories of the Norman cavalry's feigned flights, drawing some of the English out of their strong position, suggest practice on one side and inexperience on the other. Even so, the battle was fought hard and long. It was already getting dark when Harold was killed, in circumstances which remain a mystery. William of Poitiers, the contemporary writer who knew most about what happened, chose to stay silent. When the remaining English turned and fled, they were hunted down. The day ended with a massacre which shocked contemporaries. It sent a signal, no doubt deliberately. To make himself King of England, there was no step from which the duke would shrink.

The conquest of England

Their leadership dead or in disarray, and lacking a plausible candidate for the vacant throne, the English were unable to put up any significant resistance as William's army marched on London, taking a circuitous, but strategically astute, route via Dover, Canterbury, Winchester, and

Wallingford. On Christmas Day 1066 William was crowned in Westminster Abbey. Early in 1067 he returned in triumph to Normandy. But the Normans celebrated too soon. There were risings every year from 1067 to 1070: in Kent, in the southwest, the Welsh marches, the fenlands, above all in Northumbria. By 1069 William had realized that the north posed military problems well-nigh insoluble for a king of England who was also Duke of Normandy. Virtually cut off from the rest of England by the Humber marshes and the Pennines, Northumbria lay wide open to Danish and Scottish intervention. William's solution, pushed relentlessly through during the winter of 1069–70, was the 'Harrying of the North', the calculated destruction of a region's winter food supplies and seed corn: massacre by famine. The wreck of the Yorkshire economy was still visible years later in the Domesday Book (1086). In strategic terms William had solved the problem of the north, turning it into a cordon sanitaire, a wasteland of no interest to predatory neighbours. In 1070 the kings of both Denmark and Scotland revisited, and both soon went home again.

After 1071, William's hold on England was fairly secure, made more so by his policy of building castles in all towns of any importance. But the citizens of Le Mans had taken advantage of his absence to throw off Norman rule. In 1073 he returned to Maine, bringing English troops with him. In the words of the Anglo-Saxon Chronicle: 'they laid it waste, destroyed the vineyards, burned down the towns and completely devastated the countryside, bringing it all into subjection'. It was back to business as usual. As a new king of France and Count of Anjou flexed their muscles, William's homeland was much more vulnerable to sudden attack than his island kingdom. From then on diplomacy and war on the Norman frontiers took up most of his attention. As he grew older, not everything went his way. In 1087 the garrison of the French fortress of Mantes raided Normandy. While William's troops sacked Mantes in retaliation, he received the injury from which he died.

Known to his contemporaries as William the Bastard, his mastery of all the disciplines of eleventh-century warfare, the routine, the exceptional and the brutal, means that he unquestionably deserved the name by which he has been known for the last eight centuries: William the Conqueror.

BOHEMOND I

c. 1055–1111

JONATHAN PHILLIPS

BOHEMOND OF TARANTO, Prince of Antioch, was arguably the greatest soldier of the First Crusade (1095–9). When the crusaders captured Jerusalem, people across Latin Christendom perceived it as a miraculous event – 'a renewal of biblical times', as one writer exclaimed. Bohemond's skilled generalship and bravery in battle were fundamental to the survival and the success of the Crusade, and created a huge reputation in his own lifetime and for generations to come.

When he travelled to France in 1106, people crowded around him; William of Malmesbury wrote that knights wished 'to see in action at close quarters that living image of valour, whose glorious fame made him talked of everywhere'. He was a leading figure in the *Chanson d'Antioche*, one of the most popular epics of the twelfth century and a tale embedded at the heart of chivalric culture. He was also a benchmark for future crusaders: as Richard the Lionheart's dejected warriors turned back from Jerusalem in 1192, they recalled Bohemond's valour and remarked how 'God raised [his] deeds to great heights'; heights they seemed unable to attain for themselves.

Bohemond's early years

Bohemond was born in about 1055, the eldest son of Robert Guiscard, foremost amongst the dynamic Norman adventurers who carved out their lands in southern Italy. His baptismal name was Mark, but such was the infant's size that, after hearing a story about an eponymous giant, his father called him Bohemond and the nickname stuck. Bohemond was soon exposed to harsh political reality when Guiscard divorced his Norman wife to marry a southern Italian princess and it was their offspring who were designated to succeed to the duchies of Apulia and Calabria, leaving his eldest son without an inheritance. Nevertheless, Bohemond soon established himself as a warrior of great prowess and by 1081 he rose to be second-in-command to his father.

Guiscard's relentless territorial ambition turned him towards the struggling Byzantine Empire, and in 1081 he invaded Greek lands. Bohemond led much of the campaign and he gathered considerable military experience, steering the Normans to victories in Albania and Bulgaria. These were tough wars, fought in difficult terrain against a wily enemy; it required sharp leadership to counter the full range of Byzantine strategies, such as the use of fast chariots and horse-traps. The defeat of formidable opponents such as the famed Varangian Guard, and the completion of a series of sieges, further extended his military repertoire. But by 1085 a combination of sterner Greek resistance and the effects of a plague in the Norman camp saw the expedition collapse; Guiscard himself died on Corfu in July of that year. It was rumoured that he had planned to make Bohemond the ruler of the territory conquered from Byzantium, but at the time of his death no provision had been made for his eldest son.

To establish a domain for himself, Bohemond needed to fight his brother Roger, and this he duly did, acquiring lands in Apulia that included the important cities of Taranto, Brindisi and Bari. Interestingly, in 1089, 1092 and 1093, Bohemond also met Pope Urban II and became a papal vassal. Within two years of the last of these meetings the pontiff had launched the most radical and enduring idea of the medieval age – the Crusade.

The crossing of Asia Minor

Urban's appeal to the knighthood of western Europe to free the holy places from the hands of the Muslims in return for the remission of all their sins was an incredible success. People from all walks of life flocked to take the cross and grasp this chance of salvation. It is unclear from our sources whether Urban contacted Bohemond directly about his plan. The main eyewitness account for the campaign – a southern Italian cleric who wrote the *Gesta Francorum* (the 'Deeds of the Franks') – describes how his lord, on seeing a group of men heading towards the Holy Sepulchre, was inspired by the Holy Spirit to cut his most expensive coat into crosses and to join the expedition. In a climate of such intense religiosity it is inevitable that Bohemond would have been concerned to make good the many sins that he had committed; it is also undeniable that he, perhaps above all the crusaders, would have been determined to carve out a territory of his own in the Levant.

Bohemond gathered a force of several hundred knights, including his nephew Tancred, another warrior who would gain a considerable reputation on the crusade, and headed towards the Christian forces' main rendezvous, Constantinople (where Bohemond met the emperor's daughter, Anna Comnena, whose *Alexiad*, written some fifty years later, describes both his physical appearance and his presence in vivid detail). Given events in the 1080s this was a delicate diplomatic moment. The Byzantine emperor Alexius was, in part, responsible for the calling of the crusade, having sought Urban's help against the Seljuks of Asia Minor. He had not, however, anticipated that a series of armies, numbering perhaps sixty thousand in total and inflamed with religious zeal, would head towards his lands. The fact that one contingent was led by Bohemond – his bitterest enemy – was a further complication.

In the event, Bohemond kept firm discipline amongst his men and worked hard to establish good terms with the emperor. Alexius required all the crusade leaders, such as Raymond of St Gilles, Count of Toulouse, and Godfrey of Bouillon, Duke of Lower Lorraine, to swear oaths of fealty to him and to promise to return any lands that were former possessions of the Byzantine Empire. In return they would receive food, guides and military support. Some were reluctant to make such a commitment but, given the practicalities of the situation, there was little alternative.

In the early summer of 1097 the crusaders and the Greeks moved into Asia Minor. The crusaders laid siege to the city of Nicaea, but when the Byzantine army arrived with reinforcements, the defenders surrendered to Alexius. The emperor gave some compensation to the crusaders, but from this time onwards, relations between the two parties soured and the Franks (as they were collectively known) pressed on alone. As they passed near Dorylaeum on 30 June, Bohemond's camp was attacked by a force of Seljuk mounted archers. The Normans fought bravely for over six hours, but it was only the arrival of Godfrey and Raymond's contingents that enabled the crusader forces to form a new battle-line, and in a concerted charge they drove the Turks from the field.

The arduous march across the Anatolian plateau (in the height of summer) saw the loss of many valuable horses; numerous poorer people deserted, unable to endure the hardships of the journey. By the autumn of 1097, however, the crusaders reached the city of Antioch in northern Syria. This immense metropolis was the gateway to the Holy Land, and as recently as 1085 had been in Byzantine hands. Now it was the Turks who guarded its formidable walls and towers, in part skirted by the River Orontes and all over-looked by a citadel perched high above. The city was too big to surround effectively but the crusader armies settled down to try to squeeze it into submission.

The Siege of Antioch

At first, supplies of fruit, corn and wine were plentiful, but by the early winter the surrounding land was beginning to be stripped bare. It was at around this time that Bohemond's fighting capabilities most clearly emerged. His years of warfare in southern Italy and Byzantium had already gained him a formidable reputation – compared to the other leaders of the crusade he was almost certainly the man with the broadest range of military experience, which he now brought to the fore. In December 1097 he led a major foraging expedition, but near Albarra it encountered a strong Muslim force heading towards Antioch. A swift charge by the crusader heavy cavalry drove back the Muslims in disorder and brought the attackers some plunder. Hardly any food was found, however, and the continued privations in the camp led to more desertions; news of the approach of an army from Aleppo brought further gloom. Bohemond now assumed a dominant role amongst the senior nobles. Taking the initiative, he led a large cavalry contingent away from the camp to confront the Turks a few miles to the north by the Lake of Antioch.

Bohemond realized that his forces were numerically inferior. To help counter this, he positioned his troops between a river and the marshy edge of the lake. Once his scouts had ascertained that the Turks were close by, he drew the crusaders up into five contingents, holding his own at the back in reserve. The Turks began with a hail of arrows, followed by a cavalry charge. When Bohemond saw his men beginning to buckle, he hurled himself into the fray, shouting: 'Charge at top speed like a brave man, and fight valiantly for God and the Holy Sepulchre!' The *Gesta Francorum* records that Bohemond descended on the Turkish forces 'like a lion that has been starving for three or four days, and so comes out of its cave roaring and thirsting for the blood of cattle and recklessly falls upon the flocks, tearing the sheep apart as they flee in all directions'.

Inspired by the sight of their leader's banner flying

deep in the Turkish ranks, the main body of crusaders regained courage and threw their enemy back, killing the Muslims and looting from them as they fled.

Meanwhile, the siege ground on, with the Franks continuing to struggle for supplies and the prospect of further Muslim relief armies a constant threat. In the spring of 1098 Bohemond made contact with Firuz, the Armenian warden of three towers on the city walls. The crusader offered him untold riches if he would let the invaders into the city, and Firuz consented. This was, in fact, an almost identical ploy to that used by his father in 1082 at the siege of Durazzo during the campaign against the Greeks, when the prospect of an advantageous marriage induced one of the defenders to betray the city to Guiscard. At this point we can see Bohemond's political ambitions emerging. He approached the other crusade leaders and persuaded them to agree that if one of them could engineer the downfall of the city he could keep it for himself, although it would be surrendered to Alexius when, as the emperor had promised, he came to help them. On 3 June a group of Bohemond's men approached the towers guarded by Firuz. Soon the crusaders were swarming over the walls and began to descend into the city, slaughtering anyone in their path. Once the gates were opened the crusader army poured in and put the place to the sword. Antioch had not fallen entirely, however; high on the mountain the citadel remained intact.

The Battle of Antioch

In spite of the crusaders victory, their position was about to take a turn for the worse; the besiegers were about to become the besieged. The reasons the First Crusade made such headway in Asia Minor and northern Syria were, crucially, the political and religious divisions of the Muslim Near East. The years before the crusade had seen the deaths of many powerful figures and a fragmentation of central authority; the result was a series of minor lordships in competition with one another. Understandably, they had not realized that the crusaders were engaged in a war of religious colonization and the caliph of Baghdad had shown little interest in the situation. It was not until the summer of 1098 that he authorized Kerbuqa of Mosul to lead a serious response.

The arrival of Kerbuqa's huge army soon pushed the Franks back into the city and the Muslims in the citadel also began to attack. Under such pressure even more men fled. Those who remained were so short of food that they were forced to eat their precious horses, while the poor were reduced to boiling the leaves of thistles for food. The deserters met Emperor Alexius who, as he had agreed, was crossing Asia Minor to support the Christians. The deserters convinced him that it was pointless going to Antioch at all and so he turned back, a decision that would have serious consequences for Bohemond. In mid June the 'discovery' of an object recognized as the Holy Lance inspired the troops and after almost a month pinned between Kerbuqa and the citadel, it was time for the crusaders to act.

Bohemond once more acted as commander for this crucial battle. On 28 June the crusaders marched out of the city and deployed in five contingents; Bohemond again kept his own force at the rear. With few remaining horses, the Franks must have presented a sorry sight, yet in terms of discipline and coordination they were now a well-drilled fighting force; an acute sense of desperation focused their efforts to an even greater extent. Bohemond directed his troops with authority and vision and once they had resisted early Muslim attacks, the crusaders charged and drove their enemy from the field. Seeing this disaster, the defenders of the citadel soon surrendered and handed over the fortress to Bohemond himself.

Bohemond's power established in Antioch

After such a monumental effort the crusaders took months to recover. Within the crusader camp there was huge tension between Raymond of St Gilles and Bohemond, each wanting possession of Antioch for himself; the former tried to insist that it should be held for the emperor Alexius, as had been agreed, while Bohemond began to act as if he had full authority over the city for himself, issuing privileges and confirmations of rights. Further campaigning in

northern Syria – in which again Bohemond fought promi-
nently – merely postponed the dispute until, under pressure from the pilgrim masses who were intent upon reaching
Jerusalem, Raymond headed south. Although Bohemond
would miss the capture of the crusaders' ultimate goal, he
could now establish control over his new lands and begin
to call himself Prince of Antioch. He rejected requests from
Alexius to hand over the city and claimed that because the
Greeks had failed to provide the assistance they had promised, he was under no obligation to do so; one imagines a
deep satisfaction on Bohemond's part in dismissing the
claims of his old enemy. It was not until Christmas 1099
that he felt secure enough to travel south and formally
complete his pilgrimage at the Holy Sepulchre.

Over the next few months Bohemond continued to
extend his lands in the north, but in early August 1100 he
made a rare mistake. For once it seems that he let slip his
usual caution and advanced without being properly armed
and prepared for battle. The Turks ambushed the Franks
and, much to their delight, took Bohemond prisoner; 'the
whole of the Persian nation rejoiced and was happy; for the
infidels had regarded him as the veritable king of the Franks
and all of their people had trembled at his name', as Gregory
the Priest, a contemporary local Christian, reported.
Bohemond remained a prisoner for three years before his
ransom of 100,000 gold pieces was paid.

Within a year of his release, the situation in Antioch began to deteriorate rapidly. The Greeks started to make attacks from the sea and through Cilicia; the Muslims of Aleppo pressed from the east and Bohemond's old rival, Raymond of St Gilles, caused trouble to the south. Money was extremely short (partly due to the ransom), and there was a desperate lack of fighting men. In these circumstances, Bohemond decided to return west to raise support.

Bohemond's tour of Italy and France

It is in the course of this journey that we can see just how great a reputation the hero of the First Crusade had gained. Assisted by the fact that his cousin travelled ahead to conduct some canny pre-arrival publicity, Bohemond's presence induced great excitement. One reporter noted that people came to look at him 'as if they were going to see Christ himself'! Bohemond met Pope Paschal II and it is clear that he planned to launch a new campaign against the Byzantine Empire before going on to the Holy Land. Paschal gave him a papal legate to help recruitment, although – and this is a matter of ambiguity amongst contemporary chroniclers – it is unlikely that he formally proclaimed a crusade against the Greeks.

Bohemond travelled north to France where he made a high-profile visit to the tomb of the patron saint of prisoners, St Leonard of Noblat, to give thanks for his freedom.

He then moved around France presenting relics to religious houses and making what amounted to a victory tour; people flocked to hear him and wanted him to be the godfather of their children; it is said that the name Bohemond, from being virtually unused in France, was suddenly highly popular. His promises of land and money (presumably in Byzantium) lured many to join him, and by September 1107 he was ready to sail from Bari to invade Greek lands in Albania. As in 1081, he besieged Durazzo, but this time he failed; by the summer of 1108, illness, a lack of supplies and the desertion of some of his men compelled him to swear a humiliating treaty with Alexius, in which he agreed to hold Antioch as an imperial vassal and to preserve the interests of the empire at all times.

Bohemond returned to southern Italy where little is known of his final years; he was taken ill and died in March 1111. He was buried in Canosa where his tomb – a striking combination of Byzantine and Islamic styles – remains.

While his career ended in relative ignominy there is no doubt that *Boamundus magnus*, as his son styled him, was regarded as a figure of immense achievement and ability. While it was his exploits on the First Crusade that propelled him to international fame – in the Catholic west, amongst the Christians of the Middle East and in the Muslim world

– the wealth of experience that he had accrued through decades of campaigning in southern Italy and Byzantium meant that he was brilliantly prepared to take the leading part in the expedition to the Holy Land. He was brave, enormously ambitious, and at times entirely unscrupulous. He was also a sharp conversationalist and negotiator; perhaps he is best summed up by Romauld of Salerno, a southern Italian writer, who commented that he was 'always seeking to do the impossible'.

FREDERICK BARBAROSSA

1127–90

JONATHAN PHILLIPS

IN THE SUMMER OF 1190 Frederick Barbarossa battled across Asia Minor en route to the Holy Land. His relentless advance deeply worried Saladin, the conqueror of Jerusalem, because, as the most powerful warrior in the West, Frederick would present the sternest of challenges to his hold on the Holy City. The emperor had a vast range of military and diplomatic experience: a veteran of the Second Crusade (1145–9), Frederick had led six major campaigns into northern Italy; he established his dominance over the German nobility, and, in the course of the Third Crusade (1189–92), swept past both the Greeks and the Seljuk Turks.

Just when he was poised to enter northern Syria he died – probably of a heart attack – as he crossed the River Saleph in southern Asia Minor on 10 June. The relief in the Muslim world was immense: 'If the king of the Germans is broken, then after him the unbelievers will be building on a shattered foundation', as one contemporary wrote; even with the armies of Richard the Lionheart still to come, the most potent warlord of the age had perished.

Frederick's early years

Frederick was born in 1127, the son of Frederick, Duke of Swabia, and Judith, the daughter of the Duke of Bavaria. At the age of 20 he took the cross and joined his uncle, King Conrad III of Germany, on the ill-fated Second Crusade. In the autumn of 1147 the Germans attempted to force a direct route through the heart of Asia Minor, but, weakened by a lack of food and water, their footsoldiers were decimated by the Seljuk Turks' cavalry. The Germans spent the winter recovering and then linked up with King Louis VII of France in the Holy Land. In July 1148 the crusaders besieged Damascus, but after only four days, news of the imminent arrival of relief forces from Aleppo compelled them to lift the assault and return home, angry and humiliated at this dismal performance.

Four years later Conrad died and Frederick – his nephew – was elected king of Germany, thus becoming the ruler of the largest territory in Christendom. He was a cheerful, pragmatic and clever young man; tall, strongly built, with blond curly hair and a close-cropped red beard.

He was undoubtedly physically tough because, given the demands placed on him, he had to be on the move for most of his reign. He regularly attended mass and was said to be eloquent, moderate (but not frugal) in eating, drinking and entertaining, as well as a noble warrior and a keen huntsman; a contemporary described him as 'the most vigorous prince in the world'.

The kingdom of Germany was formed by a series of powerful lordships, such as the duchies of Bavaria, Saxony, Austria and Bohemia, whose leaders could (and often did) challenge royal authority. But Frederick was not just the ruler of Germany; his imperial inheritance – which had emerged from the remains of the Carolingian empire – included the kingdom of Burgundy in eastern France and much of the Italian peninsula. In addition to his election as king of Germany he was also entitled to be crowned emperor in Rome by the pope. It was relations with the papacy and dealings with the Italian city-states that would absorb most of his energy and would lead him to become enmeshed with the aggressive kings of Sicily and the mighty Byzantine Empire; his desire to extend the boundaries of Christendom into the pagan territories of northeastern Germany was a further ambition. In assessing Frederick's performance as a military leader, therefore, we have to bear in mind the extraordinary demands these challenges placed upon his political skills, and to see that he faced a massive and complex task to realize imperial authority in the form that he desired.

Frederick's first campaign in Italy, 1154–5

In 1154 Frederick marched towards Rome for his imperial coronation. He also wanted to impose his will upon the towns and cities of Lombardy, a region long accustomed to minimal interference from Germany and, in an age of growing communal identity, unwilling to acknowledge Frederick and give the rights and taxes traditionally owed to him. He took Tortona after an eight-week siege in early 1155, then continued south to confront the Romans. Hostilities broke out on the streets of the city, but he was crowned emperor on 18 June 1155 by Pope Hadrian IV (the only Englishman ever to hold the title). An outbreak of plague forced Frederick to leave Rome, although he took Ancona and Spoleto from the Sicilians before heading home. While relations between the papacy and emperor had, to this point, been reasonably cordial, in 1156 Hadrian chose to signal his disquiet at Frederick's power and signed a treaty with King William I of Sicily, a decision that would bring the pope and the emperor into direct confrontation for over two decades.

Frederick's Italian campaigns, 1158–62

Milan was at the centre of resistance to the imperial forces and its citizens constructed an enormous 3-mile-long earthen rampart, surrounded by a water-filled moat, to protect themselves. The first assault on the city, in the late summer of 1158, lasted for only a month and was characterized by exchanges of siege artillery, skirmishes and the ravaging of crops. On 7 September a truce ended the attack, but the decrees that Frederick issued at the Diet of Roncaglia in November 1158 provoked even more anger. He set out a vision of imperial rights which made plain that city consuls were subject to his authority, which required oaths of fealty from the populace, and, in addition, contained renewed financial demands. Unsurprisingly, these decrees soon provoked dissent and Milan rebelled, followed by Crema and Brescia.

Frederick increased the size of the imperial force and drew on his allies in Germany, Bohemia and Lombardy itself. The sieges of Crema and Milan required a variety of military techniques to bring them to a close – their success stood amongst Barbarossa's finest military achievements and, for a period at least, gave him the ascendancy in his struggles with the Italians.

The siege of Crema was a particularly arduous, vicious and important episode, because it paved the way for an attack on Milan itself. Crema was formidably well defended with river defences, a large moat, a double circuit of walls and good stocks of food and water. To break through these obstacles Frederick employed some highly specialized engineers, including a man from the kingdom of Jerusalem who claimed to have had a successful career in the Levant (he may have been present at the siege of Ashkelon in 1153). Frederick's Italian allies provided the money, materials and labour to build a huge oak siege-tower that stood six storeys high, at around 100 feet. The lowest level reached the height of the city walls and had a bridge; at its top, archers and crossbowmen could rain arrows and bolts down into the city below. Hides and padding protected a structure that took five hundred men to move along on giant rollers. It needed a massive *testudo*, or armoured roof, to shield the men who laid down the rollers, a covering that also gave protection to the attackers as they attempted to fill the moat in order to bring the device right up to the walls. Frederick needed more local support, and he called on the citizens of Lodi, who provided two thousand cartloads of earth and wood to be cast into the moat to create a causeway.

In September 1159 the siege intensified as the tower was inched towards the fortifications, yet the defenders were well prepared and their own artillery inflicted serious damage on the device. They also used machines, described by contemporaries as human-sized mousetraps, to harass the attackers. To try to break their morale, Frederick ordered local captives to be suspended by ropes in front of the tower. A contemporary German writer – ignoring the part his own side had played in this episode – was horrified that the Cremasce continued to fire:

This is a thing unheard of even amongst barbarians . . . And so several children died miserably, struck by the stones, while others though remaining alive, suffered yet more pitifully, hanging there . . . You might have seen children fastened to the machines beseeching their parents, reproaching them for their inhumanity . . . *[but the parents]* consoled themselves for the necessity of their act by taking thought of the miseries they must endure if they were made subject to their enemy.

Meanwhile the *testudo* was redeployed to protect a ram, which smashed a jagged hole in the outer wall. The defenders' resourcefulness was admirable; they built an earth and timber barricade and used it as a sally point to assault the *testudo*; they also set up swinging hooks and booms to hurl incendiaries, iron weights and barbs on to it. The battle became even more vicious – the Cremasce scalped one imperial warrior and made another crawl along after his hands and feet had been severed. As is so often the case in a finely balanced struggle, it took a defection to make the crucial difference. In January 1160 the Cremasce's chief engineer, Marchesius, deserted to the emperor, and he recommended the construction of another bridging platform to go alongside the existing tower. The new machine was, of course, well protected and could extend 30 feet forward, enabling archers to deliver a sustained bombardment and a sufficient numbers of knights to cross from both the tower and the new bridge to take the walls.

On 21 January 1160 the onslaught began; initial progress was good, with imperial troops seizing the outer walls; but stern resistance at the inner walls and the destruction of the siege-tower's bridge broke their momentum. None the less, with Frederick's men now inside the walls, the defenders were forced to capitulate; given the harsh treatment of captives earlier in the siege, the fear of even more terrible reprisals was a strong motivating factor. Crema surrendered on 27 January and all its fortifications were destroyed. The colossal expense of the siege (over 2,000 silver marks) and Frederick's determination to enforce it over the winter, demonstrated his ability to hold troops in the field and to keep his allies on side. To the Milanese it was a sign that he would be hard to withstand.

The emperor's first encounters with the Milanese were tentative and not especially distinguished; there was one attempt on his life by a man of exceptional size, described by contemporaries as a lunatic, and who was in the camp as 'entertainment' for the troops. But after coming to Frederick's tent and trying to drag him towards a nearby cliff, the would-be assassin tripped over the tent-ropes and was caught and killed.

The Italians had a formidable army that included a hundred chariots with scythed wheels, as well as archers and heavy cavalry, so Frederick prudently chose to avoid battle for a while. In 1161 he began his assault on Milan in earnest, his tactics emphasizing attrition rather than assault. He initiated a substantial blockade and destroyed crops and trees within a 15-mile radius, taking particular care to deny the Milanese the annual harvest. Roads were closely monitored, and anyone carrying food for the defenders was punished by having his or her right hand amputated; by 1 March 1162 the citizens were so desperate they had no choice but to surrender. Milan's fortifications were demolished, its churches destroyed, its moats filled in; the population was dispersed and the commune abolished. Once again, Frederick had managed to preserve a large army, made up of a confederation of German forces and Italian allies, for a sustained and focused campaign – a tribute to his wealth and his skills as a commander.

Frederick in Italy, 1167–76

In 1167 Frederick crossed the Alps once more. His relationship with the papacy had, by this time, deteriorated to the point whereby he had established an anti-pope to rival Alexander III (1159–81). In July 1167 the emperor entered Rome and enthroned his own candidate, Paschal III, but an outbreak of disease killed many of Frederick's senior advisors and his best knights and compelled him to retreat. More significantly, December 1167 saw the formation of the Lombard League, a confederation of sixteen cities opposed to him. Needless to say, Alexander III supported the League, as did the Byzantine emperor Manuel Comnenus (1143–80), who saw a chance to assert himself as the sole, or certainly the dominant, ruler entitled to imperial status and to be the true successor to the Roman Empire.

Six years later Frederick sent another army into Italy. The most symbolic place to attack would be the new city of Alessandria, constructed in 1168 by the Lombard League, and named after the pope himself. The city posed an unusual challenge; instead of stone walls it relied on a huge earthwork, topped with a palisade and fronted by a wide, deep, water-filled ditch. Autumn rains frustrated the Germans' early assaults because the resultant quagmire meant it was impossible to bring forward siege machinery. This time a Genoese engineer directed imperial operations and, as the weather improved in springtime, he used a huge mobile roof to allow the creation of a causeway and then sent a ram to break down one of the gates. Somehow the defenders still managed to resist, but the Germans sent in a siege tower which became the focus of the struggle. Sustained determination frustrated the imperial forces and Frederick decided to resort to subterfuge. During a truce over Easter 1175 he ordered his men to complete a series of tunnels, intending his troops to emerge within the city and open one of the gates. The Alessandrians detected the noise made by the miners, however, and quickly collapsed the tunnels; in the resulting confusion a swift foray enabled them to burn the precious siege tower and put the imperial operation in jeopardy. News of an approaching relief force compelled Frederick to leave, and a city derided for having straw roofs and mud walls was able to celebrate its resistance.

The following year saw the Battle of Legnano, on 29 May 1176. By now Frederick was facing destructive levels of dissent within the empire; Henry the Lion, the powerful Duke of Saxony, for example, had declined to fight in Italy. Meanwhile the Lombard League gathered over three thousand five hundred cavalry – a huge number for the time – as well as several large groups of footsoldiers, and challenged him to battle. The League's forces were bigger than Frederick's, but the emperor refused to lose face by avoiding the fight. Initially the imperial troops did well and a fierce struggle developed around the *carroccio*, an ox-drawn wagon on which the League's flags and priests were based. Frederick led the attack, but in their defence of this symbol of communal identity the Italians managed to unhorse him. Some imperial troops believed him dead. Unlike William the Conqueror at the Battle of Hastings, famously remounting and raising his helmet to reassure his men that he was still alive, Frederick was unable to show his troops that he had survived, and he could not, therefore, prevent their wholesale flight. The Treaty of Venice (1177) brought this campaign to an end, and six years later the Peace of Constance marked a conclusion to the imperial effort in Italy. In spite of the defeat at Legnano, Frederick's diplomatic skills ensured that by 1183 he was in a hugely powerful position, having preserved the majority of his governmental powers and secured an oath of loyalty from the League, as well as a promise of assistance if he entered its lands. In short, imperial rule in Italy was greatly intensified.

Frederick and the Third Crusade, 1188–90

The final military episode of Frederick's career was also, potentially, the most momentous. In July 1187 Saladin recaptured the Holy City of Jerusalem; western Europe steeled itself to fight back. This was an opportunity for Frederick to take on the highest aspect of the imperial dignity, the protection of the Church – to regain Jerusalem would be the ultimate expression of this and, as such, the pinnacle of his reign.

In March 1188 he held a court at Mainz, a *curia Jesu Christi*, and the emperor, his son and thousands of others took the cross. Oddly, Frederick decided to take the land route to the East, rather than sail, as Richard the Lionheart was to do; it brought a further level of complexity to the enterprise and opened up the possibility of a repeat of the troubles of 1147–8. The emperor had perfectly good relations with the Venetians, so why did he not go by sea? The size of his army may be one explanation; another is that a soothsayer predicted the emperor would die in water and he therefore wished to avoid sailing. Given his final demise, if true, this forecast would indeed be ironic. In his preparations we can see the legacy of Frederick's experiences on the Second Crusade. He made sure that only men with sufficient money were allowed to take part and he worked strenuously to establish firm agreements for markets and prices with the Hungarians, Byzantines and Seljuks. Crusaders who behaved badly were punished by mutilation or death.

The German army set out in the spring of 1189 and made excellent progress until Emperor Isaac II Angelous of Byzantium, an ally of Saladin, began to hinder the troops. Such was the size of Frederick's army, however, that he was able to compel the Byzantine ruler to let him cross into Asia Minor at Gallipoli. At this point the expedition hit trouble; relations with the Seljuks became hostile and, beset by lack of food and water, the crusaders had to mount a fighting march towards the Seljuk capital of Iconium in central Anatolia. In spite of his troops' weakened state, Frederick was determined: 'With the help of our Lord Jesus

Christ, whose troops we are, the road will have to be opened with iron', he wrote. In mid May Iconium fell to the Germans, thus avenging one of the Second Crusaders' defeats. The march towards Armenia continued successfully, but when Frederick perished in the River Saleph in June, army morale collapsed and many returned home; others, weakened by their suffering across Asia Minor, died at the siege of Acre in 1190–91.

There remains, however, a further part of Frederick's story. Legends emerged: he remains in an enchanted sleep in Mount Kyffhausen in Thuringia, waiting to reawaken on the Day of Judgement, his red beard having grown so long as to twice encircle the stone table at which he sits. Just like those surrounding King Arthur, these tales reflect a combination of nationalism and regeneration, and while they may originally have been connected with Frederick II (1198–1250) they are now firmly associated with the mighty Barbarossa and his vision of imperial glory, a vision underpinned by a long and varied military career.

GENGHIS KHAN

c. 1167–1227

JUSTIN MAROZZI

THE MILITARY RECORD OF GENGHIS KHAN places him comfortably at the top table of world conquerors, together with Alexander the Great and Tamerlane. Yet even this accolade scarcely does him justice. Genghis Khan could arguably lay claim to being the most successful commander and empire-builder who ever lived. At the time of his death in 1227, the Mongol empire he had created from nothing stretched from the Pacific to the Caspian, and covered an area four times the size of Alexander's realm. Unlike Tamerlane's empire, it proved remarkably robust and continued to expand after his death, doubling in size under his sons and grandsons.

Possessed of a savage genius both for warfare and for the civil administration of government, Genghis struck terror across Asia. Those who surrendered without opposing him could expect to be spared his trademark outrages. As a rule, though there were exceptions, they were shown mercy. But cities that chose to resist him forfeited their right to exist: they were razed to the ground, their populations subjected to hideous tortures before falling victim to whole-sale slaughter. When the indefatigable Moroccan traveller Ibn Battutah journeyed through Central Asia in the 1330s, more than a century after Genghis's ravages, many of the celebrated cities of antiquity he encountered, such as Merv and Balkh, still lay in ruins. For Muslim chroniclers, Genghis occupied the heights of infamy as the Evil or Accursed One.

A heavenly destiny

There is a good deal of obscurity surrounding Genghis's life, particularly his early years, which is not entirely unex-pected when studying a hitherto illiterate nomadic race of the late twelfth century, a people that despised the settled life of cities. The precise year of his birth remains contro-versial, varying from 1155 to 1167.

Acknowledging the difficulties of such a shadowy subject in a landmark study of the Mongols, the nine-teenth-century historian Henry Howorth wrote, 'If we wish to enter upon a branch of inquiry which seems utterly wanting in unity, to be as disintegrated as sand, and defying any orderly or rational treatment, we can hardly choose a better one than the history of the Asiatic nomads.'

In seeking to make sense of Genghis's career of conquest, historians have necessarily relied heavily on *The Secret History of the Mongols*, Mongolia's first written work, compiled by scribes in 1228 to record his momentous deeds. Although it is of questionable reliability, few contemporaries among his shamanistic brethren would have quibbled with its opening sentence, which baldly states: 'Genghis Khan was born with his destiny ordained by Heaven above.' No other possible explanation could account for Genghis's extraordinary mastery of his fellow men; nothing else could justify a wrath and destructive power that appeared almost divine in its vengeful fury.

At the height of his power, Genghis did little to discourage such suggestions of a heavenly mandate to rule. There was, according to John Man, one of his most recent biographers, 'an odd division between the arrogance of one chosen to unite, lead and conquer, who was justified in using every means to achieve Heaven's purpose, and the humility of an ordinary man awed by the inexplicable nature of his assignment'. It was this internal dichotomy, Man suggests, 'that lay at the heart of the paradoxical whirlwind of destructiveness and creativity, of ruthlessness and generosity, that constituted Genghis's character'.

From inauspicious beginnings

If heaven had marked him out for special things, it kept

such promises well hidden during his earliest years. He was born near the present-day Mongolian capital of Ulan Bator, the eldest son of a minor chieftain, Yesugey, and given the name Temujin after a Tatar captured by his father. *The Secret History* records, no doubt apocryphally, that he was born with a clot of blood in his right hand, a harbinger, according to Mongolian tradition, of future greatness.

Having noble blood conferred considerable advantages, but they proved short-lived. When Temujin was 9, Yesugey departed to find his son and heir a suitable girl to marry. The mission was successful – the girl's name was Borte – but Yesugey was poisoned on his return home, leaving his wife with six young children to bring up alone. Temujin had lost his protector. Abandoned by their relatives, the family was forced to survive by foraging for fruits and roots, fishing and hunting.

With extreme adversity came certain benefits. It was probably during this time that Temujin honed his skills in the saddle, an essential foundation for future leadership and conquest. In a desolate landscape, survival itself – primarily through the hunting of meat – demanded the same set of talents required on the battlefield. Military techniques were thus learnt from the earliest age among the Mongols. As soon as a boy could ride, he was well on his way to becoming a soldier. Temujin would have learnt to master his horse and to manoeuvre it with the greatest finesse, to gauge the distance between himself and his quarry, and to shoot with deadly accuracy. It was the perfect training for a mounted archer, the backbone of Genghis's army, equipped with the lethal composite bow of horn, sinew and wood. As the eighteenth-century historian Edward Gibbon remarked, 'the amusements of the chase serve as a prelude to the conquest of an empire'.

The Secret History records Temujin's first kill, at the tender age of 13. His victim, felled in cold blood, was his half-brother Bekter, with whom he had quarrelled over the capture of a lark and minnow. It was the first indication of a ruthlessness that came to characterize his later career. Tales of bravery and derring-do accumulated steadily during his youth. He survived kidnaps and raids, made hair-raising escapes, and on one occasion launched a daring rescue mission to retrieve his family's stolen horses, upon which its survival depended.

Once married, he began to demonstrate there was far more to his abilities than mere military prowess. Evidence of his prodigious political talents came to the fore as he assembled a coterie of allies and protectors. Already joined with his sworn blood brother Jamuka, he added a more powerful; his father's blood brother Toghrul. Together, the two men helped Temujin put a combined army of twelve thousand into the field to retrieve his wife Borte, kidnapped by a rival Mongol clan. Temujin's fame spread and soon he was emerging as much more than his family's protector. Indeed, in time both Jamuka and Toghrul would be sacrificed on the altar of his overweening ambition.

Unleashing the Mongols

By around 1200, Temujin had managed to unite about half the traditionally feuding Mongol clans under his leadership. Jamuka and Toghrul, however, stood in the way of sole command. Over the next several years, after a bewildering period of opportunistic, shifting alliances, battles, triumphs and reversals, they were finally eliminated from the field, removing the last obstacles in Temujin's rise to power. *The Secret History* shows a magnanimous Temujin allowing his defeated blood brother Jamuka a noble execution – although another chronicle says he suffered an agonizing death by dismemberment.

In 1206 a kuriltay or national assembly was summoned at the source of the Onon river. Temujin, the man who had 'unified the people of the felt-walled tents', was proclaimed Genghis Khan, Oceanic Khan or Ruler of the Universe. Though the tribes subsumed under his command were many, henceforth they came to be known simply as the Mongols. The Mongol conquests, a period of catastrophic terror and destruction for the peoples of Asia, could begin.

Genghis took immediate steps to underpin his military command, starting with a fundamental reordering of tribal loyalties. His army was organized according to the traditional decimal system of the steppe: platoons of 10, companies of 100, brigades of 1,000 and divisions of 10,000 soldiers. Genghis's radical innovation was to create these units from mixed races and tribes, thereby undermining traditional loyalties and creating a new force united in its allegiance to his person. This was in addition to a brand new creation, an elite imperial guard of 10,000. Staffed by many of the sons of his regimental commanders, it acted as an insurance policy against disloyalty in the wider army and a buttress to his unrivalled personal command. General conscription was introduced for all men between 15 and 70.

Once created, this vast fighting force, which probably numbered at least one hundred thousand at this stage, needed to be kept occupied in the field. Soldiers did not receive salaries and were only paid with plunder from defeated enemies and ransacked cities. If the army was not kept busy campaigning, the likelihood was that it would quickly fracture into the time-honoured pattern of feuding tribal factions, thereby destroying the foundation of its master's new-found authority.

Genghis looked south across his borders and decided to strike. Across the Gobi desert lay the Tanguts of Xi Xia, his weakest neighbours, and a people whose cultural obscurity to this day can largely be attributed to the genocide meted out by Genghis's ferocious army. It was, of course, a taste of things to come. The Tanguts were an easy stepping-stone towards a richer, more powerful adversary, the Jin empire of northern China.

His army, noted for its exceptional horsemanship and superb archery, swept across Asia like a tsunami, flattening every enemy it encountered. In 1209, the Turkic Uyghurs in what is today Xinjiang offered their submission. Two years later, undeterred by a Jin army numbering several hundred thousand, the Mongols invaded the northern Chinese empire.

Beijing, its capital, was one of the most powerful, heavily defended cities in the world. With 10 miles of walls, nine hundred guard-towers, and a bristling arsenal of heavy weaponry such as catapults that could hurl fire bombs at attackers, it was Genghis's greatest challenge yet. He starved it into surrender. Beijing fell in the late spring of 1215.

For the first time a civilized city felt the full destructive terror of a Mongol onslaught. Within minutes, the looted palaces and public buildings were going up in smoke and the first of many massacres was underway. The campaigns against northern China rumbled on for the next two decades. To Genghis's growing arsenal of military weapons was added the machinery and techniques of siege warfare. Once mastered, they offered him a wider canvas on which to paint the world red.

The invasion of the west

The Qara-Khitay, nomads who controlled lands from their base in the Altaic steppes of northern China, had fallen under the rule of one of Genghis's earliest enemies, Kuchluk, former king of the Naimans who was now persecuting his Muslim subjects. In 1218, Genghis's general Jebe rode to Kashgar with a corps of twenty thousand men, where he fomented rebellion by reminding the downtrodden Muslims of Genghis's precept of religious toleration and freedom. The Qara-Khitay revolted, Kuchluk was captured and killed and Mongol dominion had seeped further west with barely a sword raised.

The victory brought the frontiers of Genghis's nascent empire rubbing uncomfortably close to those of Sultan Mohammed, the Muslim Khorezmshah who ruled over most of Persia and Mawarannahr, with his capital in Samarkand. It is debatable whether Genghis was looking to fight this formidable Asian ruler at this time, but after a caravan of four hundred and fifty Muslim merchants from his territories were butchered in cold blood in Mohammed's border city of Otrar on suspicion of being spies (which they probably were), and after reparations were refused, invasion was the only course open to him. The Sultan compounded his offence with the unpardonable folly of killing one Mongol ambassador and shaving off the beards of two others. Genghis's blood was up.

This was a man who revelled in war and bloodshed, who believed, as he told his generals, that 'Man's greatest good fortune is to chase and defeat his enemy, seize all his possessions, leave his married women weeping and wailing, ride his gelding, use the bodies of his women as night-shirts and supports, gazing upon and kissing their rosy breasts, sucking their lips which are as sweet as the berries of the breasts.'

In 1219, a Mongol army of two hundred thousand swarmed into Central Asia. Otrar, in what is now Kazakhstan, was put under siege and captured. Genghis's sons Ogedey and Chaghatay seized its governor and executed him by pouring molten gold into his eyes and ears. It was the first sign of the terrifyingly vicious campaign to come. The suddenly feeble Mohammed fled in terror, closely pursued to an island on the Caspian Sea where he died in mysterious circumstances. The rest of his kingdom was not so fortunate.

Arriving in fabled Bukhara, 'dome of Islam' and richest city of the kingdom, Genghis mounted the pulpit of the Kalon mosque and warned the terrified inhabitants that God had sent him to punish them for their sins. From Bukhara, the Mongols rode southeast across the steppe to Samarkand, driving thousands of captured prisoners before them to create the impression of an irresistible army on the move. The city's defensive forces were no match for the massed Mongols, who by now had been joined by Ogedey and Chaghatay. Samarkand's speedy surrender in 1220 failed to prevent its plunder in another orgy of bloodletting. Thirty thousand artisans were deported to Mongolia and – an infinitesimally small mercy – only the clergy were spared.

North of the Oxus the Mongols fell upon the ancient city of Termez, where legend had it that a woman who begged to be spared the massacre, telling her captors she had swallowed a pearl, had her stomach ripped open and the gem removed. Genghis then ordered his men to disembowel every corpse. Balkh, the celebrated former capital of the Bactrian empire, collapsed before the Mongol onslaught, followed in 1221 by the city of Merv, where the forces of Genghis's son Tuli were said to have massacred seven hundred thousand. For four days, the captive population was rounded up and driven onto the plain. Each soldier was ordered to execute three to four hundred prisoners and bring the severed ears of the victims to their commanders to prove they had done so.

Another siege was mounted against Gurganj (Urgench), homeland of the shahs. After seven months of resistance, the city was stormed and taken street by street, Mongol troops hurling flaming naphtha into houses. A small number of artisans – and women for the harem – were spared and the rest were put to the sword. The Persian historian Juvayni records that fifty thousand soldiers were commanded to kill twenty-four prisoners each, a death toll of 1.2 million. Even allowing for the notorious unreliability of the chroniclers, the slaughter was immense.

In 1221, Nishapur fell in a frenzy of killing. The heads of men, women, children – even cats and dogs – were piled into dreadful pyramids in the streets. By the end of the year Herat and Bamiyan had fallen amid similar horrors. It was only in the dying months of 1221, when Mohammed's son Jalal al-Din was defeated at the Battle of the Indus, that the campaign was over. Genghis's empire stood poised on the fringes of Europe.

The three-year campaign was one of the most blood-soaked in history. It has been likened to the genocidal outrages committed by the Assyrians in ancient history and by the Nazis in more modern times.

Writing shortly after this campaign in the Middle East had concluded in 1221, the Arab historian Ibn al Athir was in no doubt of the magnitude of the calamity and the epochal horrors it had inflicted. It was, he wrote, 'a tremendous disaster such as had never happened before ... It may well be that the world from now until its end ... will not experience the like of it again, apart perhaps from Gog and Magog.'

Taking the scenic route home

The conclusion of the campaign against Sultan Mohammed did not spell an end to Mongol conquest in the region. The lust for blood and treasure had not been sated.

While Genghis took a break from the action, the section of his army under the generals Jebe and Subedey continued north around the Caspian Sea, rolling over every enemy in their path. Cities were razed and depopulated, prisoners slain or ordered to march as shields before the army in full battle formation. Riding through Azerbaijan, the invaders sacked the Christian kingdom of Georgia, flattening the capital of Tiflis (Tbilisi) in 1221. Through the Caucasus and the Crimea and along the Volga they advanced, routing Bulgars, Turks and Russian princes as they hugged the northern shores. Twenty nations were defeated in this aston-ishing, megalomaniacal circuit of the Caspian.

In 1225, after a couple of years hunting in the steppes of Turkestan, brushing up on his philosophy in discussions with a Taoist sage – from whom he sought the elusive elixir of immortality – and discussing religion with the Islamic priests of Bukhara, Genghis set out for home.

Although by now an old man, Genghis's appetite for war remained undimmed. By the end of 1226 he had put the rebellious Tangut capital of Ning-hsia under siege. The city, and its inhabitants, went the way all flesh did when confronting Genghis. Chinese chronicles lament the battlefields piled high with the bones of their countrymen.

He lived to see his eldest son and troublesome heir, Jochi, predecease him in 1227. The succession was bestowed upon Ogedey. Later that year, Genghis Khan, the Ruler of the Universe, died, master of an empire which spanned an entire continent from China to the gates of Europe. Rarely have the sword and sceptre been so brilliantly – and brutally – held by one man.

KUBLAI KHAN

1215–94

JUSTIN MAROZZI

MOST EMINENT DESCENDANT of the royal house of Genghis, Kublai Khan was the fifth Great Khan of the Mongols and founder of the Yuan dynasty in China. With the tumultuous conquest of China finally completed in 1279, he became the most powerful man on earth, his authority acknowledged by the junior branches of the Mongol empire throughout Asia, right up to the borders of eastern Europe.

After the barbarous savagery of his grandfather Genghis's conquests, the rule of Kublai ushered in a new era of civilization. Where Genghis had been the archetype of the nomad conqueror of the steppes, Kublai was master of a noble, sedentary society. The famous study of the emperor from the National Palace Museum in Taipei shows a benevolent old sage rather than the demonically fierce warrior that was Genghis. Heavily influenced by his cultivated Chinese court, Kublai, without ever forgetting the martial ferocity of the Mongols that was instilled into his very nature, was a lavish patron of literature, culture and science.

Though his campaigns lacked the irresistible momentum of Genghis's armies during their whirlwind conquests, Kublai's enduring triumph was the astonishingly successful incorporation of China into the Mongol realm. Completed in 1267, his magnificent new capital T'ai-tu ('Great Court'), popularly known as Khan-Balik ('City of the Khan'), was an appropriately splendid monument to the genius of Mongol military might throughout the thirteenth and fourteenth centuries. Fuelled both by the high-spirited tales of Marco Polo and, half a millennium later, by Samuel Taylor Coleridge's opium-inspired poem about Kubla Khan and his 'stately pleasure dome' in Xanadu, it gave rise to the sense of romance and wonder that still greets Kublai's name today.

Troublesome relatives

In a culture that regarded Genghisid blood as the sine qua non of military and political leadership, Kublai, second son of Genghis's son Tuli, was blessed from birth with considerable advantages. Not for him the humble scrabbling about for followers that marked the early years of both Genghis and Tamerlane. While at an age when both of these men had been grubbing about in adversity and complete obscurity, Kublai, together with his younger brother Hulagu, founder of the Ilkhanate dynasty of Persia, were joining their world-famous grandfather on his last campaign in 1226–7. Neither boy was yet a teenager. A Mongol chronicler records how Genghis singled out the young Kublai for future greatness while on his deathbed. With his father away much of the time campaigning with Genghis, Kublai learnt to ride, shoot and hunt under the watchful eye of his mother Sorkaktani, a woman of enormous political mettle.

After Genghis's death in 1227, the succession passed to Ogedey, who established the seat of the Mongol empire in Karakorum and consolidated its hold over northern China before his rule collapsed as he descended into alcoholism. After Ogedey's death in 1246, his son Kuyuk became Great Khan, a brief and unhappy reign which ended just two years later with his premature death from a fatal combination of gout and alcoholism. Sibling rivalry between the various branches of the Genghisid family now burst out into the open and rival courts were established. It was only through the deft manoeuvring of Kublai's mother, by then Tuli's widow, that Kublai's older brother Monke was installed as Great Khan in 1251, though not without more opposition from within the perennially feuding Genghisid clan.

It was not until 1251 that Kublai played any more

than a cameo role in the Mongol story. Though his blood was unquestionably noble, he had plenty of relatives who could make the same boast. Genghis had not been backward in spreading the Mongol seed. Kublai was merely part of the extended royal family, no more, no less. Critically, he was not a member of the senior Ogedey branch from which all future Great Khans had to be chosen. Monke's elevation, however – effectively a coup by the house of Tuli against the house of Ogedey – immediately tore up the old script and thrust Kublai into greater prominence.

Early glory in China

If martial success was an overriding characteristic of the Mongol khans, it was invariably twinned with an insatiable hunger for territorial conquest. With his brother Hulagu blazing through the west, Monke looked east to continue the Mongol march deep into China. The unfathomably rich, unconquered southern Sung dynasty, ruler of 50 million subjects, was an affront to a race that believed its heavenly destiny was to rule the world.

Kublai was a natural choice to prosecute this ambitious effort in the east. He owned lands around Xian and already had experience of governing in China. In 1252, Monke gave him command of an army to take the modern-day province of Yunnan. Once conquered, it would serve as the base for the conquest of the south. This was Kublai's first opportunity to prove himself on the only testing ground that really mattered to the Mongols – the battlefield.

Kublai marched south with his army more than a year after receiving his orders, accompanied by Uriyangkhaday, the son of Genghis's greatest general, Subedey, having devoted the intervening time to intensive preparations for his debut campaign. Unlike his father Tuli and Monke, who had both commanded expeditions in their teens and early twenties, Kublai was by now in his mid thirties. He was resolved to make his mark.

In the event, Kublai's first foray into war was a brilliant success. His complacent enemy was undone by a three-pronged offensive and, after a surprise night-time attack across the Upper Yangtze, the Mongols prevailed. After only a handful of executions, the capital of Dali was spared and the king became a Mongol puppet with minimal disruption. Kublai had won his spurs.

A bigger prize

In 1257, after several years of governing and extending his Chinese estates with an increasingly cosmopolitan caucus of advisers, Kublai's next commission was to lead one of Monke's four armies sent to conquer the Sung dynasty, thereby uniting the north and south under Mongol rule. The campaign was interrupted in 1259 by the sudden death of Monke, a severe blow to the Mongol body politic. It marked the collapse of unity and the end of further Mongol conquest in Asia Minor and the Middle East. For the first time, the succession from one Great Khan to the next would be decided by the use of arms.

Rather than hurrying north to press his case for supreme command of the empire, when asked to return Kublai refused, choosing instead to continue the campaign, perhaps reasoning that a military triumph would only improve his chances. The army pushed on south of the Yangtze, forcing the Sung into a defensive position. With his younger brother Arik Boke gaining ground in his bid to succeed Monke, Kublai was forced to put the campaign on hold. He called a kuriltay, the traditional national assembly convened to select a new emperor, and on 5 May 1260 in Chang-tu, or Xanadu – henceforth his summer capital – Kublai was duly made Great Khan.

Winning the civil war

A month after Kublai's coronation, Arik Boke was proclaimed Great Khan in a rival ceremony in Karakorum, Genghis's former capital. With the early backing of Berke, khan of the Golden Horde, and Alghu, Chaghatay khan of Central Asia, together with many in Monke's family, Arik had an early edge over his older brother, who could count only on Hulagu, embattled in the west. Quite legit- imately, Arik argued that Kublai's kuriltay was invalid,

since it had been convened outside the Mongolian homeland. The two men, though brothers, were poles apart.
Arik represented the traditional Mongol values of the
steppe, opposed to the despicable luxuries of settled life
and arguing that the centre of the Mongol empire should
be in Mongolia. Kublai, on the other hand, was a more
pragmatic ruler steeped in the culture of his Chinese
subjects, who recognized the need for accommodation
between the relatively small Mongol political class and the
far more numerous people they ruled.

The rivalry had to be resolved on the battlefield. Arik,
hampered by an inability to secure enough grain and
weapons for his army, ended up in a distracting fight with
his former ally, Alghu. With Chinese support behind him,
Kublai consolidated his hold over Mongolia, in 1264 forcing
Arik to make a humiliating surrender. Within the space of
a year, the deaths of Hulagu, Berke and Alghu had cleared
the diplomatic field for him. In 1266, Arik, too, died
suddenly. The unproven suspicion remains that Kublai had
him poisoned. Whatever the truth, all of the main challenges to his authority had been removed in short order.
Though his cousin Kaidu, head of the house of Ogedey,
continued to oppose him, and though there were always
Mongols who resented Kublai's Chinese ways, his position
at the helm of the most powerful empire in the world was
never seriously unsettled again.

A Chinese dynasty for China

With these internal matters resolved, Kublai could turn once more to his main preoccupation: China, specifically the incorporation of the elusive southern Sung dynasty into the Mongol realms. Part of his genius lay in the way this was accomplished. Genghis might have looked upon such an undertaking as a purely military exercise. For Kublai it was profoundly political, too.

It was for this reason that, at the outset of his reign, Kublai moved his capital from Karakorum to T'ai-tu, Marco Polo's dazzling city of Cambaluc, today's Beijing. As J. J. Saunders wrote in his classic work, *The History of the Mongol Conquests*, for a man such as Kublai, who had spent almost his entire life in China, 'it seemed natural that he should transfer the centre of empire to a Chinese city within the Great Wall and that he should aspire to reign as Son of Heaven rather than as a Mongol khan'. It was a seismic shift in the history of the empire. The imperial capital was now a settled city built by Chinese architects on Chinese soil. Under Kublai's command it grew to the height of magnificence, surrounded by 15 miles of walls 30 feet high and 30 feet thick. A second set of walls screened the Imperial City, a third hid the royal palace and a fourth created a palace within a palace. It would become the richest city on earth.

Northern China might have fallen into the hands of

foreign barbarians, but Kublai did his best to disguise this obvious truth. Hence the new Chinese name for his new dynasty: Yuan, meaning first, principal, fundamental, the ultimate source, cannily plucked by Kublai from the *I Ching*, the hallowed book of divination. A master of imperial administration, Kublai sustained his new dynasty with a subtle amalgam of Mongol and Chinese traditions and officials.

Defeating the Sung

Kublai's initial attempts to wrest control of southern China from the Sung were diplomatic. Initially, limited self-rule was offered in return for acknowledgement of his authority. The Sung were unimpressed and detained his envoy for sixteen years. Throughout the 1260s Kublai remained committed to the cause, encouraging defections from the Sung army, giving land, clothing and oxen to those who rallied to his side. It was also during this time that Kublai brought Tibet within his expanding sway, through astute patronage of a Buddhist lama and prince, Phags-pa.

Conquering the Sung was the Mongol empire's most formidable challenge to date. Unlike the steppe homeland, southern China was a land of cities and rivers. Its conquest required a mastery of both siege and naval warfare. The key to success in the south lay on the Han river, a tributary of the mighty Yangtze; it was the prodigiously strong and well-defended city of Siang-yang.

The zenith of Kublai's military career was unquestionably the conquest of southern Sung China, a victory that guaranteed his posterity as one of the Mongols' finest commanders.

The heart of the Mongols' armies had always been their superb cavalry, trained almost from birth and deployed with devastating effect across the battlefields of Asia. To take Sung China, however, required a concerted input from Kublai's infantry and an impromptu navy, allied with a breathtaking level of logistical support and the world's latest siege machinery – all of this for a campaign that would rumble along for a decade. Few, if any, Mongol expeditions had ever attempted anything so ambitious.

The siege of Siang-yang and the adjacent city of Fancheng was the longest confrontation of this sustained campaign, lasting from 1268 to 1273. It was rightly singled out for special notice by the Persian historian Rashid al-Din, Marco Polo and the Chinese chronicles. The two cities on the opposite banks of the Han river were the heavily fortified gates to the Yangtze basin and the south. Siang-yang, said Rashid al-Din, was defended by a 'strong castle, a stout wall and a deep moat'. To take it demanded a complete blockade of the Han.

The cosmopolitan background of the commanders Kublai chose to prosecute this campaign demonstrated his flair for promoting non-Mongols to important positions, which was a key factor in his military triumphs. Two were Chinese generals, including a recent defector. The chief Mongol was Aju, son of Uriyangkhaday, the grandson of Genghis's legendary general Subedey. From Persia came the siege engineers Ismail and Ala al-Din. His ships were built by Koreans and Jurchens.

An order was given to build 500 boats in order to draw a noose around Siang-yang. Next came fortifications south of the city to prevent boats bringing in supplies. There were periodic attempts to break the blockade. In August 1269, the Sung general attacked with 3,000 boats, only to be trounced by Mongol forces. In March 1270, 10,000 Sung soldiers and cavalry, together with 100 boats, tried to break through and again were defeated.

The siege, however, was drifting into stalemate. Kublai sent to his nephew Abakha, the Persian Ilkhan 4,000 miles away, for siege engineers, and in late 1272, a huge counterweight trebuchet started raining down enormous missiles on the two cities. 'These took effect among the buildings, crashing and smashing through everything with huge din and commotion,' Marco Polo wrote. With such formidable artillery support, the Mongol army was able to storm the fort at Fancheng, which quickly fell in late 1272. Ten thousand soldiers and civilians had their throats slit within sight of Siang-yang.

The city held out until the following spring, but the blockade and artillery barrage proved too fierce. The garrison, Polo wrote, 'took counsel together, but no counsel could be suggested how to escape from these engines. They declared they were all dead men if they yielded not, so they determined to surrender.' Siang-yang's fall led Kublai's army to the Sung capital Hangchow, which quickly folded. Its fall was the crowning glory of Kublai's career, a landmark conquest of the Mongols' toughest ever adversary. This triumph opened the way to the Sung capital of Lin-an (Hangchow), then the world's richest and most populous city, with a population conservatively estimated at 1.5 million.

From Siang-yang, the Mongol army turned east, commanded by Kublai's most trusted general, Bayan. Towns and cities folded before their advance, prompting the dowager empress Hsieh to sue for peace on favourable terms. But it was too late. Bayan was interested only in unconditional surrender, finally achieved in 1276. Further resistance from Sung loyalists who had been forced further south continued to test Kublai's resolve and patience. It was only when the 9-year-old child emperor Shih died, following the shipwreck of his fleeing supporters in 1278, that Kublai finally extinguished the dream of Sung independence for good.

It has been said that Kublai was emperor of a greater population than had ever acknowledged the supremacy of one man.

The later campaigns

Gloriously successful at home, where his political skills eclipsed his military talents, Kublai proved less impressive overseas. It is difficult to avoid the conclusion that his later adventures overseas, particularly his ill-conceived campaigns against Japan, Java and Vietnam, dulled the gloss on what had, until then, been an exemplary military record. So why did Kublai launch such campaigns? Because he was a Mongol and this is what a Mongol emperor instinctively did. Imperial expansion was not so much a choice as a necessity. It came almost as a hereditary obligation. It is only because they are so rare that we tend to be disproportionately shocked by Mongol defeats. If, for much of the twentieth century, the British Conservative Party was seen as the natural party of government, for much of the thirteenth and fourteenth centuries the Mongols were seen as the natural masters of warfare and empire.

Kublai's first attempt on Japan was launched unsuccessfully from his vassal state of Korea in 1274. A second attack, with an army of forty-five thousand Mongols and one hundred and twenty thousand Sino-Koreans, followed in 1281, but it was wiped out by the defenders of Kyushu and a vicious typhoon. It was Kublai's most catastrophic loss and destroyed the Mongols' long-treasured aura of invincibility in the East. A third punitive campaign was only prevented by the refusal of Chinese shipbuilders to produce the vast numbers of boats Kublai demanded. There were repeated campaigns against the recalcitrant little kingdom of Pagan (Burma) from 1277. But even when the wily king eventually offered tribute in 1287, the blood and treasure it had cost Kublai to mount these expeditions was far more than anything derived from it. Further embarrassing overseas failures followed, first in Vietnam and then, in 1292–3, in Java.

With rebellions breaking out in Tibet and Manchuria, in 1287 the 72-year-old Khan of Khans, laid low by gout and rheumatism, took to the battlefield in person to see off his cousins, rebel leaders Nayan and Kaidu. Marco Polo described the encounter as 'the most parlous and fierce and fearful battle that ever has been fought in our day'. It resulted in the capture of Nayan, who was bound and trussed, rolled inside a carpet and beaten to death in the traditional bloodless execution the Mongols favoured for a royal prince. Kaidu remained at large. The disappointments of Kublai's later years were crowned with the crushing deaths of his favourite wife Chabi in 1281 and his crown prince Chen-chin in 1285. Kublai's response was to consume spectacular quantities of food and wine, ballooning into a vastly overweight alcoholic in the process. He died in his eightieth year, diminished through age and gluttony, but with his reputation as one of the Mongols' most brilliant commanders deservedly intact.

ALEXANDER NEVSKY

1220/21–1263

ISABEL DE MADARIAGA

PRINCE ALEXANDER YAROSLAVICH NEVSKY was born in Pereyaslavl' Zalessky, in northeastern Russia. Whilst still a young man, Alexander was appointed by his uncle, Grand Prince Yury Vsevolodovich, to rule in the Republic of Novgorod, and in 1238 and 1242 commanded Russian forces in two seemingly minor engagements, both of which he won, and which later added to his great fame as saint, prince and warrior.

Russia's reigning dynasty in the early thirteenth century descended from the possibly legendary Scandinavian prince Riurik. In the late tenth century, Grand Prince Vladimir had presided over the conversion of Russia to Orthodox Christianity as practised in Constantinople. Russia's principal city was Kiev, on the Dnieper river, from whence the

Scandinavian–Slavonic settlements spread out. The number of Russian princes multiplied over the centuries, and there were frequent and violent disputes over the succession to the lands belonging to the various branches of the princely family. In a practice adopted by many other ethnic groups at this time, the throne did not normally descend from father to son but from the ruler to his eldest brother. The succession then went from brother to brother and, when there were no further brothers, to the eldest son of the eldest brother, then to his next son and, if the heirs failed, to the son of the next brother in line. Non-ruling princes were often temporarily allotted lesser principalities of their own, which they might pass to their own brothers or sons.

By the late twelfth century, Kiev had been replaced by the city of Vladimir-in-Suzdal as the stable political centre of the dynastic lands; its ruler was also called 'grand prince' and charged with appointing princes to the other princi-palities of northeastern Russia. In the early thirteenth century Yury II was grand prince, and his heir was his brother Yaroslav, the father of Alexander Nevsky.

To the northeast of the lands of the Rus' princes lay the city republics of Novgorod ('new town') and Pskov, both within easy reach of the Baltic Sea. Novgorod was a prosperous, self-governing trading community, owning vast lands that extended as far as the Arctic Ocean. Rich in furs, wax, honey and hides, it traded extensively down the Volga river to the Caspian Sea and the Far East; down the Dnieper river to the Black Sea and the Eastern Roman Empire; and through the Baltic Sea to the west, by means of its relationship with the German Hanseatic League. Novgorod had a special arrangement with the Grand Principality of Kiev, whereby it appointed a prince from the ruling dynasty, by contract, to organize and lead the defence of the city and to supervise its administration; the town assembly comprised the mayor and the wealthier citizens, and the archbishop also played a prominent political role in the government of the city.

In the early thirteenth century the land of Rus' faced serious enemies: in the north, the Swedes and members of a German crusading order in Livonia; further west, the pagan Grand Principality of Lithuania, not yet dynastically linked with Poland but advancing already against the Russian principality of Polotsk; and in the east, the even more serious threat of the Mongol empire of Genghis Khan.

The Mongol invasions

By the end of the twelfth century, the Mongols were united under the rule of Genghis Khan in his distant city, Karakorum, in what is today Outer Mongolia. A first exploratory raid on southern Russia took place in 1222–3, as part of a carefully planned Mongol attack on Central Asia which culminated in a Russian defeat on the River Kalka, on the Sea of Azov.

Although Genghis Khan died in 1227, a further assault on the West was made in 1234, the Mongols this time advancing to Moscow, which they burnt, then storming Vladimir-in-Suzdal and killing the inhabitants, including Grand Prince Yury's wife and two of his sons.

A second and more serious battle took place on 4 March 1238 on the River Sit', in the province of Vladimir, in which the Grand Duke Yury himself was killed, together with three of his nephews. With the approaching spring thaw, however, the Mongols turned south, to where they could find the vast pastures necessary for the maintenance of their huge cavalry army. After a year's rest the Mongol army renewed its assault and on 6 December 1240 stormed into Kiev, destroying the city and massacring all who lived there. The Mongol advance into Europe continued under Genghis Khan's grandson Batu, and on 9 April 1241 the Mongols defeated the joint German–Polish forces at the Battle of Liegnitz in Silesia and, continuing into Croatia, reached the coast of Dalmatia. The campaign was called off, however, on the news of the death of the Khan in faraway Karakorum in the spring of 1252.

The first appearance of Alexander Nevsky

As ruler of Vladimir-in-Suzdal, Grand Prince Yury II had occasionally sent his young nephew, Alexander, to rule in Novgorod. On the death of Yury in the battle of Sit', his next brother, Alexander's father Yaroslav, became Grand Duke, and the young Prince Alexander Yaroslavich was again sent to Novgorod. As a result, Alexander's first independent experience of battle was against the Swedes, who had been converted to Christianity by Catholic priests and monks and had been briefly under the tutelage of Cardinal Nicolas Breakspear (later Pope Hadrian IV).

Unfortunately for the Rus', the Christian Church of Rome considered the Orthodox Christians of the Church of Constantinople to be schismatics, as bad as pagans. The Catholic Swedish Vikings, in a crusading spirit, thus felt entitled to attack as heathens the small Russian settlements on the southern shore of the Gulf of Finland. Indeed, it has been suggested that the Swedes were moved at this time, by pressure from the papacy, to embark on a crusade against the schismatic Russians in order to extend the lands under Catholic control, but there seems to be no strong evidence to support this otherwise convenient theory. What is certain is that Sweden was anxious to control the narrow isthmus that dominated communication between Finland and Lake Ladoga, which would enable the Swedes to defend themselves against constant attacks by local tribes.

The evidence of events in the early thirteenth century is firstly based almost entirely on the many versions of local Russian and Livonian chronicles, produced in various redactions and at various times, usually by monks, in the interests of various princes; and, secondly, on the many versions of a 'Life' of Alexander Nevsky – part biography, part hagiography – probably composed some forty years after Alexander's death by someone who had known him personally, possibly under the supervision of Metropolitan Cyril. The most systematic chronicle, the genealogical *Book of Degrees*, dates from the mid sixteenth century, and introduces much material which emphasizes Alexander's role as a saint and a prince, but not as a military commander.

According to the 'Life' of Alexander, as remodelled in 1563, the king (Erik) 'of a land of the Roman faith' to the North (Sweden), hearing that the Rus' were suffering from the ravages of the Mongols, 'thought it a good time to conquer the rest of Rus'', to 'reduce the Slavs to slavery' and to take Grand Prince Alexander 'alive with my own hands'. The Swedish forces, therefore, with the support of Norwegian, Finnish and Karelian contingents, landed near the mouth of the River Neva in July 1240, with the aim of seizing the settlement of Ladoga, advancing on Novgorod the Great, and enslaving the people of Rus'.

Russian military organization

There was at this time no Russian national army, because there was no national centre or state. The armament reflected the time and the enemies faced by the Russians, comprising mounted and armour-clad western knights and the fleet cavalry of the steppe nomads. Russian armed forces consisted of cavalry from the local prince's personal retinue, supported by their own mounted retainers and supplemented by a locally based militia raised in the cities and the villages. The higher-ranking princes and boyars (noblemen) supplied the cavalry. They were armed with shields, helmets and chain-mail tunics; in illustrations, Russian helmets with noseguards are usually spiked and German ones round. The cavalry sometimes also fought on foot, though the militia normally supplied the foot soldiers and baggage train.

Firearms began to be used at the end of the thirteenth century. Weapons consisted of double-edged swords, sabres, long and short spears, axes, bows and arrows. Troops were divided into '*polki*', usually translated as regiments, but at this time more realistically viewed as 'units' of between five hundred and a thousand men, depending on the size of the total force, which could be stationed as three or five or more units and could be flexibly deployed around the enemy centre. There were few castles and fortified town-ships in this marshy land.

The Battle of the Neva

The 'Life' describes the young Alexander as fearing God, keeping the commandments, keeping himself clean in body and soul, and being a virtuous young man, pleasing to God. His enemies trembled at the sound of his name. In response to the Swedish challenge, Prince Alexander called upon divine help and prayed in the church of Saint Sophia in Novgorod.

There is no information about the numbers engaged on either side in the Battle of the Neva, and indeed some historians think that no such battle actually took place, since it is not even mentioned in Swedish sources. To reconstruct Alexander's strategy, Russian authors have had to rely on the various redactions of the 'Life', and on an entry in the first *Novgorod Chronicle*. They have also drawn upon descriptions of fifteenth-century conflicts.

Divine intervention

The Swedes are said to have landed on the southern shore of the Gulf of Finland, not far from the confluence of the River Izhora with the Neva. Alexander had assembled a mixed force of cavalry and foot soldiers, also mainly mounted, and by forced marches had covered the 90 miles from Novgorod to the shores of the gulf in two days. He confronted the enemy on 16 July 1240. According to historical reconstructions of his tactics, he deployed five *'polki'*, disposed in 'echelons', which enabled them to advance in waves and to re-form.

Battle began with a cavalry charge by knights armed with lances, and very fierce fighting. Alexander himself slashed the leader of the Swedish forces across the face with his sword. The battle then split up into encounters between individuals or small groups. One modern historian, drawing on the earliest version of the *Novgorod Chronicle*, has suggested that among the Russian knights there were perhaps twenty killed, and among the soldiers perhaps over one hundred; the total number of men involved in the battle could thus be counted in hundreds rather than thousands.

But Alexander had other allies: one of his scouts spotted the two Russian eleventh-century princely martyrs, the brothers Boris and Gleb, being rowed in a boat towards the land. Boris called out to Gleb to row harder so as to hasten their arrival to assist Alexander. When informed of the presence of the saints, Alexander bade his followers not to mention it, until God had proclaimed his will. Defeated by the intervention of angels, the Swedes rushed to their ships, threw their dead into three of their vessels, which they sank in Lake Nevo, and fled. According to the 'Life', great multitudes of men struck down by God's angels were found dead on the opposite shore of the Izhora, where the prince's troops had not even set foot. His victory earned Prince Alexander the name of 'Nevsky,' given to him much later.

The attack from the Catholic West

The people of Novgorod were not, however, grateful to Alexander for his victory, and the grand prince left, taking his troops and his family with him. There was always tension between Alexander and the republican city, the princes wanting to increase their rights and authority, the Novgorodians wanting to preserve their independence. But hostilities of a different kind soon broke out. The German crusading Teutonic Order (formed by the merger between the Livonian Brothers of the Sword and those members of the Order of the Temple who remained after the collapse of the crusader kingdoms at the end of the twelfth century) had undertaken the task of converting the peoples of the Baltic shore by conquest and colonization – a tale enshrined in the Livonian *Rhymed Chronicle* (1290), and in a *Novgorod Chronicle*. Grand Prince Yaroslav of Vladimir sent his second son Andrey to defend Novgorod, and Alexander and Andrey cooperated in demolishing a fortress built by the advancing Germans in Kopor'e, and in freeing Pskov, which had been seized by the Teutonic Order. Re-establishing his authority in Novgorod by executing a number of 'traitors' and advancing into Estonian land, Alexander prepared for battle against the Teutonic Order on Lake Chud (also known as Lake Peipus), which took place on 5 April 1242. The combined Russian forces numbered at least three 'regiments' according to one authority, and there was also a contingent of archers.

The Battle on the Ice

According to a recent reconstruction based on a battle in 1268, the Novgorodian troops, on reaching the shores of Lake Chud, retreated, or feigned a retreat, on to the ice on the lake. Their feint drew the German troops, drawn up in their usual 'wedge', or 'hog' form, on to the frozen surface of the lake in pursuit. The Russian archers then attacked the knights on both flanks, but left the hand-to-hand fighting to the Russian cavalry advancing on both sides. Again there is very little evidence of what actually happened, but according to the 'Life' of Alexander, there was now 'a great and cruel slaughter of the Germans on Lake Chud, and a loud noise from the breaking of spears, and the clashing of swords. The frozen surface of the lake seemed to move and the ice could not be seen for the blood that covered it.' Alexander's forces pursued the fleeing Germans on the ice for seven versts (4½ miles).

The battle did not involve large numbers. According to the first *Novgorod Chronicle* four hundred German knights were killed and fifty taken prisoner. There were, however, fewer than four hundred and fifty knights in the Teutonic Order at the time, so the figures must be an exaggeration. The Livonian *Rhymed Chronicle* speaks only of twenty knights killed, and six taken prisoner. There is still considerable disagreement between Russian historians about this battle, some arguing that, like the Battle of the Neva, it never took place at all. Yet the battle and the personality of Alexander Nevsky have become embedded in historical memory.

The actual feasibility of a battle on the ice is questionable. A group of mainly American historians has recently discussed the surviving evidence in some detail, partly because there is no mention of knights being drowned in the early sources. The 'Life' of Alexander speaks of the ice 'beginning to move' (*zadvigat'sya*) in the course of the battle, and the sixteenth-century miniatures clearly show a few knights sinking in water, surrounded by shards of broken ice. But there are mentions of battles on ice at earlier times and in different places which may have influenced the historical memory. Moreover, are historians thinking of horsemen merely crossing frozen rivers on the ice, or are they thinking of actual fighting taking place on frozen rivers and lakes? Some have argued that 'it was safe to act on the thick ice' and that the Mongol contingent of the Russian force preferred campaigning in winter because it was easier for the small Mongol horses, possibly unshod, to gallop on frozen ground and rivers. It has been suggested that the horses were equipped with crampons. The greater weight of iron carried by German knights might have reduced their mobility on ice just beginning to thaw. However, underwater investigations carried out in the 1950s in what seems to have been the right places in Lake Chud revealed no remains of dead German knights in armour in the relatively shallow waters of the lake.

Was this a turning point in Russian history?
The idea of the Battle on the Ice has fascinated subsequent

students of historical myths in Russia, and it features dramatically in *Alexander Nevsky*, Sergei Eisenstein's film of 1938 – where Alexander is hero, prince, common man, splendid general, and charismatic saviour of Orthodox Russia from German conquest and from the Roman Catholic aggression of the papacy. (The film was withdrawn during the Nazi–Soviet pact of August 1939 but released when Germany invaded Russia in June 1941.) But there is really no agreement on the significance in Russian history of these two minor battles won by Alexander Nevsky.

Alexander succeeded his father in 1252 after Yaroslav, who had been confirmed as Grand Prince of Vladimir by the Mongol overlord, died in 1246 on the return journey from Karakorum. Alexander himself journeyed twice to Saray, the Mongol capital on the Volga, and once all the way to Karakorum, also dying on the return journey. Apparently believing that Russia was too weak to oppose Mongol supremacy, Alexander pursued a policy of appeasement of the Mongols, coupled with a number of victorious engagements against western forces. He cooperated with the Khans in imposing a census on Novgorod, levying the tribute for the Mongols, recruiting Russians for service in the Tatar army and influencing the choice of princely rulers. His 'great deeds' in defence of Russia and the confidence which his charismatic personality inspired (he took the highest monastic order on his death bed in 1263) led many (though not the

Novgorodians) to overlook his pro-Mongol policies, and to regard his tomb in the church of Vladimir-in-Suzdal as a shrine. He was proclaimed a saint in Russia in 1547.

'Cet Ulysse parmi les saints'

The final apotheosis of this 'Ulysses among the Saints', in the words of the French scholar Pierre Pascal, came when Peter the Great, after his defeat of Sweden, planted wooden crosses in 1704 near the site of the Battle of the Neva, and made St Alexander Nevsky patron saint of his new city of St Petersburg, as a warrior, not a monk. His widow, Catherine I, founded the Military Order of Knights of St Alexander Nevsky in 1725 in his honour. The intimate association of St Alexander Nevsky, first with his direct descendants, the tsars of Moscow, then with St Petersburg and the Romanovs, raised him to the highest level of Russian heroism and sanctity.

BAIBARS

c. 1229–77

JONATHAN PHILLIPS

SULTAN BAIBARS CAN JUSTLY CLAIM to be the most formidable warrior of the medieval Islamic world. He rose from being a reject on the slave-markets of Syria to become the foundation stone of the Mamluk dynasty – for over two hundred years one of the world's great powers. His own career encompassed the crusade of Saint Louis (1248–54); the defeat of the previously invincible Mongols at the Battle of 'Ayn Jalut (1260) and a seventeen-year period as the ruler of Egypt and Syria (1260–77).

While Saladin (d. 1193) stands as the emblematic figure of the Muslim–Crusader conflict – as an icon of chivalric virtue in the West and, for present-day Islamists, the man who recaptured Jerusalem from the Christians (1187) – it was Baibars who really broke the Frankish stranglehold on the coast and made their expulsion from the mainland Levant almost inevitable. If it is Saladin who dominates the popular imagination of today it was, until modern times, Baibars' reputation that loomed the larger. Apart from the biographies written during and after his lifetime, it was in the fifteenth century that we find the first references to the oral folk epic, *Sirat Baibars* (*The Story of Baibars*). With the heroism, humanity and piety of its hero burnished to the dazzling levels appropriate to the genre, it remained an immensely popular work for hundreds of years; in the early twentieth century it still had at least thirty specialist reciters on the streets of Cairo alone.

The origins of the Mamluks

The principal feature of Baibars' regime – and that of his successors – was the dominance of the army; the sultan himself was the product of a military upbringing. He was born in around 1229 to a family of Kipchak Turks who had fled from the southern Russian steppes to the Crimea in the face of Mongol invasions. As a youth Baibars was enslaved, but his first purchaser returned him because of a white mark in one of his pupils, while another buyer turned him down because of his supposedly evil eye.

At the age of 14, he was purchased cheaply in the slave markets of Aleppo by a local noble, but before long he ended up in Cairo at the court of as-Salih Ayyub, the ruler of Egypt and a descendant of Saladin himself. There he was sent to join the Bahriyya Mamluks, a body created by Ayyub to be the elite force of his army. The Muslim rulers had long used Mamluks (slave soldiers, literally meaning 'owned') purchased from central Asia or the Crimea, but the youths from this particular group were separated and sent to the island of al-Rawda in the Nile, where they were converted to Islam. They lived a communal life in barracks and trained hard – the need for conversion aside, in these other respects they were comparable to the prime strike force of the Christian armies, the Military Orders. After completing their training the Bahriyya Mamluks were emancipated and formed the sultan's combat household.

One of the earliest occasions when this group came to the fore was at the Battle of Mansourah in February 1250. The previous summer King (later Saint) Louis IX of France had landed in Egypt at the head of the Seventh Crusade, the best-organized of them all; now he advanced down the Nile and threatened Cairo itself. The sultan Ayyub had recently died, and on 8 February the crusaders crossed the river and devastated the Egyptian camp, killing their commander as he took his early morning bath. The Christian cavalry thundered on towards the town of Mansourah – a fatal error; with Baibars at the head of the Bahriyya Mamluks, the Muslims regrouped. Described by a contemporary as 'lions in battle and the champions of cut and thrust' the Mamluks mounted a vicious counter-charge and the Christians scattered. Then, trapped in the dense warren of Mansourah's streets, the Muslims killed the crusaders' horses and slowly picked off the exhausted, thirsty knights. Probably fifteen hundred of the finest crusader warriors perished, including two hundred and eighty Templars. For Baibars and the Bahriyya, it was a famous victory. In a society that so valued fighting prowess this was a vital example of strength and, of course, of divine favour – two factors that would be advanced later to help justify Baibars' seizure of power.

The Mongol invasion and the Battle of 'Ayn Jalut

The Seventh Crusade eventually collapsed, although not before Ayyub's heir, Turanshah, had been murdered by the Bahriyya for failing to reward them for their efforts at Mansourah. Into this dynastic void an unsteady combination of Ayyubid and Mamluk rulers emerged, led in the late 1250s by Baibars' rival, Qutuz. It was this man who had to face the most dangerous threat of all: the Mongols. In 1258 an army of over one hundred thousand nomadic horsemen smashed their way into Baghdad, the greatest city in the Near East, and destroyed the Sunni caliphate. The Mongols were emboldened by their belief in a divine mandate, which entitled them to treat anyone who confronted them as enemies of God and deserving of obliteration. On this basis, in late 1259, they advanced on Syria, Palestine and Egypt;

some cities, such as Frankish Antioch, submitted; others, such as Muslim Aleppo, tried to fight but were crushed. In the early summer of 1260, however, a large part of the Mongol army retreated to seek better pasture and Qutuz took this as his cue to resist. With Baghdad and Syria in Mongol hands, the survival of Islam in the Near East rested with the Egyptians. Invoking the jihad, or holy war, against the Mongols, Qutuz cut their envoys in half in a brutal declaration of hostility.

In September 1260 Qutuz, now accompanied by Baibars, marched into Syria to confront the invaders. The two armies, each numbering about twelve thousand men, met on 25 September at 'Ayn Jalut – the Springs of Goliath; an appropriate place for a supposedly weaker party to take on an allegedly invincible opponent. Unlike a battle between contemporary Christians and Muslims, the two forces were relatively similar, with both sides formed principally of mounted archers, rather than the heavy cavalry intrinsic to Frankish warfare.

A crucial element in the Mamluk victory was the work of Baibars' scouting party, who repeatedly tangled with the Mongol vanguard, only to drop back and lure his opponents to the Mamluks' chosen battle-ground at 'Ayn Jalut, a valley with wooded ridges, water supply and an adjacent plain. The Muslim troops arrayed themselves on the hillside while the Mongols faced the strong early morning sun. The Mamluks marched slowly down the slope, constantly beating their drums and calling upon God's help. At first the Mongols looked the stronger, but the Mamluk left wing had been reinforced with extra cavalry and was able to push back the Mongol right. Then, on the Mongol left, the ruler of Homs, a Muslim ally of the nomads, broke and fled, leaving the centre to be surrounded. The remaining Mongols fought fiercely and tried to battle up the hill, but Baibars led the pursuit and they were routed. Ibn 'Abd al-Zahir, Baibars' contemporary biographer, described how:

He stood before the enemy and bore the first shock of their onslaught. The enemy saw his bravery, the like of which was never heard before . . . *[He]* followed them up the hill . . . People heard about his efforts on the mountain and they climbed up to him from every direction, while he was fighting like one who staked his very life. The foot soldiers began to collect the heads of those he had killed.

The Mongol general was among those slain, and his remaining contingents in Syria were swiftly driven out. For the Mamluks this was a supreme moment – the aura of Mongol invincibility was broken.

Baibars takes power

Qutuz was not able to savour his achievement for long. On the journey back to Egypt he was murdered by Baibars near Gaza on 23 October 1260. Given his own heroism in the battle, Baibars could claim a large part of the responsibility for the Muslims' victory; more importantly, 'Ayn Jalut allowed him to pose as the true defender of Islam, the saviour of the faith; usurper or not, God must have approved of the Mamluks to permit them such a famous triumph.

Baibars moved fast to capitalize on 'Ayn Jalut and had himself elected as sultan; he also initiated a clever propaganda push. Ibn 'Abd al-Zahir wrote: 'When God had granted him victory over the Tartars at 'Ayn Jalut, the sultan ordered the erection of the Mashhad al-Nasr (a victory monument) to make plain the importance of this gift of God and the spilled blood of the enemy.'

When Baibars became sultan, his absolute priority was to organize the defences of Syria and Egypt against a possible Mongol counter-attack; the continued declaration of jihad was an integral part of this. Baibars himself was a devout Muslim and part of his success came through a close identification with holy war. To assist in this he resurrected the Sunni caliphate after its destruction at Baghdad in 1258. The sultan found a 'relative' of the last caliph and in 1262 invested him with the title. The man was kept under a close watch and with such 'guidance' he provided a source of spiritual legitimacy for Baibars, who could then act in the tradition of Saladin and Ayyub as leader of the jihad.

Baibars' organization of the army

Baibars required a military machine of the highest order, and under his command the numbers of cavalry rose considerably, in part boosted by refugees from areas now controlled by the Mongols; these were trained men incorporated into existing forces. It was amongst the Mamluks themselves, however, that the most significant changes took place. From a group of about one thousand, Baibars increased the number to nearer four thousand, a substantial body of highly skilled men who were to form the backbone of his army. These troops were fully professional soldiers who received rigorous training and were imbued with the ideas of jihad. They were exceptionally formidable warriors: heavily armed, bearing a bow and arrow, a sword, an axe, a lance, shield and wearing body armour, while riding horses (also with frontal protection) that combined the mobility of Arab mounts with the sturdiness of the Cyrenaica breed that could adapt to rougher terrain.

Baibars himself ordered the construction of special hippodromes in Cairo, and inspired his men through his wholehearted involvement in drills to practise the skills of equitation, fencing (one thousand hits a day on a target), archery, and the use of the lance (seventy-two separate exercises had to be mastered). The sultan's iron discipline was also famous; he held regular inspections of the troops and anyone who failed to pass muster was executed. Political challengers to the sultan were brutally dealt with, and drowning, crucifixion, banishment and blinding were amongst the summary deterrents meted out to those who opposed him.

Baibars paid great attention to logistical matters. Immediately after he became sultan he set up a 'pony express' style system of riders who could carry messages from Cairo to Damascus in three days – a distance of over 400 miles. He also used signal fires and a pigeon post to spread news, and he ensured that land routes were in good condition, improving roads and bridges where practical. He was particularly keen on espionage and would disguise himself to discover an opponent's strengths and weaknesses. At Tripoli in 1268, for example, he dressed as an equerry to meet Prince Bohemond VI in person, although his primary aim was to 'explore the town and find the points it could be stormed' according to Ibn 'Abd al-Zahir.

Baibars' campaigns against the Franks

Baibars certainly exploited this combination of military expertise, practical support and intelligence gathering; his remarkable energy allowed him to lead campaigns in almost every year of his rule, and he took on Franks (the name given to Christian settlers in the Levant), Turks, Mongols, Arabs and Armenians with equal determination and calculated ferocity. He made a series of truces with the Franks, usually when he needed to confront other opponents, but readily broke them when it suited him.

A summary of his efforts against the Franks gives an impression of his vigour: in 1261, he raided Frankish Palestine; in 1263, he attacked Acre; in 1265, he took Caesarea and Arsuf; in 1266, he captured Safad; in 1267, he raided Acre; and in 1268, he captured Jaffa and Beaufort before marching further north and taking Antioch. In 1269, he threatened Tyre, and in 1270 he raided near Krak des Chevaliers and captured it the following year along with Safita and Akkar. This schedule was in addition to the almost annual need to visit Damascus, to inspect his other Syrian lands, and to campaign in Nubia, the Yemen and Asia Minor. In 1269 he also made the haj to Mecca and Medina.

Baibars' raids against the Franks were so harsh that even Muslim writers characterized them as malicious: harvest crops were ravaged, trees felled and villages and livestock destroyed. From time to time various tricks were employed. On one occasion his men carried banners captured from the Templars and Hospitallers so as not to alarm agricultural workers close to the city of Acre; when the defenceless peasants realized the deceit it was too late to escape and five hundred of them were killed and then scalped, the trophies being strung on to a cord and hung around a tower on the castle of Safad.

The sultan's policy with regard to Frankish castles was cited by Ibn al-Furat: 'One part of the Muslim armies uproots Frankish fortresses, and destroys their castles, while another rebuilds what the Mongols destroyed in the east and increases the height of their ramparts [compared with what they were].' The idea behind dismantling those on the coast was to deny any forthcoming crusades a bridge-head. As the writer here noted, however, fortresses inland were often repaired after the damage of a siege and could be used as a base to control the surrounding districts, to intimidate Christian lands, and to defend against possible Mongol incursions.

The capture of Safad

Probably the most important battle of Baibars' career was 'Ayn Jalut but, as we have seen, he was not yet the commander. The Mamluks' greatest victory came a couple of years after his death when they routed the Persian Mongols at the Battle of Homs in 1281, although this is generally agreed to be a consequence of the military expertise generated by Baibars. The sultan himself led his troops in many successful sieges and the investment of

Safad in June 1266 gives a sense of the formidable range of weapons – military, psychological, and economic – that he would bring to bear upon an opponent.

The Franks had spent huge sums of money on this Templar fortress in northern Palestine. Ibn 'Abd al-Zahir described it as 'a lump in Syria's throat, an obstacle to breathing in Islam's chest'. As usual, soon after the siege began, Baibars offered the defenders gifts to try to induce them to surrender; much to the sultan's fury, however, these were adopted as ammunition and hurled back by mangonels (stone-throwing siege machines). Baibars brought up his own heavy siege engines from Damascus to fire naphtha and huge stones. After a few days he took the barbican, although in doing so the Muslims suffered heavy losses. Worried by this, Baibars offered the Syrian Christians – but not the Templars – safe conduct; he then renewed the attack. Because the castle seemed about to fall, a Templar official went out to negotiate. But Baibars still nursed a grievance over the insult concerning the gifts, and in revenge for the slight to his honour, he substituted a double of himself in order to offer safe conduct to everyone but then kill the Christians. Baibars told the Templar envoy his plan and gave him a simple set of alternatives – if he wanted to live and be rewarded, he was to go along with this strata-gem, otherwise he would be killed most cruelly. The man picked the former option. The defenders duly made their agreement with the false sultan and on 22 July 1266 they surrendered. The following night, as they made their way towards Acre, the Christians were seized and beheaded. In a typically macabre display, the sultan had their bones and heads placed inside a small circular wall so that they could be seen; a gruesome example for those who presumed to defy him.

Baibars and the Mongols

The threat from the Mongols of Persia required Baibars to show flexibility and inventiveness in his warfare. In the early years of his rule, he created a scorched-earth zone in the east of his lands to deny the nomads pasture for their horses. Then, needing more time in which to build up his own forces, he used diplomacy; first, as noted above, by making treaties with the Franks, but also by working with the Mongols of the Golden Horde, a group based in southern Russia who had become Muslims. Invoking a shared faith, Baibars exploited the deep-seated rivalry between the Golden Horde and the Mongols in Persia to take the pressure off his own lands. There were occasions, however, when the Mongols did invade. In 1273 they surrounded the castle of al-Bira on the Euphrates. The sultan skirted around the enemy with camels and wagons on which were carried boats in kit form; he then reassembled the boats and launched a devastating attack that utterly routed the

Mongols. He continued to push back the nomads in Asia Minor, and victories here and in Cilicia were among the last of his career.

Baibars died on 20 June 1277. He was taken ill while watching a polo match during which he had drunk some qumiz, a highly alcoholic brew made from fermented mare's milk (not the wine he so frowned upon). Given his atrocious record of murder and deceit, rumours of poisoning abounded, but no one was identified as responsible. He was buried in the Madrasa Zahiriye (formerly the house of Saladin's father) and the domed chamber, decorated with polychrome marble and mosaic work, can still be seen today.

Both ruthless and calculating, Baibars created an empire that ran from Asia Minor, through Syria, Palestine and Egypt down to Nubia and the Yemen. He successfully resisted the most lethal military force of the day and arguably took over that mantle for his own superb armies. His skills broke Frankish Syria beyond repair, and in spite of his harsh rule he governed successfully for seventeen years – a remarkable achievement for the slave-boy from the Crimea.

TAMERLANE

1336–1405

JUSTIN MAROZZI

IN THE CLOSING DECADES of the fourteenth century, the world's greatest conqueror surged forth unannounced from Central Asia. Tamerlane blazed through the continent like a firestorm, toppling kings and empires with contemptuous ease, riding to victory after victory at the head of his ferocious army of mounted Tatar archers. One by one the great cities of the East were stormed and sacked: Antioch and Aleppo, Balkh and Baghdad, Damascus and Delhi, Herat, Kabul, Shiraz and Isfahan – all were left in flaming ruins, their populations tortured without mercy, slaughtered and decapitated. On every battlefield Tamerlane's soldiers built soaring towers from the heads of their victims, deadly warnings to anyone who dared oppose them.

With each new triumph, his sparkling imperial capital of Samarkand, Pearl of the East, grew richer and more magnificent with the treasures plundered from across Asia, a booty that included waves of captive scholars and silk-weavers, poets and painters, musicians and miniaturists, armourers, gem-cutters, masons, architects, silversmiths and calligraphers. The sweep of his conquests was staggering. By the time of his death in 1405, after thirty-five years of constant campaigning, Tamerlane remained undefeated on the battlefield and had outshone both Alexander the Great and Genghis Khan in the annals of empire-building and warfare. Little wonder that two centuries later, in his celebrated play *Tamburlaine the Great*, Christopher Marlowe should christen him 'The Scourge of God'.

That all this could be achieved by one man is astonishing. That it is the record of a military leader crippled down his right side is scarcely credible. Excellence in the martial arts was an absolute prerequisite for success and self-advancement in the turbulent world of fourteenth-century Central Asia. As a local proverb had it: 'Only a hand that can grasp a sword can hold a sceptre.'

Tamerlane's beginnings were relatively humble. Unlike Alexander, he was not the son of a mighty king, nor of royal blood. According to tradition, he was born in Shakhrisabz, south of Samarkand, on 9 April 1336 to a minor noble called Taraghay of the Barlas tribe. His name was Temur, meaning 'iron'. An injury in his youth gave rise to the Persian version Temur-i-lang, Temur the Lame, which became further corrupted to Tamburlaine and Tamerlane.

Unlike Genghis Khan and his Mongols, he did not have a homogenous people to lead to war. Central Asia was a melting-pot of feuding tribes, riven by divisions and shifting alliances. It took a leader of outstanding charisma and bravery to forge these disparate peoples into one formidable army that was to prove so irresistible in the field. Any assessment of Tamerlane's extraordinary career must take into account these important distinctions.

The sheep-rustler who would rule the world

The fifteenth-century court chronicle of Sharaf ad-din Ali Yazdi, a masterpiece of florid sycophancy, has the young Tamerlane aspiring to world dominion. A much harsher verdict comes from Ahmed ibn Arabshah, Yazdi's Syrian contemporary, who as a young boy saw Tamerlane put his native city of Damascus to the sword in 1401. Arabshah lays much emphasis on the conqueror's early years as a sheep-stealer and petty brigand. It was during one such foraging mission that Tamerlane appears to have received his debilitating injury, probably shot by arrows to his right arm and leg while roaming the deserts of southwest Afghanistan in 1363.

Though the sources are generally quiet about Tamerlane's childhood and youth, there are glimpses of the relentless cunning that throughout his life would see him outwit and outmanoeuvre opponents both on and off the battlefield. If martial prowess was a constant throughout his career, so too was a quick intelligence coupled with meticulous preparation. His army was always superbly organized and equipped. Tactically and strategically he was masterful, with a love of the unexpected. Few commanders in history have been as bold.

In 1360, he vaulted out of obscurity and into the official histories with a characteristically audacious move. His homeland of Mawarannahr, the land beyond the river, had been invaded by the Moghul khan. Haji Beg, chief of the Barlas clan that ruled the Qashka Darya valley where Tamerlane lived, decided to flee rather than fight. The youthful Tamerlane told his leader he would stay behind to prevent the invading Moghuls from seizing more land. He did nothing of the sort. Recognizing the superiority of his enemy's army, he immediately offered his services to the Moghul khan as a vassal ruler. The offer was accepted. At the age of 24, Tamerlane had successfully claimed leadership of the entire Barlas tribe.

In another, more outlandish example of his cunning in the years before he rose to power in 1370, he was summoned to pledge his loyalty to a hereditary khan or face him on the battlefield. Since he did not have an army strong enough to deploy, he pretended he was sick and drank a basinful of wild boar's blood before receiving the khan's envoys. During the interview he started vomiting blood copiously, convincing his visitors that he was at death's door. The envoys returned to their master with news of their adversary's imminent demise. Tamerlane, who was encamped nearby, chose this moment to strike. Catching the hapless khan and his courtly entourage entirely unawares, he slew them where they lay.

By 1370, the opportunist sheep-stealer had seen off his one-time ally Amir Husayn, grandson of the last Chaghatay khan. He had himself crowned imperial ruler of Chaghatay in Balkh, the celebrated seat of power that had attracted both Alexander and Genghis Khan before him. His royal titles, nothing if not premature, were harbingers of the great conquests to come: Lord of the Fortunate Conjunction, Emperor of the Age, Conqueror of the World.

The horizons expand

From 1370 until his death in 1405, en route to war with the Ming emperor of China, Tamerlane hardly stood still. Apart from a two-year stint in Samarkand from 1396–8, during which he threw himself into a grandiose building programme with a fury usually reserved for the battlefield, he was always on the move. Samarkand was the hub around which his restless campaigning revolved.

Conquest was only possible for as long as he could keep his armies in the field. Steppe tribesmen traditionally would remain loyal to a leader for as long as he proved victorious in battle. There were no salaries. Temur understood this acutely. His military career was one long campaign, punctuated with only the briefest of interludes; he needed to keep his armies on the move.

Surveying a map of his conquests, the first decade or so of his reign from 1370 looks very much like a dress rehearsal for the main performance. It was during this time that Tamerlane started to consolidate his power in Mawarannahr and the surrounding region, the necessary precursor to projecting his force much further afield. In 1379, he sacked the city of Urgench. Roving west in 1381, he added Herat to his nascent empire with barely a murmur, and by 1382 Tamerlane was lord of the Caspian.

Wars of terror

It was also during this period that he developed a style of warfare that sent collective shudders across Asia and, in many instances, defeated opponents before they had even set foot on the battlefield. His soldiers, motivated by prospects for plunder, were willing agents of this policy of inflicting terror on their enemies and the civilian population alike.

As Sir John Malcolm, the nineteenth-century historian of Persia, wrote, 'Such a leader as Timour must have been idolized by his soldiers . . . he was careless of the opinion of other classes in the community. His object was fame as a conqueror; and a noble city was laid in ashes, or the inhabitants of a province massacred, on a cold calculation that the dreadful impression would facilitate the purposes of his ambition . . .'

News of what today we would call war crimes spread fast across the Asian steppes. Kings and princes came to appreciate the wisdom of acknowledging his suzerainty quickly. Those steadfast or rash enough to challenge his might were despatched with appalling brutality.

In 1383, Tamerlane had 2,000 prisoners cemented alive into towers in the city of Isfizar to punish the rebels of Khorasan. In 1387, infuriated by an uprising in the Persian city of Isfahan, which had already surrendered to him, he ordered a general massacre, in which 70,000 were slaughtered. Poised on the outskirts of Delhi in 1398, he ordered the army to kill in cold blood the 100,000 Indian prisoners he had captured, who had made the mistake of celebrating the Tatars' initial reversals during the early skirmishes with the Indians outside the city walls. Two years later, 3,000 Armenians were buried alive in the Turkish city of Sivas, this being Tamerlane's way of honouring a promise not to shed any blood after it had surrendered. After the fall of Baghdad in 1401, as the Tigris ran red with blood, Tamerlane had another terrible girdle of 120 towers piled around the city, this time the vultures having 90,000 heads to feed on.

Though Tamerlane bequeathed a splendid architectural

legacy characterized by monumental blue-tiled mosques and madrassahs with domes of iridescent blue rising high above elaborate portals, it was neither these remarkable buildings, nor the exquisite parks and palaces he designed during his reign for which he was best remembered. The much more ephemeral towers and pyramids of human heads, often illuminated by beacons at night, the hallmark of his battlefield victories, were his most feared and dreadful signature. They represented a powerful and highly effective disincentive for an independent city to resist or a subject city to rebel.

Taking care of his nemesis

In 1386, shortly after capturing Sultaniya, Tamerlane received disquieting news. His former protégé Tokhtamish, who with Tamerlane's repeated military support in the 1370s had become khan of the Golden Horde, had sacked the city of Tabriz in a direct challenge to his one-time mentor. Tamerlane's response was swift: the three-year campaign against Persia. The army marched west from Samarkand, taking Tabriz, quickly followed by the Georgian capital of Tiflis (Tbilisi). After one of his worst massacres, Isfahan fell in 1387, prompting Shiraz to surrender (wisely) without a fight. While Tamerlane was campaigning in Armenia and Asia Minor, word came that Tokhtamish, by now emerging as a formidable foe, had been laying waste to Mawarannahr.

In the harsh winter of 1389–90, with snow up to his horses' flanks, Tamerlane ordered his army north to hunt out and destroy his rival. For five months and almost 2,000 miles his men rode across the bleak Siberian steppe in ever worsening conditions. Tokhtamish's army, retreating into the shadows, refused to engage them, luring Tamerlane to certain destruction deep inside enemy territory.

Eventually, on 18 June 1391, the two armies came face to face. In a show of calculated contempt for his adversary, Tamerlane ordered his men to unpack and erect his sumptuous, fur-lined tents and pavilions and calmly lay out his carpets. According to the chronicles, this exercise in psychological warfare had its intended effect, shattering the morale of the Golden Horde. The next day, in the heat of the battle, Tokhtamish fled, leaving Tamerlane once more victorious.

On 22 April 1395, the two rivals faced each other again for the last time. For three days, both armies manoeuvred for position on opposite banks of the Terek river in modern-day Chechnya, Tokhtamish holding the advantage. At this point, as the confrontation was drifting towards stalemate, Tamerlane played his master card. As night fell, he ordered the women in his camp to dress up as soldiers, while his men made a three-day forced march back to a ford, the only crossing point available. Battle was then joined, with Tamerlane's men having seized the advantage. For the second time Tokhtamish fled during the battle. The Golden Horde was pillaged and put to the sword.

Outdoing his predecessors

Though his enemies within the Muslim world considered him an infidel barbarian, Tamerlane was a cultured man, a keen student of history and religion, and a peerless chess player. When, in 1398, he announced a campaign against India, having just concluded the successful, blood-soaked five-year campaign against Persia and Georgia, he did so consciously, to eclipse the achievements of Alexander and Genghis before him.

His princes and amirs were aghast at the logistical challenges of moving an army of one hundred thousand across the roof of the world. How would they cross the mountains and the rivers that lay between Samarkand and Delhi, they asked? How would they overcome the Indians' terrifying fighting elephants, clad in steel armour with tusk-mounted scimitars and flame-throwers, archers and crossbowmen in protected turrets on their backs? Tamerlane silenced them. Such feeble objections counted for nothing to the man who had never known defeat.

It was a whirlwind mission. Once the treacherous route across the mountains had been negotiated, with the elderly emperor at one point having to be lowered on a litter over a 1,000-foot precipice, the rest of the campaign proceeded as though on auto-pilot. Ruthless as ever in his preparations for war, Tamerlane ordered his men to make caltrops, three-pronged iron stakes, and leave them on the plain around Delhi. Camels were loaded with bundles of dried grass and wood. When battle was joined, the Indian war elephants found themselves being charged by roaring camels on fire. Wheeling around in terror, they retreated pell-mell through their own ranks, hobbled by the deadly caltrops, scattering the Indian troops who fled in blind panic. With a tortured gasp, one of the richest cities in the world slipped into Tamerlane's dominions. The extraordinary wealth accumulated by generations of India's sultans was plundered within the space of several days. Decapitated bodies lay putrefying in the streets. Towers of skulls loomed over a scene of unspeakable carnage. Famine and disease were rife. It took more than a century for Delhi to recover.

A pilgrimage of destruction

Barely pausing for breath after his triumphant homecoming to Samarkand, Tamerlane levied his army for the Seven-Year Campaign. It would be his final push. Age had not softened him. After his burying alive of the Armenian garrison at Sivas in 1400, he continued southwest into the heart of the Egyptian empire, striking first at Aleppo, which collapsed before the onslaught. The Tatars gave no quarter. Men, women and children were cut down where they stood,

thousands of heads being piled into mounds as th...
marched further south, leaving behind them scenes of
appalling slaughter.

In 1402, he faced his most powerful enemy in the
corpulent form of Sultan Bayezit the Thunderbolt, Sword
Arm of the Faith. Tamerlane's victory over his Ottoman
rival at the Battle of Ankara would be the most triumphant
of his life.

At around 10 o'clock on the morning of 28 July 1402,
Tamerlane surveyed his army on the Chibukabad plain,
northeast of Ankara. There were up to two hundred thousand professional soldiers drawn from the farthest reaches
of his empire, from Armenia to Afghanistan, and from
Samarkand to Siberia. They had never been defeated in
battle.

The left wing was commanded by the emperor's son,
Prince Shah Rukh, and his grandson, Khalil Sultan. Its
advance guard was under another grandson, Sultan Husayn.
Tamerlane's third son, Prince Miranshah, led the right wing,
his own son, Abu Bakr, at the head of the vanguard. The
main body of the army was under the command of
Tamerlane's grandson and heir, Prince Mohammed Sultan.

The Ottoman sultan Bayezit I had put a similar number
of troops into the field. There were twenty thousand Serbian
cavalry in full armour, mounted Sipahis, irregular cavalry
and infantry from the provinces of Asia Minor. Bayezit

commanded the centre at the head of five thousand Janissaries – the makings of a regular infantry – supported by three of his sons, the princes Musa, Isa and Mustapha. The right wing was led by the sultan's Christian brother-in-law, Lazarovic of Serbia, the left by another of his sons, Prince Suleiman Chelebi.

Even before battle commenced, Tamerlane's brilliant tactical manoeuvrings had comprehensively wrong-footed the Ottomans, knocking their morale and leaving them exhausted and thirsty. Only a week earlier they had occupied the higher ground on which their adversary's army now stood. Feigning flight, the Tatars had outmanoeuvred them, diverted and poisoned their water supply, doubled back, plundered their undefended camp and taken their position.

From the first blows struck the fighting was ferocious. Charging across the plain came the formidable Serbian cavalry. Under pressure, the Tatar left flank retreated, defending itself with volley after volley of arrows and flames of naphtha. On the right wing, Abu Bakr's forces, advancing against Prince Chelebi's left wing under cover of a cloud of arrows, fought like lions and finally broke through their enemy's ranks.

Bayezit's Tatar cavalry chose this moment to switch sides, turning suddenly against Chelebi's Macedonians and Turks from the rear. It was a decisive moment, which broke the Ottoman attack. Tamerlane had engineered the defection of the Tatars in the months before the battle by playing on their sense of tribal loyalty and holding out the prospect of richer plunder. Chelebi judged the battle lost and fled the field with the remainder of his men.

The elite Samarkand division, together with a body of the emperor's guards, charged the Serbian cavalry, who buckled under the attack and followed Chelebi in retreat towards Brusa. Bayezit's infantry were now the only forces left intact. Worse was to follow. The Tatar centre now moved forward to settle the affair with eighty regiments and the dreaded war elephants. The Ottoman infantry was routed.

Bayezit's forces defended their sultan valiantly to the last, but the Tatars' greater numbers eventually told. For the first and only time in Ottoman history, the sultan was captured in person. Tamerlane's greatest victory was complete.

Having sacked Asia Minor, he stood on the shores of the Aegean with Europe at his mercy. Instead, he set his eyes east towards the greatest prize yet: the Celestial Empire of China, the only significant adversary against which he had yet to test himself.

In the winter of 1404, the Tatar army marched from Samarkand with the wizened 68-year-old emperor at its head. Temperatures plummeted, winds gusted and the snows fell. Beards and moustaches froze on men's faces, said the chronicles. In Otrar, in what is today Kazakhstan, Tamerlane fell ill. Court doctors attended to him with hot drinks laced with drugs and spices but still the fever worsened. At 8 o'clock at night on 18 February 1405, he breathed his last. His blood had barely cooled when the internecine conflicts that he had warned against on his deathbed exploded. The empire he had laboured so carefully and cruelly to build started crumbling away. Within a century of his death it had vanished altogether.

THE BLACK PRINCE

1330–76

JONATHAN SUMPTION

EDWARD, PRINCE OF WALES AND AQUITAINE, the eldest son of Edward III, has been known as the 'Black Prince' since at least the sixteenth century. To his contemporaries, however, he was simply 'the Prince', a man whose fame in his own time was so great that no other description was called for. If generalship is the art of winning pitched battles, then Edward was unquestionably the greatest general of his day, and one of the greatest of the European Middle Ages. He commanded the Anglo-Gascon army which defeated and captured John II of France at the Battle of Poitiers in September 1356, one of the most complete military victories of the Hundred Years War. Eleven years later, at Nájera in northern Castile, he led another Anglo-Gascon army to overwhelming victory against Henry of Trastámara, the pretender to the throne of Castile. These were remarkable battles. If they were not decisive, it was because generalship is more than battlefield tactics and politics more than force of arms.

The Prince was born into a world in which military methods were evolving rapidly. For several centuries, the chief instrument of war had been the heavy cavalryman, mounted on a powerful charger, protected from head to toe by chain mail, and armed with lance and buckler, axe and sword. Yet however powerful the impact of their charge, heavy cavalry were generally ineffective against disciplined men fighting on foot in prepared positions. Moreover, they were vulnerable to mass archery, which could wreak havoc among the dense mass of unprotected horses, breaking up their formations and inflicting heavy casualties. In 1302, in a remarkable and widely noted demonstration of the superior strength of defensive formations of infantry, the army of the Flemish towns destroyed the chivalry of France at the Battle of Courtrai. The suicidal charge of the English cavalry against the disciplined squares of Scottish pikemen at the Battle of Bannockburn in 1314 was an awesome lesson, better learned by the English, perhaps, than by any other European nation.

Over the next half century, the English devised battle tactics which revolutionized European warfare. The hallmark of the English method was the use of dismounted cavalry fighting on foot, both defensively and offensively. The horses were taken to the rear at the outset of any engagement, to be used only for the rout at the end and the pursuit afterwards or, if things went badly, for flight.

At the same time, dismounted infantry formations were supported by dense lines of archers, generally at least a third of their strength, rising to two thirds by the end of the fourteenth century. The English, alone among European nations, made the longbow a formidable battlefield weapon. With their longer range and rapid rate of fire, longbows completely outclassed the crossbows which had become the standard item of equipment in other European armies. Traditional infantry was gradually eliminated from English armies, and had almost vanished by 1350. It was the co-ordinated use of dismounted cavalry and longbowmen that enabled Edward III to destroy a Scottish army at Halidon Hill in 1333 and a French one at Crécy in 1346. Crécy taught the French the lesson that they had failed to learn at Courtrai. In the second half of the century, their military method developed along English lines, with smaller, all-mounted armies fighting on foot, and increasingly composed of full-time professionals.

These developments taxed the skills of generations of army commanders to come. The co-ordinated deployment of dismounted men-at-arms and archers called for commanders to exercise a far greater degree of control over formations in the course of the battle than had been necessary before. Manoeuvring large bodies of men-at-arms who had never trained together was one of the perennial problems of medieval battlefields. It required not just outstanding judgement but battlefield staff, a rudimentary chain of command, and some means of communicating with subordinates. These requirements presented a considerable challenge at a time when orders were transmitted to section commanders by trumpet, occasionally by messenger, and thence by shouting. Signals could be complex, and difficult to hear inside a vizored helmet. The Prince rose to the challenge better than any of his contemporaries.

The Battle of Crécy, 1346

The Prince first saw action in 1346, when he took part, under his father's command, in the campaign in northern France which culminated in the Battle of Crécy on 26 August. He was then 16 years old, and in nominal command of one of the three divisions which made up an English army of about fourteen thousand men. They had fought a difficult campaign, landing from the sea in southern Normandy, and making their way first to Paris, then across the Seine west of the city, and finally, hungry and exhausted, across the great plain of Picardy. At Crécy the Prince, guided by experienced military commanders in the king's confidence, commanded the vanguard. We cannot know what impact the experience made on the young man. But some lessons must have been learned, for the battle was perhaps the classic demonstration of the English tactical method at a time when it was new to continental warfare, as well as a terrible warning of the consequences of a commander losing control of his own army.

The first division of French cavalry charged en masse with neither warning nor orders, trampling their own archers underfoot. The rest of the cavalry careered pell-mell after them, and ran into the rear of the first division. The English bowmen, stationed at the wings of the army, inflicted carnage on the Genoese crossbowmen – who provided the archery arm of the French army – before they could even come within range. They broke up the lines of the approaching masses of heavy cavalry, the latter being finally stopped by the lines of dismounted men-at-arms. The French horsemen repeatedly wheeled and charged, but without regard to what was happening elsewhere on the field. As a result, they were overwhelmed by a smaller but more skilful and disciplined enemy.

The Poitiers campaign

After the battle, the Prince played an increasingly promi-nent part in his father's wars against France. He served in the eleven-month siege of Calais which followed the Battle of Crécy, fought in the battle outside Calais in January 1350 and fought again in the great sea-battle off Winchelsea later that year. But he did not exercise an independent command until 1355, when he served as his father's lieutenant in the English duchy of Aquitaine in southwestern France. The

Prince arrived in Bordeaux by sea in September 1355, accompanied by a small English army of eight hundred men-at-arms and fourteen hundred mounted archers. Most of his strength was to be recruited after his arrival from the Gascon nobility. Between October and December 1355, the Prince's variegated army got used to fighting together in the course of a long and spectacular raid into the French province of Languedoc, which took them from the Atlantic coast at Bordeaux to within sight of the Mediterranean at Narbonne.

The real purpose of the Prince's presence in Aquitaine, however, was to take part in the great offensive against the heartlands of the French kingdom which had originally been planned for the autumn of 1355, but in the event had to be deferred to the following year. In its final form this plan had been formulated by the fertile strategic minds of King Edward III and his cousin Henry of Grosmont, Duke of Lancaster. It called for the co-ordinated invasion of France by three separate armies. The Prince was to advance north from Bordeaux. A small English army was to land in the Cotentin peninsula under Lancaster's command, and join forces with English garrison troops in Brittany and a substantial contingent of men loyal to Charles of Evreux, the French King of Navarre, then embroiled in a bitter civil war with the French monarchy. A third, much larger army, was to cross to Calais under the command of the king himself and come down from the north. All three English armies would join up in the Loire valley.

The Prince set out with his own army at the beginning of August 1356. Allowing for troops that had to be left behind to guard the marches of Aquitaine, he must have had between six and seven thousand men at his back, at least two thirds of whom were Gascon cavalrymen. There were about one thousand English archers. The army reached the Loire at Tours on 7 September, only to find that the northern claw of Edward's pincer movement had failed. The king had been forced to cancel the army of Picardy. Lancaster had set out from Normandy, but the great barrier of the Loire prevented him from joining forces with the Prince. Every crossing of the river was either broken or heavily defended, and Lancaster was obliged to retreat. The French king, John II, had collected an army of about eight thousand heavy cavalry and three thousand infantry. If the three English armies had been able to join up, he would have been seriously outnumbered. As it was, he was able to confront the Prince's army on its own. The Prince, concerned about numbers, supplies and communications with his base in Gascony, appears at first to have tried to retreat to Bordeaux. But the French king crossed the Loire and came south in pursuit. On 16 September 1356 he caught up with him in the great plain east of Poitiers. There, his army was defeated and largely destroyed in a great battle on the following day.

When dawn broke on 17 September 1356, the English

were dug in to a strong defensive position on gently rising ground south of the French army. Their front was protected by a thick hawthorn hedge. Their archers were stationed in their traditional position on the army's wings, their flanks protected on one side by deep trenches, and on the other by a marshy expanse of ground by the banks of the River Miosson. The French had decided on their tactics at a quarrelsome council of war the previous evening. They resolved to abandon the mass cavalry charge which had been the main feature of their battle tactics for more than two centuries, and deploy the greater part of the cavalry on foot. Interestingly, these dispositions were made on the advice of the Scottish knight, William Lord of Douglas, who was fighting with the French army and who reminded his colleagues of the fate of the English at Bannockburn.

The first French attack was a cavalry charge by two small formations, directed against the English wings. It was designed to scatter the archers and open the way for the main force. It came at the worst possible moment for the English. A short time before, the Prince and his advisers had decided to retreat, mainly, it seems, because they had run out of food. The force of the initial French cavalry charge struck the two flanks of the English line just as the retreat was beginning. However, regrouping with great difficulty, the archers succeeded in inflicting terrible casualties on the approaching horsemen and their mounts. All this was hidden from the lines of French men-at-arms by the brow of a hill. Ignorant of the fate of the cavalry, their first line was already advancing on foot towards the English positions under the young Dauphin of France. When they reached the hawthorn hedge, they crammed into the gaps to attack the enemy. After two hours of fierce hand-to-hand fighting, they were forced into retreat. In order to protect the Dauphin, he was hurried from the field with most of his men. The second French line took this as a signal to withdraw and followed after them. It was left to King John II to try to save the day by leading the reserve against the triumphant English. Attacking the whole of the English army with just a third of his own, John was driven back down the hill and over-whelmed in the fields below. At the critical point, one of the Prince's Gascon captains remounted about one hundred and sixty of his men and took them round the rear of the French to attack from behind. Another cavalry force, commanded by Sir James Audley, attacked from the side, completing the rout. Among the many famous French pris-oners of the day was John II himself.

The outcome of the Battle of Poitiers was largely deter-mined by differences at the level of command. The French king, although he had the larger army, tried to attack a strong defensive position without any local superiority of numbers, and proved incapable of modifying his plans as the battle developed. His divisional commanders had received their orders before the battle, and carried them out with grim persistence and outstanding courage, regardless of what was happening elsewhere. By comparison, the Prince was able to improvise plans in the heat of battle, and redeploy formations, communicating his orders with impressive speed to those who had to act on them. It was an outstanding demonstration of courage, discipline and generalship.

Yet it went a long way to show how evanescent were even the greatest victories if there were no means of following them up. The English in France in the fourteenth century never had the financial or administrative resources to occupy and hold enemy territory for more than short periods. They relied on the moral impact of defeat on their enemies, and on the sheer scale of physical destruction that they were able to inflict, rather as advocates of area bombing did in the Second World War. After the battle, the Prince returned with his army and his prisoners to Bordeaux. Even the capture of the king of France was an advantage that ultimately proved hard to exploit. The battle provoked a prolonged and bloody political crisis in France. Yet it took nearly four years to force the French to ransom their king and agree terms, and even then these terms proved to be short lived.

Prince of Aquitaine

It is perhaps unfair to blame the Prince for the limitations of medieval warfare or the failure of a strategy devised by his father. Yet when his own turn came to govern, he showed much the same inability to grasp the political framework in which all military action occurs. Between 1364 and 1371, the Prince was the independent ruler of the English principality of Aquitaine, a vastly enlarged territory comprising about a quarter of France which emerged from the treaties of 1360. In one sense it was the reward of his victory at Poitiers. Yet it was thrown away by a series of political misjudgements. Characteristically, the greatest of these misjudgements was about what could be achieved by mere force of arms.

In 1366, the Prince agreed with the deposed king of Castile, Pedro I, to invade Castile in order to restore him to his throne. It was essentially a financial transaction, under which the Prince was putting his army at Pedro's service in return for his expenses and a suitable fee. The Prince does not seem to have asked himself whether Pedro could afford to pay him, or how he would enforce the debt if he had to. He did not consider how Pedro could be maintained on his throne once the army which put him there had gone. He did not wonder what impact the venture would have on the future relations between England and the Iberian kingdoms.

The Battle of Nájera

Nájera is a small town of northern Castile, a short distance south of the River Ebro. West of its walls is the site of the Prince's last great battle, which was fought on 3 April 1367. His army was slightly larger than the one he had commanded at Poitiers, about eight to ten thousand men. Its make-up was very similar, consisting of a core of English men-at-arms and archers, with a much larger number of Gascon cavalry. The army ranged against him, however, was a good deal less formidable than the host of John II in 1356. The Pretender of Castile, Henry of Trastámara, had gathered together an army which was rather larger than the Prince's, but weaker in cavalry and both technically and tactically backward. Its main strength lay in the presence in its ranks of about one thousand experienced French veterans commanded by the future Constable of France, Bertrand du Guesclin. Like the Prince, they were there for money.

Henry was wrong-footed from the outset when a large section of the Anglo-Gascon army approached his forces by an unexpected route, from behind a line of hills beyond their left flank. Attacked from two directions at once, the Castilians and their French auxiliaries tried to take the offensive, only to be met by a rain of arrows from the English lines which broke up their formations and enabled them to be defeated in detail. It was all over in minutes. The Castilian light cavalry, which refused to demean itself by fighting on foot, was wiped out. As at

Poitiers, the Prince's victory was due mainly to his intelligent exploitation of the lie of the land, his willingness to try an unconventional manoeuvre, and his ability to follow and control the movements of his dispersed forces.

Decline and death

As after Poitiers, however, the Prince was unable to exploit his victory. In spite of an attempt to occupy territory in Castile as security for his claims, he was forced to return, bankrupt and ill, to Aquitaine. Henry of Trastámara himself barely escaped alive from the field of Nájera. Yet three years later, he had defeated and killed his rival, and permanently secured his possession of the Castilian throne. The financial claims of the Prince's Gascon followers, aggravated by his own lack of political finesse, ultimately led to a major rebellion against the Prince in Aquitaine which enabled Charles V of France to recover all the territory that France had lost in 1360. Weakened in body and mind, the Prince's one attempt to command his armies in person was the siege of the rebel city of Limoges in 1370. The siege became notorious for the massacre of the inhabitants that followed the successful assault, but had almost no impact on the inexorable advance of the French into his principality. The Prince returned a broken man to England at the end of 1371. He died at Westminster on 8 June 1376, a year before his father. Such was the prestige enjoyed by the profession of arms in the late Middle Ages, that no one recalled his political incompetence or questioned what his victories had really achieved. It was enough that the Prince had been physically impressive, courageous in the face of danger, and had won every battle that he had fought.

HENRY V

1387–1422

ROBERT HARDY

'"THOU LIEST, THOU LIEST, MY PORTION IS WITH THE LORD JESUS CHRIST!": the dying cry of one of the greatest commanders in the long history of English wars. He had been confronted in his sleep by a demon of doubt and fear that all he had achieved was evil, and damned him to Hell, in which he certainly believed. That cry had brought him upright in his bed; but then he lay back in his confessor's arms and a little later murmured "In manus tuas, Domine, ipsum terminum redimisti", and died "as if he slept".'

(Thomas Rymer x. 253, Vita Henrici Quinti, Monstrelet, et al.)

It was midnight, 20 August 1422, that Henry Plantagenet, King of England, heir of France, father of a baby boy who would be crowned King of France and England, died in the Château de Vincennes, outside Paris, a few weeks short of his thirty-fifth birthday; in another six weeks and a day he would have outlived his troubled and defeated rival, Charles VI of France, and become by solemn treaty inheritor of the crown of France.

Henry, Shakespeare's Hal – which let us call him for the moment – was born on 16 September 1387 in Monmouth Castle, the first surviving child of Henry Bolingbroke and grandson of John of Gaunt, Duke of Lancaster. The facts of his early upbringing are few. By the time he was 11, Hal's father had been banished by their cousin, King Richard II, partly because Bolingbroke had ousted some of the king's favourites, partly because of a dangerous quarrel with the Duke of Norfolk whom he accused of treachery, but also because his father was John of Gaunt, the king's uncle, whom Richard loathed and whose brother Gloucester the king had had murdered at Calais the year before. Hal was called to Court, as hostage for his father's good behaviour abroad, where Bolingbroke was now nursing his anger and planning revenge.

Gaunt died in 1399 and his absent son should have become Duke of Lancaster, but the king declared both title and lands forfeit to the Crown. Fortified with this extra money to pay his troops, Richard invaded Ireland, taking young Hal with him and dubbing him knight for a conspicuous piece of bravery during the abortive campaign.

Enraged by Richard's denial of his rights, Bolingbroke

landed in England. The news reached the king in Ireland, who called Hal to him, and said, 'Henry, my boy, see what thy father hath done to me ... through these unhappy doings thou wilt perchance lose thine inheritance.' The 'doings' gathered pace and power; Bolingbroke said he had only come to claim his rights, but the speed of chance and events bore him faster and further than that, and in that same year, 1399, Richard was deposed, 'uncrowned' in Westminster Hall, and Bolingbroke became King Henry IV of England.

From the first Bolingbroke insisted his sons should succeed him, in a strong Lancastrian dynasty, so Hal, sent for by his father from Richard's side, though pleading his loyalty to Richard, met Henry at the Tower of London. Later, seated next to his father at the coronation, he was declared Prince of Wales, Duke of Cornwall, Earl of Chester, and soon afterwards, Duke of Aquitaine. In November he inherited the dukedom of Lancaster; he was heir to the throne a mere two months after his twelfth birthday.

But all was troubled, and Hal was in for a hard and insecure life. His father was a usurper; deposed Richard was in prison and shortly murdered at Henry's command; a growing number resented the usurpation. The new monarch was short of money, short of support beyond his rigidly controlled adherents, there was a threat of civil war and the Welsh were already in arms, with a new and splendid leader,

Owain Glyndwr, who in September 1400 proclaimed himself Prince of Wales and invaded England. In October the king and Prince Hal led an army into Wales to meet him. As would happen so often in these wars, the Welsh melted away among the mountains. Hal was put in charge of his principality with a council of which another Henry, Henry Percy (called Harry Hotspur), son of the Earl of Northumberland, was the principal member. Hal became his friend, and learned from him much of military matters, though he soon began to have his own ideas of strategy and tactics in the field. He took from Hotspur much of the fierce courage of the older man, but not the reckless, dangerous bravura that cost Hotspur his life.

Hal wrote frequent despatches to his father, in precise forthright style, usually begging, often without result, for troops and money to pay them, having pawned all his own 'little jewels'. He witnessed all the horrors of war, the barbaric executions after battle. He did not shrink from it; 'War without fire', he once said, 'is like sausage without mustard.' He could be cruel, certainly to our eyes, but even the French, after his death, said he was 'ever just'.

Those battles were in March 1404. Two years before, Hotspur, returning north to repel a Scottish invasion, had a great victory, won entirely by his longbowmen. But this had led to a profound dispute between the Percies of Northumberland and the king, the several reasons for which led to a massive rebellion which came to a head in 1403.

Hal, as commander in chief of the forces on the Welsh border, was at Shrewsbury. Hotspur marched south, on his way gathering large forces from counties still loyal to Richard's memory. He aimed to capture the prince before aid could reach him, but the king, hearing the news at Nottingham on 12 July, by remarkable forced marches arrived just before the rebels, so that when Hotspur and his uncle Worcester caught sight of the walls of Shrewsbury on 20 July, they saw the royal standard flying beside the prince's above the castle. The rebels' hope had been to join with Glyndwr's forces before any battle, but the Welsh prince was far distant at a siege and never arrived.

Hotspur chose his ground well, a long, south-facing slope 2 miles north of the town, ideal for his archers looking down on the enemy below. Henry's army, approaching from the southeast, had to be content with the low ground. The battle was the first fearsome fight between two armies with equal numbers of skilled longbowmen, and a grim encounter it was, a foretaste of the horrors to come in the Wars of the Roses.

Early on, Hal, in command of the royal left wing, was wounded in the face by a rebel arrow; his companions tried to persuade him to leave the field, but he would not, and went on to alter the balance of the battle, which was going badly for the king. Moving his wing round Hotspur's right, Hal outflanked him, bringing on the final mêlée in which

Hotspur was killed, possibly by an arrow in the face, or more likely struck down in the thick of battle in his last desperate charge at the king.

Shrewsbury Field must have been a grievous one for Hal; he was 14, he had been a leader of those forces that caused the death of his friend and old tutor, Henry Percy, and he was badly wounded. His courage in refusing to leave the field is the more extraordinary when you hear the extent of the wound from the surgeon, John Bradmore, who operated on him days later in Kenilworth Castle; his royal patient 'was struck by an arrow next to his nose on the left side . . . the which entered at an angle, and . . . the head of the arrow remained in the furthermost part of the bone of the skull for a depth of six inches'.

The manner of a prince

So what did this calmly determined, strange young man look like? A monk of Westminster with frequent opportunity to observe him tells us that his limbs were well-formed, his bones and sinews firmly knit together, he had a broad forehead, a spherical cranium, brown hair, cut short all round, above the ear (for ease in a hot helmet), with a straight nose, eyes bright, large and hazel, teeth 'even and white' and his chin 'divided'.

Maître Jean Fusoris, an eminent French savant who came with the last French embassy before the war of 1415, saw Henry at Winchester and said that though he had the manner of a prince, he seemed more like a priest, less a soldier than his brother, the Duke of Clarence. This was a misjudgement of real character. Clarence was a sort of Hotspur soldier, later killed in a rash attack, Henry a superb and meticulous planner, strategist and tactician. He treated all men equally, with courteous affability but never wasting words; to any who failed him he was ice and fire.

We must leap over the years of Hal's well-substantiated wildness when not engaged in Wales; the years when he rose to power, with his own allies, a power often exercised against his father's rule, which became so dangerous to the king's government that he was dismissed from the Council; the prince's virtual rule of England during his father's illness, the quarrels between father and son; the king's death; these must fly past, until we see that an astonishing transformation came over him on his accession as Henry V in 1413. He now prepared to put the kingdom in order, dealing with those disloyal to his father either by stern action or by restoration of deprived lands and titles on condition of loyalty to himself.

Preparing for war

In 1414 Henry demanded from France the restoration of all lands granted to his great-grandfather, King Edward III, at the Treaty of Brétigny in 1360, following the English victories of Crécy in 1346 and Poitiers in 1356, and soon pushed further: he claimed, like Edward, his right to the throne of France. If any Englishman could make such a claim, it was Edward, Earl of March, through Edward III's mother, the daughter of King Philip IV of France. But Henry was a visionary. He was destined, he believed, to unite the warring factions in France, the Burgundians and Armagnacs, unite all Christendom under one pope as a defence against the Infidel, and finally unite the armies of all Europe to recapture Jerusalem. It was even a possibility. France's king was mad a good deal of the time, religious and dynastic divisions were tearing the country apart; there were two, at one time three, popes; now Henry must step in and make an empire under his rule.

There was much diplomatic activity, spying, promising and reneging until a gross insult by the Dauphin, accompanied by a gift of tennis balls, as appropriate to his youth, offered an excuse for Henry to declare himself at war with France.

Immense preparations were made under Henry's supervision, backed by a nobility hungry for conquest and honour, and a country with a newfound sense of itself and a feeling of patriotic confidence. Soldiers by thousands, weapons of war in vast quantities, tens of thousands of yew longbows, millions of arrows, ships built or impressed, guns such as never seen before, men and still more men for all the tasks of war; and in July and August 1415, a massive army moved towards Southampton, to await the fleet there.

All was ready, the king was in Southampton, when suddenly the Earl of March, the rather fearful claimant to the throne, revealed to Henry a plot to kill the king and install March in his place. Henry acted fast: the ringleaders were arrested, summarily tried, and executed. That done, fair stood the wind for France. On Sunday 11 August 1415 the ships of the expedition moved into Southampton Water. One ship caught fire, which spread to two others alongside, probably started either by French spies, or remnants of the late plot. The joyous mood fell at this omen. Henry made much of the better augury of a group of swans among the ships. Then trumpets blew, the sails unfurled, and a fleet of ships bearing some 2,500 men at arms and lances, 8,000 archers, horses, grooms, varlets, cooks, esquires, and the king, set sail for the open sea; their secret destination Harfleur, on the coast of Normandy.

Two days later, in the afternoon of 13 August, the armada sailed into the estuary of the Seine and anchored off the Chef de Caux, which the soldiers christened 'Kidcocks'. The next morning, after a reconnaissance, the landing commenced. There was no sign of French resistance, though from the shore to the city of Harfleur defensive ditches and dykes had been built. By Saturday 17

August the unloading was complete and the advance began towards the city, over the marshes and mudflats in broiling weather. The king sent a message through the ranks: 'fellows be of good cheer; breathe you and cool you and come up with your ease, for with the love of God we shall have good tidings.'

Henry kept strict control of his army; there was to be no looting, no mistreatment of the inhabitants; women, priests and churches were to suffer no harm, and army discipline was severe – all on pain of punishment, even death. Though some French talked later of devastation, others admitted that French armies behaved far worse. By Sunday night, 18 August, the city was encircled. Henry was to prove from then until his death in 1422 that he was a Caesar in siege warfare, and after one great battle whose name resounds today, most of his campaigns in France were a series of sieges, planned with meticulous care, with a Caesarian eye for detail and the morale of his men.

The surrender of Harfleur

The city did not surrender until 22 September, when its leaders, with ropes around their necks, were received by Henry, who was clad in cloth of gold, and seated on a throne. Henry entered the city barefoot, went to the church and gave thanks to God who had delivered Harfleur 'to its rightful owner'. The question was, what next? His army was

depleted by casualties, disease and desertions, and a fleet
with relief forces had been scattered by a storm. Should he
march on Paris? Return home to raise more money and
troops? His Council advised return to England; the siege
had taken too long, the season was late, the weather turning
bad. Yet Henry's belief in his own destiny put aside all argu-
ment. He would march north to Calais, by treaty an English
town, and show his banner through France. Some say it
was a retreat, but as Winston Churchill and others have
contended, 'his decision shows his design was to tempt the
enemy to battle'. Henry said, 'We will go, if it please God,
without harm or danger, and if they disturb us on our
journey we shall come off with victory, triumph and very
great fame.'

On 8 October the army marched north, with eight
days' rations. It was a dreadful march in foul weather,
denied by the French any crossing of the Somme, having
to march inland to find an unguarded ford, kept going by
the will and determination of a leader who somehow maintained the spirits and discipline of his men. At last they
reached two fords, at Voyennes and Bethencourt, where
Henry himself supervised the crossing.

On 20 October he let the army rest and rode ahead,
to be met by a French party, whose leaders 'inform thee
that before thou comest to Calais they will make thee to
fight with them'. Henry replied calmly, 'without his face

changing colour', that he would march straight to Calais. They moved on, dogged now by the French, and sixteen days after leaving Harfleur, on 24 October, crossed their last river, the little Ternoise at Blangy, soaked, cold, hungry and exhausted.

Preparing for battle

Henry was called to the advance guard at the top of the slope beyond the river. He saw the French, as his chaplain described it, 'in compact masses, battles and columns, their numbers not comparable to ours . . . they took up a position facing us, a little more than half a mile to our right . . . and there was only a little valley, not so very wide between us.' The valley can be seen today, to the right of the Calais road, not a mile above the river. Here Henry

> very calmly and quite heedless of danger, gave encouragement to his army, drawing them up in their battles and wings to go at once into action . . . then the enemy withdrew to the far side of a certain wood, and our king believing they would either circle it and attack us by surprise, or else move behind woods in the distance and completely encircle us, immediately moved his lines again, always positioning them so that they faced the enemy.

But the light was gone. In the dark, in incessant rain, Henry quartered his army in and around the tiny village of Maisoncelles. Whether, as Shakespeare has it, he went among his men we do not know, but it was his constant practice. He forbade the army to make any noise, and in their silence they could hear the French camp half a mile away.

The Battle of Agincourt

Before dawn on 25 October Henry was up and armed; he heard three masses, then with his captains drew up his army, men-at-arms four deep in a single line, divided in three battalions; his longbowmen, five times more numerous, were grouped between the battalions and thrust forward on the wings of the army, and probably deployed across the front of the host, but able to withdraw among the armed men when the armies clashed. Before their main groups, archers hammered stakes into the ground, their sharpened points chest high to horses.

Henry rode among them on a little white horse, without his spurs – he would not run, but die with them – inspiring them; warning the archers that the French would cut off the first two fingers of the right hand of any captured. He dismounted, then went to the centre of his army, beneath his banners, on foot as they all were.

Across the flat, soaked fields between the woods of

Tramecourt and Agincourt, glinting with armour and weapons, bright with banners, was the massed French host. Yet nothing happened.

The only movements among the crowds of French were to do with breakfast, and arguments about positions; their archers and crossbowmen and gunners were being pushed to the back. Henry could not stay still; his army would starve. He ordered the archers to pull up their stakes, and the whole force to advance. They trudged through the mud, stopping several times to maintain formation. Within bowshot of the French – 250–300 yards – they halted. Henry watched for any movement from the enemy while so many of his men had their backs to them, as they drove in their stakes again, and then re-formed. The marshal of the army, Sir Thomas Erpingham, hurled his baton into the air; the army gave wild shouts, and five or six thousand archers let fly into the French.

This stinging, murderous cloud of arrows forced the French to attack, first with cavalry on the wings, ploughing through thick mud, aiming to roll up the wing archers; they came slowly, floundering into the stakes, and as they laboured, the archers shot and shot, wounding and killing until the maddened horses that still lived, arrows wagging in their wounds, turned back, and crashed into their crowded vanguard, pushing forward on foot. Disorder made the crowding worse, but they came on, the narrowing woods pressing them inwards, heads down against the rattling arrows, until their vast weight of numbers hit the English and drove them back. But Henry's line held, and held; he was in the thickest of it; the archers, now too close to shoot, threw bows behind them and joined the men-at-arms, with swords and battle hammers, killing without pause, until great heaps of dead and wounded French were piling in the mud, on which the archers climbed, dinging, thrusting, slashing at those below, who, pressing up behind the French front ranks, forced an ever tighter pack, unable to use their weapons freely, endless victims of their hacking enemy.

The French were surrendering in droves and, pushed behind the English line, stood, numbed by defeat. Word suddenly came that the French rear was mounting a fresh attack; the English baggage had been raided, its treasure stolen, unarmed people killed. Henry saw a fearful danger: hundreds of French captives could pick up weapons that strewed the ground and attack his rear. He ordered that the prisoners be killed; many were, until it was clear there would be no more fighting. To us, an infinite cruelty, to contemporaries, in England and in France, merely logical. The battle was over by about two o'clock, and Henry named it after the nearest little castle – Agincourt. It was a long way from Monmouth.

It was a victory of discipline and calm, fearless command, which Henry continued to exercise for seven successful years of campaigning in France, and organization at home. What would have happened if he had lived another twenty years? That fine medieval historian Bruce MacFarlane said of him: 'Take him all round he was, I think, the greatest man who ever ruled England.'

JOAN OF ARC

c. 1412–31

ANNE CURRY

JOAN OF ARC IS UNIQUE. In this collection of great commanders she is the only woman, and one of only two saints. These characteristics suggest that there is something very special – if not odd – about Joan as a military leader. She was not canonized because of her role in saving France from English rule, of course, but her achievements in that context are substantial. After raising the siege of Orléans in early May 1429 and defeating the English at the Battle of Patay on 18 June in the same year, she then led the Dauphin Charles to his coronation at Reims on 17 July and to the reconquest of many towns previously held by the English and their Burgundian allies, until her capture by the latter at Compiègne in May 1430.

That she was not made a saint until 1920, almost four hundred years after her condemnation for heresy and her burning at the stake in Rouen on 30 May 1431, demonstrates that Joan was as controversial in death as in life. After all, few whom the Roman Catholic Church has condemned as heretics have been made saints by that self- same body.

Joan's military career was fleeting, yet we know more about her than her gender and social status might have predicted. She speaks to us directly in response to questions at her trial in 1431 (the *procès de condemnation*), the procedure and outcome of which were nullified at a second trial in 1456 (the *procès de nullification*, later called 'the Rehabilitation') at which no fewer than 115 of those who had known her gave testimony. These witnesses included childhood friends as well as companions-in-arms and the commanders of the French army. At a time when 'women were excluded from the deeds of men', as one late fourteenth-century military treatise put it, she was a phenomenon: not surprisingly, then, her deeds were recorded in chronicles, letters and governmental records. Even so, it remains difficult to 'explain' Joan. Much ink has been spilled in attempts to do so, but we need to strip back the accretions of later centuries to find the real Joan and to understand her place as a military leader.

Joan the woman

We do not know when Joan was born. When asked at her trial, she replied that 'as far as she knew, she was around

19 years old'. At the time that she relieved Orléans in 1429, therefore, she was no more than 17. Although there are examples of those who were military commanders at an early age, these are men of royal or noble status whose birth committed them to leadership. Joan was of humble birth. Admittedly her family were not impoverished: they were middling farmers, and an uncle had entered the priesthood. Joan's father was the *doyen* or sergeant of Domrémy (now in the *département* of Vosges), responsible for representing his fellow villagers and for assisting in the collection of the taxes they owed to the Crown. After her military successes Joan remembered not only her family – two brothers who served alongside her were elevated to noble status on 25 December 1429 – but also her community. Two weeks after his coronation on 17 July 1429, Charles VII removed Domrémy's tax liability 'in honour of and at the request of Joan La Pucelle considering the great and profitable service which she has done and does each day'. For each year until the French Revolution, the tax registers record simply '*néant* (nothing) – La Pucelle'.

Joan appears to have been an ordinary village girl in upbringing and interests. Asked during her trial if in her youth she had learned a craft, she said 'yes, to sew linen and to spin', and she 'did not fear any woman in Rouen when it came to sewing and spinning'. Here is a brief glimpse of the bravado and self-confidence that assisted her later military command. As she herself explained, her 'voices' had told her that she should leave home and come to the French king to save the kingdom. A witness in the Rehabilitation said that Joan first approached Robert de Baudricourt, her local lord and captain of Vaucouleurs, in May 1428, but he sent her packing. Two months later, her patriotism, and her determination to serve, were heightened when she and her family were forced by incursions of Burgundian soldiers to flee their village and take temporary refuge in the nearest town, Neufchâteau. When the siege of Orléans, laid by the English in October 1428 as a major push into the Dauphin's territory south of the Loire, dragged on into the New Year, her voices spoke of a more specific intention: she would raise the siege. De Baudricourt was finally persuaded, and provided a sword, horse and escort as she set out for the Dauphin's court in Chinon on 22 February 1429. It was at this point that she adopted male clothing and cut her hair short.

The making of Joan the warrior

Joan had no experience of war, and no experience of leadership. She was, like all women of the day, excluded both in theory and practice from the world of the warrior. How, then, did she become a commander at all? The answer must be found not only in the military and political context but also in contemporary religious sensibilities. The English had suffered a setback at the start of the siege of Orléans with the death of their commander, Thomas, Earl of Salisbury, who was an early victim of gunshot. They had strained their resources to keep an army surrounding the city over the winter, but thanks to Sir John Fastolf's victory at the 'Battle of the Herrings' near Rouvray on 12 February, they managed to bring in much-needed supplies to continue the siege. Faced with this situation, the Dauphin's advisors looked for other solutions. An embassy under Poton de Xaintrailles (one of Joan's later companions) was sent from Orléans to the Duke of Burgundy, trying to persuade him to drop his alliance with the English in return for a power-sharing arrangement with the Dauphin. Nothing came of this, but shortly afterwards a dispute between the duke and his allies prompted him to withdraw his troops. The moment was therefore ripe for a French attempt to raise the siege.

Arriving in Chinon on 4 March 1429, and meeting the Dauphin two days later, Joan had appeared at exactly the right time. This may not be coincidence. Charles was known to be fascinated with signs and predictions. Historians have suggested that Joan was put forward by one of the factions at court, the Angevins, who were related to his wife, Marie of Anjou. We know that before Joan's last interview with de Baudricourt she had visited the Duke of Lorraine, father-in-law of Duke René of Anjou, asking him to persuade his son-in-law to give armed support. When Joan arrived at the Dauphin's court, the other factions were not impressed with her, but Charles was soon in her thrall. All that was needed was proof of her virginity: a brief physical examination carried out by his mother-in-law reassured him. He decreed that Joan should be allowed to go to raise the siege, 'to show a sign of divine approval before Orléans'.

Whilst an army of several thousand was gathered under the Count of Dunois, Joan prepared herself – and was also coached – for her intended role. She had told her voices that 'she was a poor girl who did not know how to ride on horseback or lead in war'. Yet by 22 April, the Lord of Roteslar could write that 'the Pucelle every day rides on horseback, armed with a lance in battle, as all the other armed men guarding the king are accustomed to doing'. The Duke of Alençon, himself a patron of astrologers and one of Joan's main supporters, also reported in 1456 that he had seen her at Chinon riding before him with a lance, and was so impressed by her skills that he gave her a horse. Unless Joan had been practising in Domrémy (which is highly improbable given medieval gender expectations), we can envisage a crash course in basic military training where she proved an eager, if not star, pupil. 'Designer armour' was provided by the king. That Joan was new to wearing it may be suggested by the observation of one of her companions-in-arms in 1456 that she was very bruised on her arrival at Orléans because she had slept fully armed the night before. An 'Excalibur' was found for her, somewhat predictably, perhaps, buried behind the altar at the church of St Catherine de Fierbois on 2 April. But in Joan's own words, she loved her standard forty times more than her sword. It bore 'the image of our saviour sitting in judgement on the clouds of heaven . . . an angel holding in his hands a fleur-de-lys which the image of Christ was blessing', alongside the names 'Jesus Maria'. The standard was a symbol of Joan's purpose as a spiritual as well as military leader. As she herself said at her trial, she 'carried her standard to avoid killing anyone'. In all of her successful engagements, her presence with this standard – its image created to show God's approval for the French cause and for Joan herself – was vital. Time after time, in chronicles and in the testimonies of 1456, we are told that French soldiers were hesitant and anxious until she appeared with her standard and encouraged them to advance, in the name of God as much as of the French king.

Through Joan, the rescue of Orléans, and the war against the English as a whole, was made a religious as much as a military mission. The intention was made clear in a letter dictated by Joan on 22 March urging the English to surrender not simply the city but all their conquests. It was not couched in the standard terms of a commander but in those of an impassioned teenager and fervent believer:

God will send greater strength to the Pucelle, both
to her and her good men-at-arms than you English
could overwhelm in all your assaults. The one who
has greater right from God in heaven will be
revealed by this exchange of blows.

Although Charles did not give her formal command, his
captains were subordinated to her because, as one contemporary observer put it, 'counsel from God supersedes any
judgement from a military council'. When the advance
guard set off for Orléans she had priests walk ahead singing
veni creator spiritus ('come, holy spirit').

The siege of Orléans

By the time Joan arrived at Orléans in April 1429, the
English-laid siege, now in its seventh month, was flagging.
The city was too large and well defended to surround
completely. Burgundian troops had already been withdrawn.
The English army was distributed in a series of specially
constructed temporary fortresses. They were particularly
weak on the eastern side. At the Rehabilitation, the crossing
of Joan and her men to the north bank of the Loire was
ascribed to a miracle, in which God responded to her prayers
that the wind change direction to help them to sail across
the river. In reality, it was more likely the *sortie* of the
defenders of Orléans against the English at the outwork of

Saint Loup, launched once they heard of the imminent approach of French troops and supplies, that enabled Joan to enter the city on 29 April. According to Dunois' testimony in 1456, she was furious that there had not been immediate engagement with the English. Indeed, there is evidence to suggest that Dunois was initially hostile to her involvement in the proposed action. How could she fulfil her mission if he would not allow her to fight?

In the early days of May, Joan harried the English with religious invective, targeting particularly William Glasdale and his men, who were defending Les Tourelles, the southernmost defence of the bridge over the Loire. She also rallied support within the city itself as well as reconnoitring the English defences. Meanwhile, Dunois sought reinforcements at Blois. Once achieved, Saint Loup could be captured on 4 May. Two days later, Augustins was captured. This assault was Joan's first experience of action and it was exhausting and costly. But she urged that the next day, on 8 May, an attack should be launched on Les Tourelles. She was wounded by an arrow 'which penetrated her flesh between her neck and her shoulder for a depth of half a foot', as Dunois later recalled. The fight went on almost all day and Dunois advised withdrawal. But Joan asked him to wait until she had prayed. Returning, 'she took her standard in her hands and placed it on the side of the ditch, and instantly, once she was there, the

English became afraid and trembled, and the soldiers of the king regained their confidence and began to climb up'. According to her own testimony, she was the first to put her ladder against the wall. After hard hand-to-hand fighting, the English were defeated. Those in the remaining defences chose to withdraw from the siege. Orléans had been saved. For the next two days, its streets resounded with cheering for Joan and her troops, and its churches with prayers of thanksgiving.

From success to failure

Despite her success at Orléans, Joan could not continue her action against the English without more men. Once reinforcements arrived, she moved against the other English-held strongholds on the Loire since until the whole area was secured and the enemy driven back towards Normandy, it was dangerous for the Dauphin to attempt a move to Reims for coronation. What is clear, however, is that Joan's success at Orléans boosted confidence in her and her mission. Troops rallied to her support, and in their turn the English were afraid to offer resistance. We can only imagine the psychological effect of Joan's presence on the English. She was linked to the worst military disaster they had faced since their king, Henry V, had reopened the war in 1415, thereby putting into their minds the notion that God had deserted their cause for that of the French. Joan was now joined by the Duke of Alençon, who proved the most enduring of her supporters. At the Rehabilitation he told how some of the French captains, despite the success at Orléans, were reluctant to chance an attack on Jargeau because of the strength of the English garrison, and that it had been Joan who had persuaded them that all would go well because 'God was conducting their work'. In fact, it seems to have been French artillery that softened the town enough to allow an assault. Other successes followed at Beaugency and Meung-sur-Loire, and advance was begun towards Reims. The French constable, Arthur de Richemont, then arrived with more troops, making it possible to confront the English at Patay. Joan's role here is uncertain, a reflection, perhaps, that her limited military skills were adequate for encouraging soldiers in a siege but not for pitched battle.

Joan continued to regard the war as a religious mission. As she wrote to the inhabitants of Troyes on 4 July, 'Joan the Maid commands you on behalf of the King of Heaven our rightful and sovereign lord in whose royal service she serves each day, that you should obey and recognize the gracious king of France'. But opposition to her within the French command was increasing even before the entry into Reims and the coronation of the Dauphin as Charles VII on 17 July. Although at the crowning she stood by his side carrying her banner, the anointing of the king transformed him into God's chosen one as well as the supreme military commander. From that point onwards, Joan was surplus to requirements. Whilst she lobbied for the continuation of the war, Charles preferred a political solution through negotiations with the Duke of Burgundy. He also refused to heed her increasingly desperate urgings to move quickly against the English in Paris. She was determined to take the city, but underestimated how difficult this would be. If Orléans could not be taken by siege, there was little chance Paris could be, and the English had drawn back into it many of their troops from the Loire valley and Normandy as well as bringing a new expeditionary force from England. On 8 September she launched a premature attack against the St Honoré gate to the west of the city. Struck by a crossbow bolt, she urged her men on, but this time, unlike the action at Les Tourelles, her men were disheartened by her wounding and withdrew. Within a few days the king ordered the attacks to cease, and brought his army back to the Loire, discharging the Duke of Alençon. Joan's enemies had triumphed. The king no longer had confidence in her: she had prophesied that he would enter Paris, but her predictions had proved untrue.

Joan fought on in the upper Loire, but now with what were little more than mercenary companies and without much role in command. Although Saint-Pierre-le-Moutier was taken, the king refused to send more men or supplies to continue the advance, so that her attempt shortly before Christmas 1429 to besiege La Charité-sur-Loire failed. It is unlikely that after this point she was ever in the royal presence again. The remainder of her career saw further failure. She rushed to the defence of Compiègne when she learned that the Burgundians had defaulted on their rapprochement with King Charles and were preparing to lay siege to the town. She arrived in time to enter the town, but on the very next day, 23 May 1430, she led an ill-advised sortie in which she was captured. There is even some suggestion that she was betrayed by the French captain of Compiègne, Guillaume de Flavy, who, according to the chronicler, Perceval de Cagny, 'had the bridge raised and the gate shut' so that she could not return to the town. A few days later, the University of Paris demanded that she be handed over to the Inquisition. Sold to the English in November, she was taken to Rouen just before Christmas 1430. The preliminaries of her trial for heresy began in early January, with Joan being presented to the court on 21 February. Her last battle began, not against soldiers and fortifications, but against theologians. As an uneducated woman, and a woman who had usurped a male role, this was a battle she had no chance of winning. Yet she remained steadfast in her support for her king. Intriguingly, at her trial she denied that she had called herself a 'commander of war' in the letter sent to the English before her arrival at Orléans, but she never denied her belief that she had acted in God's name. Her war was a religious mission. As much as serving the king of France, Joan of Arc, the maid of Orléans, saw herself as serving the king of Heaven.

SULTAN MEHMET II

1433–81

JOHN JULIUS NORWICH

SULTAN MEHMET II – always known to modern Turks as Fatih, *the Conqueror – changed the course of history. In May 1453, after a furious siege of fifty-five days, he and his army smashed their way through the great land walls of Constantinople, captured the city and so put an end to the Byzantine Empire. That empire had lasted for 1,123 years, a period of time comfortably longer than that which separates us from the Norman Conquest; and as it was essentially only a continuation of the old Roman Empire, Mehmet could be said to have destroyed that also. It was an astonishing achievement for a young man not yet 22 years old.*

Few people in Europe knew much about the inscrutable young prince who had recently succeeded to the throne of the Ottoman Turks. Born in 1433, Mehmet – the name is the Turkish form of Muhammad – was the third son of Sultan Murad II. He had had an unhappy childhood. His father had made no secret of his preference for his two elder half-brothers Ahmet and Ali, both children of well-born mothers, whereas Mehmet's own mother had been a mere slave-girl in the harem and probably – though we cannot be sure – a Christian to boot. At the age of 2 he had been taken from his birthplace at Adrianople (the modern Edirne, on the present Turkish–Bulgarian frontier) to Amasa, a province in northern Anatolia of which his 14-year-old brother was governor; but Ahmet had died only four years later and Mehmet, now aged 6, had succeeded him.

Then, in 1444, Ali was found strangled in his bed, in circumstances still mysterious. Mehmet, now heir to the throne, was summoned back urgently to the capital, now at Adrianople. Hitherto his education had been largely neglected; suddenly he found himself in the care of the greatest scholars of their day and with them, over the next few years, laid the foundations of the learning and culture for which he was soon to be famous. At the time of his succession he is said to have been fluent not only in his native Turkish but in Arabic, Greek, Latin, Persian and Hebrew.

'But,' wrote Edward Gibbon, 'it cannot be denied that his passions were at once furious and inexorable; that in the palace, as in the field, a torrent of blood was spilt on the slightest provocation; and that the noblest of the captive youth were often dishonoured by his unnatural lust.' Twice, in the last six years of his life, Sultan Murad had abdicated in favour of his son; twice – knowing these faults all too well – his Grand Vizir Halil Pasha had persuaded him to continue. After Murad's second reluctant return to power he gave up all thoughts of retirement and settled down again in Adrianople, banishing his son to Magnesia in Anatolia; and it was there that news was brought to Mehmet that his father had died, on 13 February 1451, of an apoplectic seizure.

The young sultan

It took Mehmet just five days to travel from Magnesia to Adrianople, where he held a formal reception at which he confirmed his father's ministers in their places or, in certain cases, refused to do so. At this time Murad's widow arrived to congratulate him on his accession. He received her warmly and engaged her for some time in conversation; when she returned to the harem it was to find that her infant son had been murdered in his bath. The young sultan, it seemed, was not one to take chances.

Some days later there arrived an embassy bringing congratulations from the Byzantine emperor Constantine XI. To this Mehmet is said to have replied almost too fulsomely, swearing by Allah and the Prophet to live at peace with the emperor and his people. Perhaps it was this that put Constantine on his guard; immediately he began to strengthen the city's defences. He seems to have been one of the first to sense that the sultan was not all that he appeared – that, potentially, he was very dangerous indeed.

All too soon, the emperor's suspicions were confirmed. By autumn, Mehmet had decided to build a great castle on the Bosphorus, at the point where the channel was at its narrowest. Another castle, built by his great grandfather Bayezit I, already stood on the Asiatic side; with the two opposite each other he would have complete control of the strait. There was one small technical objection to the plan: the land on which his castle was to be built was Byzantine. But this he ignored. All that winter he collected his workforce, with a thousand professional stonemasons. In the early spring all the churches and monasteries in the neighbourhood were demolished to provide additional materials, and on Saturday, 11 April 1452, the building operations began.

The castle of Rumeli Hisar still stands, essentially unchanged since the day it was completed – Thursday, 31 August – just beyond the village of Bebek. It is hard to believe that its construction took, from start to finish, only nineteen and a half weeks. When it was ready the sultan mounted three huge cannon on the tower and decreed that every passing ship, whatever its nationality, must stop for examination. That November a Venetian ship failed to obey. It was blasted out of the water; the crew were all executed, the captain impaled on a stake and publicly exposed as a warning to anyone else who might think of following his example.

The preliminaries

The Ottoman fleet assembled off Gallipoli in March 1453. It seems to have comprised no fewer than six triremes and ten biremes – vessels with respectively three and two rowers per oar – fifteen oared galleys, some seventy-five fast longboats, twenty sailing-barges for transport and a number of light sloops and cutters. A week or two later it made its way slowly across the little inland Sea of Marmara, to drop anchor beneath the walls of Constantinople.

The army, meanwhile, was gathering in Thrace. Turkish sources suggest it comprised some eighty thousand regular troops and up to twenty thousand irregulars, or *bashi-bazouks*. Included in the former category were about twelve thousand Janissaries. Though legally slaves, these elite troops had been recruited as children from Christian families, forcibly converted to Islam and subjected to rigorous military training. Mehmet was proud of both his army and his navy; but he was proudest of all of his cannon. Cannon, in its primitive form, had been used for a century or more; but it was not until 1452 that a German engineer named Urban sought an audience with the sultan and offered to build him a weapon that would blast the walls of Babylon itself.

This was just what Mehmet had been waiting for. He gave Urban four times his requested salary, and was rewarded only three months later by the fearsome monster at Rumeli Hisar that had accounted for the Venetian ship. He then demanded another, twice the size of the first. This was completed in January 1453. It is said to have been 27 feet long, with a barrel 2½ feet in diameter. The bronze was 8 inches thick. When it was tested, a ball weighing 1,340 pounds hurtled through the air for well over a mile before burying itself 6 feet deep in the ground. Two hundred men were sent out to prepare for its journey to Constantinople, smoothing the road and reinforcing the bridges; and at the beginning of March it set off, drawn by thirty pairs of oxen, with a further two hundred men to hold it steady.

On 5 April the sultan joined his army before the walls of the city. Under a flag of truce, he at once sent the emperor the message that was required under Islamic law, undertaking that he and all his subjects would be spared, with their property, if they made immediate and voluntary surrender. If on the other hand they refused, they would be given no quarter. As expected, he received no reply. Early in the morning of Friday, 6 April his cannon opened fire.

The defenders

To defend Constantinople and his empire (and by now that empire amounted to little more than the city itself), Constantine's forces were pathetically small. Moored in the Golden Horn – that long, narrow, deep-water creek that runs northwest from the city and provides it with a superb natural harbour – were just twenty-six ships, including eight Venetian, five Genoese and one each from Ancona, Catalonia and Provence. Where manpower was concerned, the situation was even worse. To defend 14 miles of land and sea walls against an army of a hundred thousand, the population, dramatically reduced after nine separate visitations of the plague, yielded – including monks and clerics – rather less than seven thousand able-bodied men.

The land walls, on the other hand, first built more than one thousand years before, running from the Marmara shore to the upper reaches of the Golden Horn, formed the most elaborate and impregnable bastion ever constructed in the Middle Ages. Both inner and outer walls boasted ninety-six towers, and outside them lay a deep ditch some 30 feet across, which could be flooded to a depth of about 30 feet in an emergency. But the builders had reckoned without the sultan's cannon. The great walls were now subjected to a bombardment unprecedented in the history of siege warfare. On the very first day, a central section was reduced to rubble. The Turks repeatedly tried to smash their way through, but were always forced to retreat under a hail of missiles until nightfall sent them back to their camp. By morning the wall had been completely rebuilt.

The siege

On 11 April the last cannon was trundled into position, and the bombardment resumed, to continue uninterrupted for the next forty-eight days. Although some of the larger pieces could be fired only once every two or three hours, the damage they did was enormous; and although the defenders worked ceaselessly to repair the damage behind makeshift wooden stockades it was clear that they could not continue indefinitely. None the less, a surprise attack on the night of 18 April was courageously beaten off; after four hours' heavy fighting the Turks had lost two hundred men, at the cost of not a single Christian life.

At sea, too, the Byzantines scored notable successes. Two attempts by heavy galleys failed miserably to break the heavy chain across the entrance to the Golden Horn; soon afterwards, four ships hired by the Pope and one sent by the King of Aragon appeared in the Marmara. The sultan personally gave strict orders to his admiral: they must be captured or sunk before they reached the city. The admiral did his best, but the superior height of the Christian ships saved the day. The small cannon mounted on the Turkish galleys lacked the necessary elevation; the balls all fell short. Grappling and boarding an enemy vessel that stood substantially higher in the water was virtually impossible, involving as it did a climb up the side under showers of arrows, while the defending crews wielded heavy axes that lopped off heads and hands indiscriminately.

The sultan had watched every moment of the battle from the shore, occasionally in his excitement riding his horse out into the sea until his robes were trailing in the water. He was famous for the violence of his rages; such was his fury as he watched the humiliation of his fleet that those around him began to fear for his sanity. The unfortunate admiral was bastinadoed and deprived of both public offices and private possessions. He was never heard of again.

From the beginning of the siege, Mehmet knew that somehow he must gain control of the Golden Horn. Having failed to break the chain across the harbour mouth, he had set his engineers to work on a road running from the Bosphorus shore just to the east, behind the suburb of Galata, over the hill (near today's Taksim Square) and down, meeting the Horn beyond the chain. Metal tracks had been laid and iron wheels cast. His carpenters, meanwhile, had been busy fashioning wooden cradles large enough to accommodate the keels of medium-sized vessels. It was a Herculean undertaking; but the sultan had enough men and materials to make it possible. On 21 April 1453 the work was complete; and on the 22nd the Genoese colony in Galata watched dumbfounded as some seventy ships were hauled by innumerable teams of oxen over a 200-foot hill and then lowered down to the water.

The Byzantines had known nothing of the sultan's plan. Seeing the Turkish ships in the Horn, they found it difficult to believe the evidence of their own eyes. Not only was their major harbour no longer secure; they now had 3½ more miles of sea wall to defend. They were still hoping for a relief expedition from the west; but even if it were to arrive, how could it now be received in safety?

Mehmet now compounded the insult by throwing a pontoon bridge across the channel. Previously all messengers between his army beyond the walls and his fleet at the entrance to the Bosphorus had to make a long detour around the top of the Horn; henceforth they would be able to complete the journey in less than an hour. The bridge had other uses too: broad enough for a regiment marching five abreast, it could also accommodate heavy carts and – on special rafts attached at intervals to the sides – cannon which could be used either to cover the army's advance or to bombard the sea walls of the city. Now, if not before, Byzantium's fate was sealed.

The final assault was planned for Tuesday, 29 May. At

half-past one in the morning, the drums, trumpets and blood-curdling Turkish war-cries signalled that the attack had begun. The sultan knew that he must attack in wave after wave, allowing the exhausted defenders no rest. First he sent in the *bashi-bazouks*, then his trained Anatolian regiments, finally the Janissaries. It was still early morning when the wall was finally breached – there is a theory that a small postern had been insecurely bolted – and the Turkish army poured into the city. The emperor, seeing that the battle was lost, plunged into the fray where the fighting was thickest. He was never seen again.

By noon the streets of Constantinople were running red. Houses were ransacked, churches razed, women and children raped and impaled. Sultan Mehmet had promised his men the traditional three days of looting; but after an orgy on such a scale, there were no protests when he brought it to a close soon after sunset. He himself waited till the late afternoon before entering the city. Then he rode slowly down the principal thoroughfare to the great church of St Sophia. Dismounting outside the central doors, he stooped to pick up a handful of earth which, in a gesture of humility, he sprinkled over his turban. He had already decided that the Church of the Holy Wisdom should be converted into the chief mosque of the city; he now entered, and touched his head to the ground in prayer and thanksgiving.

The later years

Four years later the sultan was once again on the march in Europe. By the end of 1462 he had eliminated the last vestiges of an independent Serbia – though the vital bridgehead of Belgrade had been saved by the Hungarian John Hunyadi – seized the principal islands of the northern Aegean, then swept southward to expel the Florentine dukes of Athens and the brothers of the last emperor, who had established themselves in the Peloponnese. Two years later he was master of Bosnia, and in 1480 a separate expedition (of which he was not in personal command) captured the important Venetian colony of Negropont – the modern Euboea.

By this time his health was failing, and when in the same year he attacked the Knights of St John on the island of Rhodes, he once again delegated the command. The Knights had summoned the greatest architects of the day to ensure that the fortress city of Rhodes was as near impregnable as any city could be; but they were hopelessly outnumbered, and after a two-month siege the Turks had actually broken through the walls when, in the face of a massive counter-attack, they suddenly turned and fled. Why they did so remains a mystery.

For Mehmet, triumph was from one moment to the next transformed into disaster. Furious, he immediately began preparing a fresh army, which he resolved to lead in person against Rhodes the following year. Had he done so, the Knights would have stood no chance; their defences could never have been repaired in time. But in the spring of 1481, as he was riding through Anatolia on his way to take up his command, he was stricken by a sudden attack of dysentery. A day or two later he was dead.

It is, in more ways than one, a tribute to Sultan Mehmet II that his portrait by Gentile Bellini should hang in the National Gallery in London; for the painting commemorates not only him but the breadth of his culture. No other Muslim ruler for centuries would summon a European painter to his court and then sit for his portrait; but if contemporary evidence is to be believed, Mehmet was almost certainly the most civilized man in his empire. Of course he was cruel; had he not been, he would never have survived. But he was a great ruler, and a superb commander. He captured Constantinople at the age of 21, and the world was never the same again.

HERNÁN CORTÉS
c. 1484–1547

FELIPE FERNÁNDEZ-ARMESTO

HERNÁN CORTÉS had, as far as we know, no innate or early vocation for war, and never served as a professional soldier. As strategist and tactician, he was at best unremarkable and sometimes inept. Yet, from 1519 to 1521, he led an expedition of a few hundred adventurers – ragged, ill equipped, cut off from all hope of retreat and reinforcement – against the orders of his superiors and the laws of his king, through the perils of previously unexplored environments and unknown enemies, to the conquest of one of the most dynamic and aggressive empires of the day. The outcome was startling because of the disparity of the forces and the disadvantages under which the victorious commander laboured. It was world-transforming, because Cortés's victory established the first substantial overseas land empire in what was to become a long history of European imperialism. The annals of warfare record no story harder to understand or more compelling to investigate.

Cortés was born probably in about 1484 in Medellín in southwest Spain – a nursery of conquistadores. His family belonged, technically, to the nobility, but suffered derogating poverty. Cortés's parents wanted him to be a lawyer: he acquired rudimentary legal training and a smattering, at least, of Latin in his teens. But something held him back – maybe poverty, maybe lack of aptitude. In 1506 he took the obvious route out of a society of restricted social opportunity: he crossed the Atlantic to Hispaniola, the island of adventure that Columbus had discovered and colonized in the previous decade.

It was an option many *pícaros* tried. Most settlers were more or less desperate; they had to be to cross 3,000 miles of barely explored ocean and face a future in a land notorious for savagery and sickness. For Cortés, the fact that a distant relative was governor of the island raised hopes of patronage. He became the town scribe of a new Spanish settlement – a few huts on the south coast – before escaping again, as secretary to a conquistador. When Diego Velázquez set off on the conquest of Cuba in 1509, Cortés accompanied him. There he acquired substantial property, a native mistress, and a Spanish bride, whom he married only after being gaoled for breach of promise. But his ascent was precarious. He fell out with Velázquez, who suspected his loyalty, mistrusted his ambition and doubted his reliability.

The early conquistadores

Voyages of reconnaissance across the Gulf of Mexico failed to find anything worth conquering, exploiting, or raiding – only rumours of wealthy places further west. So when Velázquez appointed Cortés to lead a third reconnaissance in 1519, it was more like a pretext for getting rid of the commander than an occasion to honour him. Cortés had to pay most of the cost of the expedition himself, but he was forbidden to trade, or engage in hostilities, or even to explore inland from the shore. The orders showed ignorance of the lands for which the ships were bound, and speculations that arose from fantasy: Cortés had instructions to check on the whereabouts of monsters of ancient and medieval legend – the Amazons, the dog-headed Cynocephali, and the Pitones, who supposedly went about wrapped in the folds of their gigantic ears. Despite – or because of – these prospects he raised a surprisingly large force of over five hundred adventurers, with an unknown number of slaves. But they formed a scrappy band, with only sixteen horses and a dozen firearms between them – a sure sign of the poverty of most of the participants, who were required to supply their own equipment. Thirty were crossbowmen. The rest were armed only with swords or pikes. Cortés raised his men by shamelessly promising to exceed orders and attempt a conquest. When Velázquez responded by appointing a new commander, Cortés evaded the consequences by putting to sea at once – leaving his superior, according to legend, raging on the shore.

Turning to conquest

Cortés had little incentive to obey orders. If he returned to Cuba without further risk, he would be poorer than before and would probably face further victimization at Velázquez's hands. If he turned his reconnaissance into a conquest, he might encounter monsters or riches or both, and become the real-life hero of a chivalric romance, of the kind he and most other modestly literate people read. Tales of knightly derring-do, involving fantastic voyages, contests with monsters and conquests of fabulous realms were the late medieval equivalent of station-bookstall pulp fiction today. He landed at what is now Veracruz in August 1519. Abjuring Velázquez's authority, he constituted his men as a civic community and had himself elected mayor. As a device for self-legitimization, it was little more than a fig-leaf. But it was almost a reflex action in the circumstances. Whenever Spaniards met on a wild frontier, they founded a city, just as Englishmen, in similar circumstances, might found a club.

Beaching his ships, Cortés proceeded 'with no fear

that once my back was turned, the people left in the town would betray me'. Rumours of Aztec wealth steeled a resolve, which, with the ships grounded, was literally to conquer or die. 'Trusting in God's greatness and in the might of their Highnesses' royal name', 315 Spaniards struck inland to seek Motecoçuma, the Aztec paramount, 'wherever he might be'. Some of the men claimed later that the boat-beaching was the result of a collective decision. But it was important for the conquistadores' self-esteem to represent themselves as acting in knightly companionage, consistently with their self-perception as heroes of chivalric romance. The real decision-making, however, lay with Cortés.

To the Aztec city of Tenochtitlan

The state for which he was bound was one of the most rapidly expanding conquest states in the world. The Aztecs' principal city, Tenochtitlan, was perched like an eagle's eyrie, 7,500 feet above sea level in the central valley of Mexico, in the midst of a lake surrounded by mountains. Like an eyrie, it was strewn with its victims' bones – literally so, because the Aztecs made human sacrifices of thousands, perhaps scores of thousands, of their captive foes, piling their skulls at the foot of the great temple. Tenochtitlan was a robber-city of enormous dimensions – probably of some eighty thousand inhabitants, despite the unconducive altitude and site. The lakebound position made it impossible to grow enough food for such a huge metropolis. The location was too high for the cotton on which the community depended for clothes and quilted armour. It was far from the source of the tropical luxuries – chocolate, rubber, exotic plumage, ocelot pelts, jade, incense – on which the elite way of life depended. Only war and tribute could supply the city with what it needed. This was both the weakness and the strength of the Aztec system. The tribute exhibited the reach of Tenochtitlan's power. But it also showed the vulnerability of Aztec hegemony to the dissolution that must ensue if tribute were withheld.

Dependent on war to replenish supplies of tribute and sacrificial blood, the Aztec state was expanding faster, perhaps, than almost any other political community in the world at the time: only the empires of the Inca and the Ottomans were comparable in their dynamism. During the reign of Motecoçuma, the Aztecs conquered forty-four communities, spread over vast distances from the Pánuco river in the north to what is now the Guatemala frontier, raising the number of tributary cities within the system to nearly three hundred and fifty. The empire was, perhaps, over-extended, but it was confident, dynamic and aggressive. The encounter between Aztecs and Spaniards was a clash of rival imperialists.

The land of Tlaxcala

Cortés's route inland was, presumably, one recommended by the native hosts – enemies of the Aztecs – who welcomed him on the coast. It seemed consciously chosen to penetrate the most inaccessible patches of the Aztec world, where Tenochtitlan's most reluctant tributaries and most defiant enemies would be found. The Spaniards climbed from Jalapa by a pass 'so rough and steep that there is none in Spain so difficult', emerging with the conviction that they were now in the Aztec realm. 'God knows,' wrote Cortés, 'how my people suffered from hunger and thirst and . . . hailstorms and rainstorms.' They fought their way through the land of Tlaxcala, home of the Aztecs' most implacable enemies. Though the battles seemed fierce enough to the Spaniards, the Tlaxcalan forces were seeking only to test them to see whether they would make worthy recruits for their war against the Aztecs. As a reward for their courage, the Spaniards acquired the alliance of the fiercest pocket of resistance to the Aztecs between Mexico and the coast.

The thread on which their morale hung frayed quickly. They were thousands of miles from home. They were cut off from hope of help and knew that if a force followed them from Cuba it would be to punish rather than assist. They were surrounded by a hostile and awe-inspiring environment and hundreds of thousands of menacing 'savages' whom they could not understand. They had to breathe an unaccustomed, rarefied atmosphere; to endure extremes of heat and cold; to eat a debilitating diet without the red meat and wine that Spaniards considered essential for health and high status. They were at the mercy of native guides and interpreters who might choose to betray them at any moment. At Cholula, Cortés resorted to terror. To pre-empt, he said, an Indian conspiracy, but, more convincingly, to alleviate the Spaniards' stress, or simply *pour encourager les autres*, he massacred, by his own account, more than three thousand people. Most indigenous sources cast a different light on the massacre: the Tlaxcalans, they maintained, induced Cortés to undertake it, making him an agent of their own vengeance against neighbours they detested.

Meeting Motecoçuma

Most Mesoamerican cultures venerated strangers. When he arrived at Tenochtitlan in November, Cortés was honourably received. Traditional explanations of this are incredible. It is nonsense, for instance, to suppose that the Aztecs mistook him for a god or the envoy of a god: there is no contemporary evidence for this legend, which myth-makers extemporized long after the conquest. In his own account of his meeting with Motecoçuma, Cortés put a fanciful speech into the paramount's mouth, resigning sovereignty in favour of the ruler of Spain: this obviously self-interested bit of propaganda deserves no credence. Even more ridiculous is the early colonial myth that corroded morale undermined Aztec resistance. The so-called portents that are supposed to have influenced them derived not from Aztec tradition but from ancient Roman and Jewish traditions about the fall of Rome and Jerusalem. The simplest explanation for Cortés's reception is the best: decision-makers at the Aztec capital wanted to detach Cortés from his alliance with Tlaxcala. They therefore showered him with the gold he demanded, even after he had taken advantage of their hospitality to make a prisoner of Motecoçuma and – in effect – to hold him to ransom. It was a characteristically bold strategy. How practical it was in the long run is doubtful, as it was vexatious to the Aztecs, unprofitable to the Spaniards' native allies, and unsatisfactory to Cortés's men, who squabbled over the division of the spoils.

In April 1520, when the situation was already tense, a force of nine hundred men arrived in Mexico from Cuba, with a commission from the crown, to arrest Cortés and restore the expedition to obedience to its official superiors. Cortés responded with customary resolution. He mustered a force of three hundred, subverted the newly arrived army with bribes, and launched a surprise attack that resulted in the capture of the leaders and the incorporation of the task force into his own army. His absence from Tenochtitlan, however, had left his garrison there dangerously weak. The commander, egged on perhaps by Tlaxcalan admonishers, attempted a pre-emptive strike against the Aztec leadership; when Cortés returned, the situation was desperate. Motecoçuma died – perhaps in an accident of war, perhaps murdered by Spaniards who realized that he had outlived his usefulness to them. Cortés felt obliged to save as much as he could of his garrison by evacuating the city with heavy losses.

Doña Marina's man

Cortés's native allies seemed to lose confidence in him after this humiliation. Had they turned against him, the Spaniards would have been massacred. But the Spaniards enjoyed the favour of a native leader whose influence proved decisive. A native woman whom the Spaniards called Doña Marina had joined the expedition in its early days as an interpreter and as Cortés's concubine. She hailed from central Mexico, perhaps from Tlaxcala itself. Long captivity near the Gulf Coast had made her fluent in the only native tongue which any of the Spaniards knew. She rapidly learned Spanish, and used her unique position to mastermind the negotiations that put together a coalition capable of overthrowing Tenochtitlan. Indigenous sources show her, rather than Cortés, in control of the anti-Aztec forces. She appears both in a central diplomatic role, and as a field commander, directing operations – massacres included. Most natives called Cortés by a name which meant, in effect, 'Marina's man'.

Cortés's resolve and his mistress's diplomatic skill proved to be a successful combination. After much hesitation, Tlaxcala held firm on the Spaniards' side. The next most important adherents were the Huexotzinca, whose own records show their contingents marching out to support Cortés, with vast quantities of supplies and *matériel*, for the siege of Tenochtitlan. Cortés spent the next few months putting together an alliance that eventually encompassed all but one of Tenochtitlan's tributary neighbours.

The Siege of Tenochtitlan

The interruption of Tenochtitlan's tributary lifeblood made the outcome of the siege a foregone conclusion. But it took a long time, owing to ferocious resistance. The defenders launched a fleet of canoes, drove stakes into the lake to trap Spanish vessels, mustered a large garrison and made deadly sorties. Ultimately, they armed women rather than surrender.

Spanish technology had little influence. Horses (even though reinforcements had brought their numbers to forty) are useless in street-fighting in the middle of a lake. Heavy Spanish armour was an embarrassment in the rarefied air of Mexico: Spaniards largely discarded it in favour of the quilted cotton armour of the natives. Guns are of marginal value without access to renewed powder and shot.

In any case, native allies did most of the Spaniards'

fighting. Reinforcements had expanded Cortés's Spanish contingent to over a thousand men, with ninety horses; but the native allies, by Cortés's own reckoning, numbered one hundred and fifty thousand. In one respect, however, Spanish ingenuity was important: Cortés had twelve brigantines built, each of 50 feet or more in length, which dominated communications across the lake.

In April 1521, the reduction of outlying lakebound and lakeside outposts began. Cortés only just eluded capture in the battle for the first of them, Xochimilco. For the next two months, progress was slow, for the attackers, under constant harassment, were unable to rebuild a causeway for an assault across the lake. On 1 June, the defenders, using hundreds of canoes, mounted a concerted attack on the brigantines. They drove the flagship aground, boarded it, and almost succeeded in capturing it. In general, however, the Spanish craft outclassed the canoes, scattering and overturning them with ease. From this point, command of the lake was so complete that the Spaniards could protect the engineers who were at work on the causeways, use the brigs as pontoons, and get close enough to the city to set parts of it on fire.

On 10 June the attackers at last managed to cross the lake and penetrate the city, but the defenders drove them back. After a further attempt a few days later, Cortés resorted to demolishing the city bit by bit in order to deny the rooftops to enemy snipers. The desertion to Cortés's coalition of all the remaining neutrals in the region showed how the battle was unfolding. By the end of June, Tenochtitlan stood virtually alone, with only the neighbouring community of Tlatelolco fighting alongside it. Yet street fighting raged for two more gruelling months, until typhus, dysentery, starvation and, perhaps, smallpox brought resistance to an end. On 13 August, the Spaniards found no defenders in the streets – only frantic, often suicidal refugees, and piles of the dead.

The glory of conquest

For the rest of his time in the New World, Cortés remained a participant in – and a major beneficiary of – internecine indigenous wars, collaborating with some of his allies, turning against others, extending control over the whole of the former Aztec realm, and into what are now Honduras and Guatemala. He ended enriched, ennobled – and embittered, dissatisfied with his rewards and frustrated at finding no more gold-rich empires to conquer.

However deficient he was in military experience, tactical sagacity, strategic mastery, or battlefield prowess, Cortés had shown outstanding qualities of leadership – which are, perhaps, nine-tenths of what it takes to be a great commander. By striking out for the conquest of Mexico on his own initiative, he showed how quick and bold he was in decision-making, as did his breathtaking insubordination and his decisions to beach his boats, capture Motecoçuma, and follow up the fall of Tenochtitlan with a series of ever wider-ranging expeditions of conquest. His men were under his spell. One memoirist, who resented the way Cortés garnered all the glory of the conquest, and much of the profit, admitted that there was never a better leader in the world, and recounted how the men would sing his praises around their campfires.

Cortés inaugurated a new era in world history by acquiring the first of many great European overseas land empires. His efforts extended contact between the different civilizations in world-changing fashion. Formerly, Spanish outposts in the New World had been of marginal importance: only modestly productive, barely significant for the lives of most people in Eurasia. Cortés put them in touch with one of the most populous and productive regions on earth. The great belt of rich sedentary civilizations that stretched across Eurasia could now begin to exchange life-forms and culture with those of the Americas. A line of communications – still imperfect, still precarious – was beginning to bind the world together.

SÜLEYMAN THE MAGNIFICENT

1494–1566

JOHN JULIUS NORWICH

DURING THE FIRST HALF of the sixteenth century, four giants bestrode Europe. They were the Habsburg Emperor Charles V, King Henry VIII of England, King Francis I of France and the Ottoman Sultan Süleyman the Magnificent. Of the four, Süleyman was arguably the greatest. He was, like the others but in his own oriental way, a son of the Renaissance: a man of wide culture and a gifted poet, under whom the imperial potteries of Iznik (the ancient Nicaea) were at their most inspired and the imperial architects – above all, the celebrated Sinan – adorned the cities of the empire with mosques and religious foundations, schools and caravanserais, many of which still stand today.

Like his Ottoman forebears, however, he was also a conqueror, whose overriding ambition was to achieve in the west victories comparable with those of his father Selim the Grim in the east, simultaneously extending ever further the frontiers of Islam. Thus he was to swell his already vast empire with conquests in Hungary, the Balkans, Central Europe, Persia and the Mediterranean.

The bombarding of Belgrade

Succeeding to the throne in September 1520, the 26-year-old Süleyman was the only member of his family whom his father had left alive: on his own accession Selim had his two brothers and five orphan nephews – the youngest of whom was aged 5 – strangled with a bowstring. (He was also suspected of having poisoned Bayezit II, his own father.) The young sultan, confident of his own position, was thus free to begin his programme of conquest. His first objective was the kingdom of Hungary – which was, since the collapse of the Bulgarian and Serbian empires and the fall of Constantinople, his major enemy in eastern Europe. Reaching Belgrade, that vast fortress at the confluence of the Sava and the Danube, he bombarded it for three weeks, until at last, after a huge explosion had destroyed the largest tower, the garrison surrendered. Most of the captured Hungarians were put to the sword; the Serbs were rounded up and taken back to Istanbul, where they were settled in a nearby forest, still known today as the Forest of Belgrade. This was Süleyman's first great victory, opening up as it did not only Hungary, but also Austria and even Germany and northern Italy to Turkish raiding parties.

The capture of Rhodes

Encouraged by his first success, Süleyman now turned to the Christian enemy that had always been a thorn in Ottoman flesh: the Knights Hospitaller of St John – who from their headquarters on Rhodes, only 10 miles off the Anatolian coast, continued to harass Turkish shipping. They were comparatively few, with neither an army nor a navy that was any match for his own, but – as his great-grand-father Mehmet had discovered to his cost forty years before – they were determined fighters. In those forty years they had worked unceasingly on their defences, building huge angled towers and strengthening the ramparts against the heavy cannon which had smashed those of Constantinople in 1453 and by which they themselves had been so nearly defeated in 1480. They would be hard indeed to dislodge.

On 26 June 1522, their Grand Master Philippe Villiers de l'Isle Adam having ignored the sultan's letter demanding the island's surrender, the first ships of the Ottoman fleet appeared on the northern horizon. They were joined a day or two later by the flagship carrying Süleyman himself and his brother-in-law Mustafa Pasha, who had marched down with the army through Asia Minor. Against this host of perhaps two hundred thousand were only some seven hundred Knights – even after their numbers had been swelled by contingents from their commanderies throughout Europe – together with five hundred Cretan archers, some fifteen hundred other mercenaries and the Christian people of Rhodes. On the other hand their defences were as near as possible impregnable, and they had laid in supplies of food, water and munitions to hold out for months.

By the end of June the heavy bombardment had begun in earnest. The Turkish sappers, too, were busy. Within weeks they had drilled some fifty tunnels running in various directions under the wall, and it was not long before a mine exploded, creating a gap 30 feet across. The Turks poured in, and there followed two hours of bitter hand-to-hand fighting before the Knights somehow prevailed and the surviving attackers retired exhausted to their camp. Gradually, however, the defenders weakened. Süleyman's cannon were even more powerful than those of Mehmet, capable of hurling stone balls a yard in diameter a mile or more. By December the Knights were at breaking point, with well over half their fighting force dead or disabled. Although the sultan offered honourable terms, the Grand Master favoured fighting to the last; it was the native Rhodiots who finally persuaded him that continued resistance would mean a massacre, of Knights and people alike. And so he invited the sultan personally into the city to discuss terms – and Süleyman accepted. As he approached the gates he is said to have dismissed his bodyguard with the words: 'My safety is guaranteed by the word of a Grand Master of the Hospitallers, which is more sure than all the armies of the world.'

On the day after Christmas, de l'Isle Adam made his formal submission. The sultan treated him with all the respect he deserved, congratulating him and his Knights on their tenacity and courage. A week later, on the evening of 1 January 1523, the survivors sailed for Crete. For the next seven years they wandered homeless; then, in 1530, Charles V gave them the island of Malta. There, after a still greater siege in 1565, they were to inflict upon Süleyman his last defeat.

The Hungarian campaign

At some time in 1525, the sultan faced a revolt by his crack fighting troops. As the result of a rumour that he had decided against any further military expeditions, the Janissaries, who lived for war and plunder, had ransacked the Jewish quarter of Istanbul. Süleyman acted fast, person- ally killing the three ringleaders with his bare hands; many senior officers were also put to death.

The rumour was in any case untrue. The sultan was already preparing his next campaign. Europe was once again to be his battlefield; it was there that he could extend the territory of Islam, there that his three great rival sovereigns could be brought low. As always, the key to Europe was the kingdom of Hungary. In the days of the great John Hunyadi and his son Matthias Corvinus, it had served as the continent's principal bulwark against the Ottomans; but now, after two feckless rulers, it was hopelessly divided. The *voivode* (governor) of Transylvania, John Zapolyai, was intriguing for the crown; the Magyar nobles felt little loyalty to the reigning king, Lewis II, and were violently anti-German at a time when they needed all the imperial help they could get.

And so Süleyman, together with his brother-in-law and Grand Vizier Ibrahim Pasha, left Istanbul on 21 April 1526 at the head of one hundred thousand men, together with three hundred cannon. The weather was dreadful; storms had swollen the rivers, washed away the bridges, flooded the roads. But discipline was never relaxed. All provisions were paid for; soldiers trampling on sown fields were executed. At Osijek a 1,000-foot bridge was thrown across the Drava river in five days; as soon as his army was safely across, Süleyman had it destroyed, making it clear that there was no question of retreat. From there it was only some 40 miles to the plain of Mohacs, where King Lewis was waiting.

On 29 August 1525 Ibrahim Pasha took up his position with the Rumelian troops in the front line; the sultan, with the Anatolian divisions and the cannon, were directly behind him. Rather than making a direct head-on attack on the Hungarian cavalry, Süleyman's basic strategy was to open his own ranks, let the Hungarians through and then close in on them. This tactic brought the Hungarians very close to Süleyman himself; had it not been for his Janissaries, who surrounded him and hamstrung his assailants' horses, he is unlikely to have survived.

The second phase of the battle belonged to the cannon. It was this that proved decisive; the Hungarians had nothing to match the power of the Turkish artillery and were blown to pieces. They fought furiously, none more courageously than their commander-in-chief Paul Tomori, Bishop of Kalocsa; but finally they fled the field, many of them – including King Lewis – drowning in the surrounding rivers and marshes.

On the following morning two thousand heads, including those of seven bishops, were piled in a pyramid before the sultan's tent. The total number of the dead was estimated at thirty thousand; Hungary never completely recovered. An old Hungarian folk song tells of a series of domestic disasters; after each comes the chorus: *'But no matter: more was lost on Mohacs field.'*

The result of the Battle of Mohacs was a foregone conclusion. Like the last two Byzantine emperors in the previous century, Lewis had appealed to all western Europe for help against the Ottoman threat; like theirs, his appeals had been largely ignored. When the moment came, he refused to wait for the reinforcements promised by Zapolyai, or even for another detachment of Croatians known to be on its way; despite a small contingent provided by King Sigismund I of Poland, his army of some thirty thousand was consequently outnumbered by more than three to one. Finally, there was the factor of discipline. That imposed by Süleyman was, as always, stern and unbending; the Hungarian knights scarcely knew the meaning of the word. They fought with immense courage; but heroism was powerless against Turkish cannon.

The Vienna expedition

Three years later, Süleyman was again at Mohacs, investing Zapolyai as his vassal-king of Hungary. He then continued to Buda, at that time occupied by the troops of Charles V's brother Ferdinand. The city fell in less than a week, and the new king was formally enthroned; but now the sultan made his fatal mistake. Had he continued his advance immediately, he could hardly have failed to take Vienna. Instead, he delayed until the high summer. Throughout his life he was unlucky with the weather; and the summer of 1529 in Central Europe was even worse than that of 1526. Not until 27 September were his one hundred and twenty thousand men and three hundred cannon all in place before the walls.

The siege continued for nearly three weeks. On 7

October the sultan was within sight of victory when the Austrians mistimed a sortie and paid the usual price – that evening saw a heap of five hundred Christian heads outside the Carinthian Gate – yet somehow the defences held. Then the foul weather returned; a week later it snowed uninterruptedly for eighteen hours, and the snow was followed by incessant rain. It was a long way back to Istanbul, and the Janissaries – deprived of their expected plunder – were growing restive. Reluctantly but wisely, Süleyman gave the order to return.

The Persian campaign

Süleyman had long been considering a campaign against Shah Tahmasp, the Safavid ruler of Persia; by 1533 it was clear that this could no longer be postponed. Over the past decade the Shah had grown steadily more powerful, intensifying his persecution of the Sunnis of Mesopotamia; executing their leaders, destroying their shrines and converting their mosques to Shia use. That autumn the army under Ibrahim Pasha set off across Anatolia, making straight for Tahmasp's capital, Tabriz. It fell without a struggle, the Shah having fled only a few weeks before. Ibrahim then settled down to await his master, who joined him two months later. Together they then headed southward to Baghdad.

It was an appalling journey. Winter was approaching, the weather deteriorating fast. The Zagros mountains took their toll on the animals, and caused the heavy cannon to be abandoned. Now the Turks' principal enemies were cold and hunger, for in that barren terrain food was desperately scarce; one of their officers was actually to die of starvation before the army finally reached the Mesopotamian plain. There Süleyman expected to find Tahmasp's army, which he was determined to bring to battle; but it never appeared.

The sultan entered Baghdad on 4 December 1534. The city was but a shadow of what it had been in the days of the Abbasid caliphate three centuries before; but he immediately initiated an ambitious programme of restoration and reconstruction, returning all the mosques to the Sunni rite. He repaired the defences, instituted a survey of property and distributed fiefs. By his departure in April 1535, Baghdad was well on its way to a new period of prosperity.

Kheir-ed-Din Barbarossa

For the previous thirty-odd years, the Barbary coast of North Africa had been dominated by a number of corsairs, led by Kheir-ed-Din Barbarossa. Son of a Greek-born Janissary, Barbarossa and his brother Aruj had conquered most of what is now Algeria, and after Aruj's death Barbarossa dominated the central and western Mediterranean. By 1533, after the Genoese admiral Andrea Doria had won several sea victories over the Turks, Süleyman summoned Barbarossa to Istanbul and commissioned him to reorganize his entire navy.

Barbarossa did so, with remarkable success. His last years were spent not as a corsair but as admiral of the Ottoman fleet, operating above all against Venice. Hitherto, Venice had pursued her mercantile activities virtually unopposed – thanks, it was said, to the goodwill of Ibrahim Pasha; but in 1536 he was murdered at the instigation of Süleyman's wife Roxelana, and his successor felt very differently. Although the Turkish siege of Corfu failed – largely, once again, owing to the appalling weather – other Venetian islands and harbours were less fortunate: Skyros, Aegina, Patmos, Ios, Paros, Astipalaia and the Peloponnesian ports of Nauplia and Malvasia (Monemvasia) fell one by one. It was the end of Venice's hegemony in the Mediterranean.

Persia and Prince Mustafa

Since the previous campaign against Tahmasp, there had always been unrest along the Persian frontier. Safavid agents were still active, spreading Shia propaganda throughout eastern Anatolia, where Ottoman authority was growing ever more uncertain. In spring 1548 the sultan took personal command of his army. His first objective was the lake fortress of Van, which he had taken in 1534 but which the Shah had since regained. It soon surrendered and Süleyman moved on to Aleppo for the winter. The following year saw the capture of 31 towns, the demolition of 14 fortresses and the construction of 28 others. His twenty-month campaign had successfully consolidated his authority, but he had failed in his main objective: to destroy Tahmasp's army once and for all. He was to make one more attempt, in 1552; but this was interrupted by a crisis which ended in the execution, on his own orders, of his eldest son.

Mustafa was 37, capable and intelligent: he would have made a worthy successor to his father. Unlike his three surviving brothers, however, he was not the child of Roxelana, and he knew that on Süleyman's death he would be in mortal danger: either he must – in traditional Ottoman fashion – kill his brothers, or they would kill him. Whether or not he was actually planning a coup is unknown; but Süleyman summoned him to his Anatolian headquarters and accused him. Mustafa protested his innocence, and was still doing so when his father raised his hand in a signal to a party of mutes who were waiting in readiness. A minute later the prince was dead. His young son Murad soon followed him to the grave.

Apparently unmoved, Süleyman continued his campaign. Once again, the Persians refused to meet him in the field; he was allowed to advance virtually unhindered, ravaging and plundering as he went, until finally Tahmasp had had enough. An ambassador was despatched to the sultan's headquarters at Erzurum with proposals for an armistice. Süleyman, equally tired of the war, accepted at once. The resulting treaty, signed in May 1555, put an end to the long quarrel. The Shah agreed to stop his propaganda campaigns; the sultan promised unrestricted entry for the Shia into the holy shrines of Islam.

The invasion of Malta

Süleyman had plenty of time to regret the mercy he had shown to the Knights of St John after his capture of Rhodes. They had promised never again to take up arms against him; never had a promise been so repeatedly broken. Furthermore, Malta promised to be a useful stepping-stone between Turkish-held Tripoli and Spanish Sicily, on which he had long had designs. His immense invasion fleet sailed in May 1565 with well over two hundred ships, carrying some forty thousand men, plus horses, cannon and ammunition. But the sultan made one mistake: regretfully deciding that at 71 he was too old to lead it in person, he divided the command between two men who detested each other and quarrelled constantly.

The three-month siege has gone down in history. It nearly succeeded – and, under Süleyman's leadership, almost certainly would have. Malta was saved by the heroism of the Knights – as always, hopelessly outnumbered – and by the dysentery that spread through the Turkish camp. When, on 7 September there arrived the *Gran Soccorso*

– the Great Relief – of nine thousand men sent by the Spanish Viceroy of Sicily, the surviving Turks saw that they were beaten and returned to their ships.

The last campaign

Scarcely had the army returned to Istanbul when war broke out again in Hungary. Süleyman had not led an expedition for ten years, but he desperately needed a victory over the Christians to expunge the shame of Malta. He could no longer ride a horse, and the rough roads made travelling by carriage a nightmare; even when the stops, on his orders, were as few and as short as possible, the journey to Belgrade took seven weeks. From there he marched on Szeged; the city fell in early September 1566, but Süleyman never knew it: he had died on the night of the 5th, in his tent.

GONZALO DE
CÓRDOBA
1453–1516

NICCOLÒ CAPPONI

GONZALO FERNÁNDEZ DE CÓRDOBA was born on 16 March 1453 in Montilla, near the city of Córdoba, with cold steel running through his bloodline. Ever since the kings of Castile had reclaimed most of Andalusia from the Moors in the thirteenth century, Gonzalo's family had been fighting the Muslims of the kingdom of Granada, and, more often than not, rival Christian lords in the area. Gonzalo's father, Don Pedro Fernández de Córdoba, Count of Aguilar, died when his son was 2 years old, leaving his widow, Doña Elvira de Herrera, to rear his children in the true Fernández de Córdoba tradition. Sharing her former husband's mettle, the Countess of Aguilar – connected by blood to some of the most powerful Castilian families – raised Gonzalo and his elder brother to be warriors and accustomed to danger from their earliest years.

Gonzalo took eagerly to soldiering, and years later would describe his attitude to martial training: 'I would take a sword and for hours fence in a room alone, away from the gaze of others. Swordsmanship came to me naturally as walking or running, and I perceived it as perfectly suited to the natural movement of the body.'

As soon as he could sit on a saddle, Gonzalo participated in raiding expeditions or joined in the relief of some beleaguered ally. The counts of Aguilar carried on a long-standing feud with the Fernández de Córdoba counts of Cabra, and minor *hidalgos* living on the Andalusian border, often related by blood to both factions, frequently changed sides at whim. Usually, but not invariably, the warring parties closed ranks when facing the Grenadine Muslims. Gonzalo mastered the hit-and-run tactics typical of border warfare and learnt how to survive the vagaries of frontier politics. The guerrilla and diplomatic skills he developed during this period would serve him to no small degree in later years.

Once Gonzalo reached the age of 14, his mother sent him to train at the court of Castile, royal service being an acceptable profession for a younger son. He was originally attached to the household of Don Alfonso, the king's brother, but after his master's untimely death Gonzalo became a retainer of Princess Isabella, heir presumptive to the Castilian throne and the wife of Ferdinand of Aragon.

Returning to Córdoba in 1473, Gonzalo became one of the officials in charge of the municipality's administration, and it was whilst he was in office that civil war broke out in the city between the *conversos* (Jews who had converted to Catholicism or their descendants) and the so-called 'Old Christians'. The origins of the upheaval were both social and religious: the 'Old Christians' not only resented the fact that the *conversos* occupied political offices, but also doubted the validity of their Christian beliefs. On Good Friday 1474, an incident occurred during a procession between 'Old Christians' and *conversos* that rapidly escalated into violent street fighting. Gonzalo, himself of *converso* descent, fought against the 'Old Christians' until he and his brother Alonso were forced to retreat to Córdoba's citadel. Eventually the two had to fight their way out, pursued by the troops of the Count of Cabra. Retreating to his fortress of Santaella (a gift from Alonso), Gonzalo eventually fell into the hands of his enemies and was carried off to Cabra in shackles.

His imprisonment lasted until the end of 1476, when he regained his freedom thanks to the personal intervention of Isabella of Castile, now queen following the death of Henry IV. Gonzalo participated in the last stages of the war of Castilian succession against the supporters of the late king's illegitimate daughter Juana, commanding a company of 'lances' (heavy cavalrymen with their retinue) and earning the praise of the grand master of the Order of Santiago, Alonso de Cárdenas, for his performance at the Battle of Albuera in 1479. He had, by this time, earned a well-deserved reputation for personal bravery and for being a careful, calculating commander.

The ten-year war for Granada brought Gonzalo more laurels, his reputation boosted by a series of skilful and daring exploits, including that of saving Queen Isabella and her retinue from a Moorish sortie. When the last Muslim stronghold in Spain finally capitulated in January 1492, he was one of the officers selected to arrange the surrender, being rewarded for his services with an estate in Loja. In the course of the conflict Gonzalo not only refined his guerrilla tactics, but he also gained knowledge in the use of artillery and field fortifications. Moreover, Ferdinand and Isabella's employment of Swiss mercenaries allowed Gonzalo to see at first hand their revolutionary fighting techniques, which were far removed from those traditionally used – and cherished – by the Spaniards.

Defeat and reform

Gonzalo did not have to wait long to put his newly acquired knowledge into practice. In September 1494, a strong French army under Charles VIII of Valois descended on Italy, with the aim of conquering the kingdom of Naples from the Aragonese of Sicily. An adroit use of diplomacy, military might and terror tactics, coupled with the indifference –

when not the open complicity – of the majority of Italy's governments and of the Neapolitan ruling elite, enabled Charles to conduct the equivalent of a blitzkrieg campaign, entering Naples at the end of February 1495. The dispossessed Neapolitan king, Ferrante II, appealed to his cousin Ferdinand of Aragon for help in the name of mutual dynastic interests, with the understanding that the latter's son Juan would be the next ruler of southern Italy should Ferrante die without legitimate male offspring.

Ferdinand of Aragon was only too happy to oblige his cousin's request. Charles VIII's high-handed behaviour had managed to alienate practically everyone in his newly conquered territories; moreover the creation by Italy's rulers of an anti-French league had forced the Valois king to retreat home leaving a reduced military presence in the kingdom of Naples – too small to control it efficiently. The man chosen to lead the expeditionary force to succour Ferrante was none other than Gonzalo Fernández de Córdoba, thanks to the influence of Isabella of Castile. The queen could not forget her former retainer's long-standing devotion and his exploits during the siege of Granada, and considered Gonzalo, a relatively junior commander, to be the right man to manage a campaign requiring diplomatic skills as much as brute force. Ferdinand and Isabella realized that without the support of the slippery Neapolitan nobility, any victory in the field would be useless.

Gonzalo sailed for Italy in May 1495 with a small army of about eighteen hundred men, mostly sword-and-buckler infantrymen, plus a small contingent of crossbowmen and harquebusiers and a few hundred light cavalrymen. He linked up with Ferrante in Calabria, discovering to his dismay the king determined to deliver a knockout blow to the French forces in the region. Ignoring Gonzalo's warnings never to fight on ground chosen by the enemy, Ferrante led the joint Spanish–Neapolitan army to Seminara, confident that his 6,000 men would easily defeat the 4,000 fielded by the French commander Robert Stewart d'Aubigny. Gonzalo knew better, for if about half of d'Aubigny's soldiers were Calabrian militiamen of dubious quality, the same could not be said of his 1,000-strong Swiss contingent and the 1,200 French cavalrymen – 300 of whom were heavily armoured gendarmes. Initially, Gonzalo's horsemen met with some success, but Ferrante's Neapolitans mistook the Spaniards' hit-and-run for a rout and retreated in panic from the field. The attack by the French gendarmes and Swiss infantry smashed the enemy line to pieces and Gonzalo and Ferrante barely escaped with their lives. Gonzalo retreated with his remaining men into the hills, from where he conducted a vigorous guerrilla-style war, pinning down the enemy and at the same time avoiding pitched battles, carefully husbanding his meagre monetary and human resources. Through force and treaty, he slowly brought over to his side the cities and towns of the region. In July 1496 Ferrante retook Naples after a daring amphibious operation, and helped by the willingness of the Neapolitans to be rid of the French for good.

Ferrante's sudden death two months later put Gonzalo in an awkward position, since his successor was the king's illegitimate uncle Federico and not – despite all previous agreements – Ferdinand of Aragon. Gonzalo therefore eagerly accepted Pope Alexander VI's request to help him expel the Valois troops occupying Ostia, at the mouth of the River Tiber, and distinguished himself by being one of the first into the breach, earning both the pontiff's gratitude and a spectacular entry into Rome at the head of his troops, which now included infantrymen carrying 10-foot pikes.

The lessons of Seminara had not been lost on Gonzalo. He realized that for Spanish soldiers to be successful in the field, their traditional fighting methods had to be drastically reformed. This implied not just a change of practice, but also, for the rank and file, absorbing and integrating the changes brought by the military revolution in Europe. The Spanish sword-and-buckler men were excellent troops, but alone could do little against Swiss-style infantry or heavily armoured horsemen. Gonzalo's reform implied integrating them with pike-wielding footmen and an increased number of harquebusiers instead of crossbowmen, backed by heavy cavalry units. Such changes required time, but to implement his reorganization Gonzalo could rely on a core of professional junior officers, many coming from the ranks of the *Santa Hermandad* (the Spanish royal police force) and veterans of the Moorish wars. While it would be wrong to attribute these military reforms solely to Gonzalo, his drive and determination accelerated a process already under development at the time of the Granada war.

Kingdom come

Gonzalo sailed back to Spain in the summer of 1498, having earned from the Italians the sobriquet of '*il Gran Capitano*' ('*el Gran Capitán*' in Spanish). Isabella and Ferdinand rewarded him with land, titles and honours, before sending him off to quash a Muslim rebellion in Andalusia. In September 1500 he sailed for the island of Cephalonia, at the head of an expeditionary force to help the Venetians recapture the island from the Ottomans. No sooner had he completed the task than he was once more ordered back to Italy. Unbeknown to him, Ferdinand of Aragon had signed a secret treaty with King Louis XII of France, aimed at the joint conquest of the kingdom of Naples. Against such formidable foes, Federico of Aragon, after putting up no more than token resistance and agreeing to become one of Louis' pensioners, could do little but surrender. However, the ambiguous wording of the Treaty of Granada caused the French and the Spanish to quarrel immediately over the partition of the newly conquered kingdom.

Confronted by French superior forces, led by the Duke of Nemours, Gonzalo once more resorted to guerrilla-style tactics and the stubborn defence of key strongholds in Calabria and Apulia. But now he could also count on the aid of the powerful *condottieri* of the Colonna family; moreover, the alliance between Ferdinand and Emperor Maximilian I meant the arrival of reinforcements in the form of two thousand landsknecht heavy infantry. A relief at a time when he did not trust his own infantry to defeat the French alone.

On the morning of 28 April 1503 the Spanish army marched out of Barletta towards the French-held stronghold of Cerignola. The Great Captain had about nine thousand five hundred men under his command, including the landsknechts, about eight hundred Spanish–Neapolitan heavy cavalry under Prospero Colonna and as many light cavalrymen under Fabrizio Colonna. The latter troops proved to be particularly useful, screening the advance of Gonzalo's main force and thus preventing the enemy from seeing its strength and advance route. Arriving in front of Cerignola, Gonzalo deployed his troops on a vine-covered ridge behind an irrigation ditch, which he immediately proceeded to excavate and strengthen. He placed his pikemen and swordsmen at the centre of the line, with harquebusiers in front and on the sides. Behind stood half his heavy cavalry, the rest being used as a tactical reserve. Fabrizio Colonna's horsemen covered the Spanish left flank, while Gonzalo's sixteen field pieces guarded the right.

Nemours arrived some time later and, seeing Gonzalo's deployment, hastily convened a war council. Many of the most experienced commanders advocated prudence, but Nemours nevertheless decided to fight, having confidence in his Swiss pikemen and French heavy cavalry. He placed his Swiss, Gascon and Italian infantry at the centre, flanked by two wings of respectively heavy and light cavalry. Behind the main line stood the twenty-six French field pieces. Nemours planned to attack first with half his cavalry, immediately following them with the infantry grouped in three squares, and keeping the remaining horsemen for the decisive blow – a total of nearly eleven thousand men. With dusk fast approaching, Nemours gave the order to attack.

As the French men-at-arms approached the ditch they were met with the withering fire of Gonzalo's harque-busiers. Unable to jump the trench, the heavy cavalrymen fell in droves, Nemours among them. Fabrizio Colonna's horsemen repulsed the French light cavalry's attempt to turn the Spanish left flank, as Gonzalo's hand gunners opened gaping holes in the advancing Valois infantry. Falling back, the French infantry collided with the rest of their mounted troops, as the Spanish infantry moved in for the kill. In only half an hour the French had suffered a crushing defeat, leaving four thousand men on the field against about two hundred Spaniards.

Years later Fabrizio Colonna would comment that the ditch had been the real victor at the Battle of Cerignola. While partially true, it is without doubt that the Great Captain's adroit use of technology had inaugurated a new season in the history of warfare.

The defeat by his lieutenants of the French forces in Calabria allowed Gonzalo to take Naples the following month. Louis XII still held the Neapolitan territories north of the Garigliano river, having built a series of formidable field fortifications along its banks and receiving constant reinforcements from the nearby port of Gaeta. Undaunted, and despite his inferior numbers, Gonzalo followed the advice of the Italian *condottiere* Bartolomeo d'Alviano, and on the night of 28 December 1503 crossed the river on a hastily built pontoon bridge and took the French by surprise. In the ensuing running fight Louis' soldiers were utterly defeated; the surrender of Gaeta a few days later meant their complete eviction from southern Italy.

Thanks to Gonzalo, the kingdom of Naples had been permanently conquered and would remain a Spanish possession for the next two hundred years. Moreover, he had completely transformed the structure of Spain's armies, a process finalized in 1503 by his creation of large tactical formations called *coronelías* (roughly, regiments) composed of 3,000 infantrymen, 400 men-at-arms, as many light cavalrymen and 11 field guns. By pairing two such units, Gonzalo created the first divisions – effectively small, self-contained armies much like the old Roman legions. Added flexibility was obtained by dividing each regiment into companies with a proportion of one harquebusier for every five foot soldiers – half of the remaining troops being pikemen and the rest armed with swords and bucklers. This combination of shot and shock would eventually develop into the famed Spanish *tercios*, the dominators of European battlefields until the mid seventeenth century.

The Great Captain's accounts

Gonzalo de Córdoba received the title of Viceroy of Naples for his exploits, but the death of Isabella of Castile in 1504 deprived him of his strongest patron. By then his fame had aroused the jealousy of Ferdinand of Aragon, who in 1507 replaced him as viceroy and, according to a well-known if uncorroborated story, asked him to show his accounts. A miffed Gonzalo delivered a sarcastic breakdown of his expenses, ending with: 'One hundred million ducats for the patience needed to listen to a King who asks accounts from the person who gave him a kingdom'. In truth he did present detailed accounts of his spending over the years;

none the less, Ferdinand recalled the Great Captain to Spain, conferring on him the dukedom of Sessa and promising him the Grand Mastership of the Order of Santiago. It was not long before the king reneged on the latter commitment, granting him instead the town of Loja as a fief. Gonzalo moved there with his wife and daughter, remaining loyal to his unfaithful monarch even during the 1508 rebellion of the Andalusian nobility. Never receiving further military employment, he died peacefully in Loja on 1 December 1516.

The Great Captain's military heritage would survive him for another century and a half, his military reforms allowing Spain to dominate European battlefields until the Thirty Years War. In addition, a number of the conquistadores who conquered large swathes of America for the Spanish crown had previously served under Gonzalo de Córdoba, thus carrying his legacy to the New World.

AKBAR THE GREAT
1542–1605

FRANCIS ROBINSON

JALAL AL-DIN MUHAMMAD AKBAR was the most successful military leader of the able line of 'Great Mughals' who ruled in India from 1526 to 1540 and from 1555 to 1707. The grandson of Zahir al-Din Muhammad Babur (1483–1526), who founded the Mughal dynasty in India, and the son of Humayun (1508–56), whom he was to succeed as Mughal emperor, Akbar was profoundly aware of his family's traditions of conquest and empire, which reached back through his ancestor Timur (Tamerlane) to Chinghiz (Genghis) Khan.

He was still a teenager when he began what was to be a continuing series of successful military campaigns, which first consolidated the Mughal empire in the quadrilateral formed by the north Indian cities of Agra, Ajmer, Lahore and Allahabad, then expanded it, so that by the end of his reign the empire stretched from Afghanistan's Helmand river in the west to Bengal's Brahmaputra in the east, and from the Deccan's Godavari river in the south to the Himalayan mountains in the north. Akbar's success flowed in part from his qualities as a leader on the field of battle, and his willingness to develop gunpowder technology; but in part, too, from his gifts as an administrator and ruler. His regime played an important role in creating the circumstances whereby the subcontinent came to support one-third of the world's Muslims.

Akbar was 13 when he came to the throne, after his father died in January 1556 as a result of falling down the stone steps of his library. In the previous year Humayun had restored Mughal power to northern India; the immediate problem after his death was to sustain it. At this stage, rule was in the hands of Bayram Khan, a successful commander whom Humayun had appointed to be Akbar's guardian, but the regime was soon threatened by a vastly superior combination of Afghan and Rajput forces; in November 1556, however, assisted by fortune, these were defeated at Panipat, north of Delhi.

Akbar's development into a ruler

As Akbar progressed through adolescence he clashed increasingly with Bayram Khan, eventually aligning himself with a court faction opposed to his guardian, led by Adham Khan, the son of his wet nurse. In 1560, Akbar dismissed Bayram Khan, who was subsequently assassinated. As Adham Khan and his mother began effectively to wield power, the young Akbar again asserted himself by appointing his own prime minister, whom Adham Khan then killed, violating the privacy of the harem in order to do so. Akbar immediately had him thrown to his death from the harem balcony. A further incident in which Akbar demonstrated his growing authority took place in 1561, when two victorious generals refused to send him the treasure and war elephants won in conquest, as they were required to do. Akbar immediately marched several hundred miles to their camp and forced them to submit. From then on, aged 19, Akbar was firmly in charge.

Akbar spent much of his time in the field. Successful campaigning kept the treasury full and the people reminded of his power. Akbar had no fixed capital city. During his reign his armies set out first from Agra, then Fatehpur Sikri, then Lahore and then again from Agra. The Mughal court travelled in Akbar's highly organized camp, in which the whole administrative apparatus of empire, registers and ledgers and so on, would be carried by elephant, camel and bullock cart. The use of different bases at different times followed the changing strategic emphases in the expansion of Mughal power.

Akbar's campaigns from Agra, 1564–71

Akbar's first major campaign from Agra began in 1564, when his Uzbek nobles revolted and invited his half-brother, Hakim, who ruled Kabul, to invade India in 1566. Matters worsened when a group of Timurid princes (that is, descended from Tamerlane) also challenged him. Akbar ignored the princes, moved quickly to confront his half-brother at Lahore, who retreated to Kabul, and then turned to drive the Uzbeks from the cities and fortresses they occupied east of Agra. The key to his success was speed and daring. Before the Uzbeks realized what was happening, he had arrived on the banks of the Ganges opposite their encampment. Although this large river was swollen by monsoon rains, Akbar led a surprise night river-crossing and attacked the rebels at dawn. The Uzbeks were overwhelmed, and the Timurid princes promptly fled, to take refuge with the Sultan of Gujarat.

These rebellions of Uzbeks and Timurids from outside India convinced Akbar of the need to enlist indigenous nobles. Some were recruited from Muslim families but significant numbers came from the Hindu Rajput clans, the heads of whom gave him their daughters as wives. The Rajputs surrendered all control over their territories, and revenues from them were collected by Mughal administrators and adjusted against their salaries. This alliance between the emperors and the Rajputs was one of the great pillars of

Mughal rule. Not all, however, gave in without a fight. In 1568 Akbar was forced to besiege the Rana of Mewar in his great fortress of Chitor, and in 1569 Rai Surjan was besieged in his fortress of Ranthambor. These two forts controlled the trade route to the Arabian Sea, and their capture underlined the will and power of Akbar, as well as the futility of resistance. The sieges have been described as 'spectacular public events'.

The Siege of Chitor

Akbar's successful siege of Chitor, which lasted from 20 October 1567 until 23 February 1568, was the key victory. Chitor was the fortified capital of Udai Singh (r. 1540–72), the Rana of Mewar, who as head of the Sisodia clan had the highest status of all the Rajput princes and chiefs. Once he had submitted, the others would duly follow.

Chitor stood on a rock outcrop $3\frac{1}{4}$ miles in circumference and rising over 600 feet above the Rajasthan plain. As Akbar approached, Udai Singh withdrew, leaving eight thousand troops with supplies to withstand a long siege. After devastating the surrounding country, he then fled to the hills. Forty thousand peasants took refuge in the fortress.

On investing Chitor, Akbar encircled it with batteries and even had a massive mortar cast on the spot to intimidate the defenders. His bombardment, however, was ineffective. In addition, despite all precautions, it was undertaken at the cost of two hundred Mughal lives a day. Despite many being killed around him, Akbar exposed himself to enemy fire without evident fear.

Faith was then placed in mining the walls. On 17 December Akbar asked that two separate gunpowder charges be placed under them, but the engineers chose to connect them. In consequence, when after the first explosion, the flower of young Mughal nobility charged through the breach, two hundred of them were then killed in the second explosion. 'Though the garrison showed exultation', Abul Fazl tells us, 'H.M. the Shahinshah was tranquil, for he knew that there had been a want of plan and gradual progress in regard to the siege . . . patience and planning were necessary . . .'

Akbar now placed his faith in a *sabat*, a covered way wide enough for ten horsemen to ride abreast and tall enough for a man on an elephant to hold a spear erect. Its side walls were made of rubble and mud to absorb cannon shot, and its wooden roof was held together with ropes of hide. Screens of hide concealed those building the *sabat* in the very dangerous position at the front. The *sabat* took a sinuous course to the foot of the wall, at which point those inside it began to tear the wall down, Akbar himself directing operations from a small pavilion on top of the structure.

In February 1568 the *sabat* reached the wall and a

breach was created. Akbar noticed Jaimal, the Rajput commander, in the breach directing operations and killed him with his favourite musket 'Sangram'. Realizing that it was all over, the Rajputs burned their women to death, the act of *jauhar*, and prepared to sell their lives dearly. On 23 February the Mughals charged through the breach with fifty elephants in the van, killing thirty thousand Rajputs. Udai Singh remained at large but ineffective; whereas Akbar, at the shrine of Muin al-Din Chishti at Ajmer, gave thanks for his victory.

Akbar's campaigns from Fatehpur Sikri, 1571–85

In 1571 Akbar moved his capital 26 miles west from Agra to Fatehpur ('City of Victory') Sikri, which he was building in order to reflect the cultural inclusiveness and Islamic legitimacy of his regime. He became interested in linking Gujarat, the province on the Arabian Sea to the southwest, with its rich agriculture, textile production and busy seaports, to his territory in the fertile Indo-Gangetic plain. He was also interested in suppressing the Timurid princes who had established themselves in the south of Gujarat. In July 1572 he occupied Ahmadabad, the capital, and by January the following year he had received the submission of the sultan and all the Muslim nobles. The Timurid princes fled south to the Deccan.

Then, three months later, the nobles of Gujarat, disap-

pointed because they had not been incorporated in the imperial service, allied with Afghans and Rajputs to drive out the
Mughals. The crisis showed Akbar at his best. He put together
a contingent of three to four hundred men who, mounted
on swift camels, rode 500 miles to Ahmadabad in nine days
– a distance that caravans would then have taken two months
to travel. On reaching the rebel army of twenty thousand
men at Sarnal, he ignored the objections of his officers and
immediately attacked, using the advantage of surprise to
force the rebels to submit. Although the respective sizes of
the two armies are those given in the *Akbar Nama*, the official history of Akbar's reign, other sources suggest the more
believable figures of three thousand Mughal troops and fifteen
thousand rebel troops. Whatever the precise figures, however,
it is clear that Akbar achieved another great feat of arms in
which speed and daring were vital. Forty-three days after
he left, he was back in Fatehpur Sikri, his reputation for
invincibility much enhanced.

In 1574 Akbar turned east to Bihar and Bengal, where
Afghan nobles and Hindu rajas still held power. He besieged
and captured the Afghan-held fortress of Patna and then
forced the Afghan Sultan of Bengal to retreat before him,
and eventually to flee to Orissa. Akbar then left the consolidation of the Mughal position to his able revenue minister,
Todar Mal, although it was not until the late 1580s that
all opposition was extinguished.

Akbar's campaigns from Lahore, 1585–98

In February 1581, Akbar's half-brother, Hakim, invaded northwest India from Kabul and took Lahore. Akbar immediately set off from Fatehpur Sikri with a major force of fifty thousand cavalry, five hundred war elephants and vast numbers of infantry. As soon as his forces approached Lahore, Hakim fled. Akbar pursued him into Afghanistan, defeating his army outside Kabul. In August, Akbar held court in Kabul. A proposal was put forward that Hakim should be executed, but Akbar showed his half-brother mercy, restored him to the throne of Kabul and returned to India.

This campaign in the northwest was the overture to thirteen years spent campaigning in order to establish Mughal power firmly in the region. The spur was the death of Hakim in 1585 and the conquest by the Shaybanid Uzbek ruler, Abd Allah Khan, of the northeastern Afghan province of Badakshan, thus threatening Kabul. Akbar responded by sending an army to occupy Kabul and by bringing the region under Mughal imperial administration. To consolidate and expand Mughal power further in 1585, he moved his capital to Lahore.

One of Akbar's major concerns in the northwest was to foster the rich caravan trade between this region and Iran, Central Asia and China. In one direction came goods such as textiles and spices from India; in the other, horses, silks and porcelain. The trade was particularly vulnerable to lawless Afghan tribes, in this case, the Yusufzais. In 1586 a royal army which recklessly attacked the Yusufzais was ambushed in the mountain passes, and eight thousand Mughal soldiers were killed, including one of the two commanders, Akbar's friend and court wit, Raja Birbal. Over the next six years Akbar responded by building a military system to control the region and protect the caravan trade. He succeeded in doing what few others have been able to do since that time.

In 1585 Akbar sent an army north to invade Kashmir which, by June 1589, he brought fully under Mughal control. In the following year, he sent another army into the lower Indus valley to conquer Sind. By 1593 its ruler had made a formal submission to Akbar in court at Lahore and his lands had become the Mughal province of Thatta. Finally, in 1595, Akbar was able to round off his control of the northwest by retaking Kandahar, when its disgraced Safavid commander surrendered to him. This important city, which had long been out of Mughal hands, controlled the caravan route which skirted the south of Afghan territory on the way to Iran.

Akbar's campaigns from Agra, 1598–1605

In 1598 Abd Allah Khan died. Akbar clearly thought that this event, together with his own military and administrative achievements, left the northwest secure enough for him to move the capital once more to Agra. One of the reasons he may have chosen his original capital over Fatehpur Sikri was the fact that he was now faced with an increasingly rebellious eldest son, Selim – and Agra was well defended.

Akbar now turned his full attention to the five Muslim sultanates in the Deccan to the south. Indeed, his armies had already been in action there, leading in 1596 to the incorporation of Berar into the empire. Subsequent Mughal armies under his sons, Murad and Daniyal, achieved only moderate success, so in September 1599 Akbar took control of operations in person, with notable results. In August 1600, Mughal forces stormed the fortress of the Sultan of Ahmadnagar; then in January 1601, after his last major military operation, Akbar secured the surrender of the great fortress of Asirgarh and the submission of the Sultan of Khandesh.

Akbar's last years were clouded by the deaths of his sons Murad and Daniyal from alcoholism and by major acts of rebellion from Selim, with whom, however, he was reconciled before his death in Agra on 25 October 1605.

Akbar's gifts as a ruler

Akbar's achievements as a commander owed much to his gifts as a ruler. To some degree his armies helped to pay for themselves through treasure captured from defeated enemies. But they were also maintained by able revenue administration. Akbar and his ministers created a system based on accurate statistics of production, which was measured field by field and crop by crop. The Mughal state levied between one-third and one-fifth of the value of the harvest as tax. Accurate measurement, and the use of averages over a ten-year period, enabled the state to achieve the desirable end of extracting a high proportion of rural productivity while leaving enough to encourage the cultivator to produce more. By the end of his reign the Mughal treasury was producing annual surpluses of between 4 and 5 million rupees.

Important, too, were Akbar's inclusive religious policies. As a Muslim he made men of all faiths welcome as contributors to his imperial project, his leading Hindu commanders, for instance, including rajas Todar Mal, Birbal and Man Singh.

Especially important in holding the imperial framework together were the nobles who filled the senior administrative and political positions in the system, and whose bureaucratic skills, military prowess and entrepreneurial abilities made it work. They all had rights to receive revenues from land assigned to them, in return for which they maintained contingents of cavalry, according to their rank – war horses, elephants and so on – all of which were at the disposal of the emperor. Managing the nobles was crucial to Akbar's success: they were moved frequently from post to post; court ceremonial required frequent acts of submission; and towards the end of his reign their loyalty was encouraged by membership of his Din-i Ilahi cult, which entitled them to wear his portrait on their turbans. At this time the nobles were responsible for one hundred and forty thousand cavalry and consumed 82 per cent of the imperial budget.

These policies enabled Akbar to fashion and maintain an effective war machine, the major features of which were organization, discipline and gunpowder technology. Observers were astonished by the size and symmetry of the imperial camp. Arranged with streets and bazaars, it was the same wherever it was pitched, with an immense white royal pavilion at the centre. The army on the march operated under rules designed to maximize its security and to minimize its impact on the local people, providing they were acquiescent. Disobedience in the ranks met with instant and exemplary punishment. Although the cavalry and composite bow remained staple weapons, gunpowder technology, in which Akbar took much personal interest, was important to its success. Indeed, so important was it to Akbar that the *Ain-i Akbari* describes it as 'a wonderful lock for securing the August edifice of royalty and a pleasing key to the door of conquest'. The royal household maintained a monopoly over artillery, which was parked in front of the emperor's pavilion in camp. In 1596 the army comprised one hundred and forty-seven thousand cavalrymen and thirty-five thousand musketeers.

At the head of this war machine Akbar won victory

after victory and fashioned what was, along with Ming China, the greatest of the early modern Asian empires. In measuring his achievement we must realize, as historian John F. Richards states,

> that the Mughal empire met determined enemies who commanded substantially well-equipped, well-motivated armies. Most battles were desperate and bloody; the sieges difficult and lengthy. On numerous occasions Akbar could have been wounded or killed when leading his troops in battle. Luck and his military skills saved him. The builder of the Mughal empire was undoubtedly a superb military commander in a generally bellicose society.

ODA NOBUNAGA

1534–82

STEPHEN TURNBULL

VILIFIED BY GEORGE SANSOM in his History of Japan *as a 'cruel and callous brute', Oda Nobunaga is still a controversial figure in Japanese history, a man whose military genius remains his only undisputed quality. Nobunaga embraced western military technology with an enthusiasm that none of his contemporaries could match, applied it with an eye for strategy and tactics that others lacked, and achieved results with an utter ruthlessness that others only feared. Through a series of military victories, achieved by a loyal and well-organized army, Oda Nobunaga began the process that was eventually to lead to the reunification of Japan, a goal that only an untimely and violent death prevented him from achieving for himself.*

The violent episode by which Nobunaga met his end – he was ambushed by the army of a treacherous subordinate while resting overnight in a temple – was no more than typical of the age into which he had been born. Since the tragic Onin War of 1467–77, the central authority of the Shogun, Japan's military dictator, had rapidly declined in favour of a number of independent *daimyō* (warlords). Nobunaga's father, Oda Nobuhide, provides a classic example. His family had overthrown the Shogun's provincial deputy, after which they ruled much of their native province of Owari. When Nobunaga succeeded to the family headship in 1551 he inherited a reputation for valour and daring, two qualities that he required in abundance when he united the province under his rule. This process, which involved fighting members of his own family, was an almost exclusively military undertaking, small in scale but indicative of the challenges that he would face from the powerful enemies who surrounded him. Their first major move in 1560 was to mark the emergence of Nobunaga's military career on to a national stage.

The Battle of Okehazama

The most powerful *daimyō* among Nobunaga's near neighbours was Imagawa Yoshimoto (1519–60), who controlled the provinces of Mikawa, Tōtōmi and Suruga. In 1554 and 1558 Nobunaga had suffered attacks from Yoshimoto, whose growing confidence, boosted by judicious alliances, was such that by 1560 he was contemplating a march against Kyōto, Japan's capital. The first unfriendly territory that Yoshimoto would have to cross in his drive against the Shogun's rule was Oda Nobunaga's province of Owari.

Contemporary accounts of the resulting Battle of Okehazama, Oda Nobunaga's first significant military victory, paint a picture of a battle won against overwhelming odds. Ota Gyūichi, the author of *Shinchō-kōki*, Nobunaga's first biography, written in 1610, may be exaggerating somewhat when he states that Imagawa Yoshimoto marched west with an army of forty-five thousand men against his master's two thousand, but the discrepancy was certainly considerable. Yoshimoto's first objective was to capture Nobunaga's frontier forts, which he did with ease, after which he rested his army while he performed the traditional ceremony of viewing the severed heads of the defeated.

The place chosen for Yoshimoto's temporary field headquarters was a small gorge with restricted access near to the hamlet of Okehazama. It was an area Nobunaga knew well, so after rigging up a dummy army of flags a safe distance away he led his men around the hills to within close distance of the unsuspecting Imagawa army. His final movements were concealed by a fortuitous thunderstorm and a fierce downpour, at the end of which Nobunaga's men attacked. Yoshimoto's guards were caught completely by surprise and could not prevent Nobunaga's raid from sweeping right into the inner circle of Yoshimoto's body-guard. Yoshimoto initially thought that a brawl had broken out among his own men, but no sooner did he discover the truth than his head was sliced from his body.

The death of Yoshimoto set in motion the rapid collapse of Imagawa influence and the consequent rise to power of Oda Nobunaga, whose willingness to take on overwhelming odds and to act swiftly and decisively confirmed his unique military skills. One response to this demonstration of talent was the recruitment of more followers to his flag and the considerable enhancement of his original *kashindan* (retainer band). The way in which Nobunaga organized his army around a nucleus of devoted followers, adding to it by incorporating defeated enemies into its ranks, was one reason for his continued martial success. Contrary to the popular image of the vanquished samurai seeking nothing but death, it was common practice for entire armies to enter a victor's service when a *daimyō* was eliminated. The distinguished Shibata Katsuie (1530–83), for example, was in joint command of an army that supported Nobunaga's younger brother for leadership of the family. He was defeated in 1556 and went on to become one of Nobunaga's most trusted generals. Similar considerations were made when the province of Mino passed into Nobunaga's control in

1567, although it became the practice to place most of these later newcomers under the command of existing generals in a subordinate role known as *yoriki*.

The *Shinchō-kōki* account of the Battle of Okehazama records the active part played by Nobunaga's *o uma mawari* (horse guards), who formed the core of his army. As his elite mounted force, the horse guards had responsibilities that went beyond guarding Nobunaga's person. In 1568, for instance, they were to lead the attack on Mitsukuriyama castle, and enjoyed a unique social status. (As shown by a bizarre account of a New Year reception Nobunaga held in 1574, when, after dismissing his ordinary retainers, Nobunaga continued with a second party for the horse guards, whose sake drinking was enlivened by a private viewing of the severed heads of the Asai and Asakura *daimyō*, nicely presented with an attractive coating of gold paint.)

The other main divisions of Nobunaga's army consisted of his *ichimon* (kinsmen) and his *koshō*, a word best translated as pages or squires. The latter tended to be young men, often the sons of senior retainers who served in the Oda Nobunaga household. Along with an emerging officer corps they went to make up a trusted leadership under a charismatic commander.

The master of musketry

Perhaps because of the heavy rain, there seems to have

been little use made at Okehazama of harquebuses, or *teppō*, the weapons with which Nobunaga is most closely associated, although Yoshimoto's troops had used them during their advance. These simple muskets were fired by dropping a lighted match on to the touch hole. First introduced by Portuguese traders in 1543, the *teppō* was soon copied and mass-produced by those *daimyō* who understood its potential. Oda Nobuhide, Nobunaga's father, was one of these, and arranged for his son to receive instruction in firearms techniques from a certain Hashimoto Ippa. He also arranged Nobunaga's marriage in 1549 to the daughter of Saitō Dōsan, and it was on a visit to his father-in-law that Nobunaga was able to demonstrate his early appreciation of the value of firearms, when he paraded in front of Dōsan with five hundred of the weapons.

By the mid 1550s the *teppō* had become widely disseminated throughout Japan. In 1555, for example, Takeda Shingen (1521–73) sent three hundred harquebuses to help in the defence of Asahiyama castle. It was Oda Nobunaga's early appreciation of the best way in which these clumsy weapons could be used, however, that was his outstanding contribution to the development of firearms in Japan. In contrast to the bow, which could deliver more missiles in a shorter space of time, the harquebus required less training but more discipline. To entrust simple *ashigaru* (foot soldiers) with the weapons, to place them en masse at the front of an army – the place traditionally occupied by the bravest and most noble mounted samurai – and then to control them to deliver organized volleys, was a considerable conceptual leap for any general to make. Yet Nobunaga seems to have achieved all three by the year 1554, when he attacked the Imagawa outpost of Muraki on the Chita peninsula.

The *Shinchō-kōki* account tells us that Nobunaga set up his position on the very edge of the castle moat, and ordered three successive volleys against the loopholes in the castle defences. The harquebusiers appear to have been organized in squads that fired in succession, confirming Nobunaga's sophisticated battlefield control, and it has been further argued that the Muraki action represents the first use of rotating volleys in Japanese history, a technique with which Nobunaga is credited during his epic Battle of Nagashino in 1575.

Victory at Nagashino

The Battle of Nagashino, Nobunaga's operational master-stroke, came about as a result of a move to lift the siege of the castle of the same name. Nagashino, which stood on a promontory where two rivers met, had been holding out against the army of Takeda Katsuyori (1546–82), the heir of the famous Shingen. The great strength of the Takeda lay in their mounted samurai, whose ability to overrun and disorder foot soldiers, even when they were armed with harquebuses, had been demonstrated as recently as the Battle of Mikata ga Hara against Nobunaga's ally Tokugawa Ieyasu in 1572.

On approaching Nagashino, Nobunaga made his plans accordingly. First, instead of simply falling on to the rear of Katsuyori's army, he took up a planned position a few miles away at Shidarahara, where the topography enabled him to restrict enemy cavalry movement. Bounded by mountains to the north and a river to the south, Nobunaga's position was not susceptible to outflanking manoeuvres. Second, Nobunaga erected a loose palisade of lashed timber that provided protection to his army while allowing some gaps through which a counter-attack might be launched. Third, he arranged a welcome for Takeda Katsuyori in the form of massed ranks of harquebusiers.

The popular view of Nobunaga's victory at Nagashino is that it came about entirely as a result of the third of these factors. A. L. Sadler credits Nobunaga with choosing 'three thousand specially selected marksmen' who would 'pour in alternate volleys. It was the machine gun and wire entanglement of those days'. This latter quotation, and Sansom's conclusion that 'the musketeers were divided into three sections, firing in rotation', has become the accepted view of Nagashino, and the notorious final scene depicting the battle in Akira Kurosawa's film *Kagemusha* makes the action look as though the bullets were indeed delivered by machine guns.

The reality of the situation is somewhat less dramatic, yet it detracts nothing from Nobunaga's generalship on the day. The first point concerns the number of harquebuses deployed. *Mikawa Go Fudoki* (Sadler's source) says three thousand. The more reliable *Shinchōkōki* has one thousand. Nor need we necessarily conclude from the observation that different squads of harquebusiers fired alternate volleys, that this was an early application of the system of rotating volleys. Such a scheme, associated in particular with the military innovations of Maurice of Nassau, required the front rank to discharge their pieces then move to the rear to allow the second rank to do the same, a manoeuvre known as the counter-march. Yet even the Dutch were to discover that a minimum of six ranks, and preferably ten, were required to keep up a constant fire.

At Nagashino, Nobunaga did not possess the resources to mimic machine guns. Many of the harquebusiers he arranged behind the palisades were not his own troops but had been supplied by allies and subordinates a few days before the battle took place. There was therefore no time to drill them in the counter-march. Alternate volleys were certainly delivered, but should be understood as a response to the successive waves of attack launched by the Takeda cavalry under the iron discipline of the five *bugyō* (commissioners) whom Nobunaga had placed in command of the squads. *Shinchō-kōki* records each of the five attacks, naming the Takeda generals who advanced to the beat of drums and were met by gunfire. *Mikawa Go Fudoki* breaks the action down further, noting that three hundred harquebusiers in the sector held by the Okubo brothers faced a charge by three thousand men under Yamagata Masakage. Interestingly, this is precisely the situation illustrated on the contemporary painted screen of the Battle of Nagashino owned by the Tokugawa Art Museum in Nagoya. Horses are shown falling dead and throwing their riders, in classic images of a broken cavalry charge. Yet the Battle of Nagashino still had several hours to run, and from this point onwards the spears and swords of the samurai came into their own. Protected by the long spears of other foot soldiers, whose contribution to the battle was in no way inferior to their harquebus-firing colleagues, Nobunaga's armies took on the Takeda on a battlefield of their own choosing. Takeda Katsuyori was decisively defeated by a skilled general who used a combination of arms to its best advantage.

Nobunaga the Ruthless

Nobunaga's appreciation of the potential of massed harquebuses in the hands of lower class warriors had not escaped the attention of the leaders of the armies who were to prove to be the deadliest enemies of his entire career. Over a period of ten years between 1570 and 1580, Nobunaga was frequently occupied in fighting the Ikkō-ikki, the fanatical warriors drawn largely from the lower echelons of the samurai class and farming communities who were united by their religious affiliation to the True Pure Land sect of Buddhism. Motivated by a belief that heaven was the reward for being killed in battle, and contemptuous of the authority over them that the samurai assumed, they ruled territories comparable to those of the *daimyō*, from self-governing communities with well-stocked arsenals. In 1570 Nobunaga led an attack on Noda and Fukushima, two outposts of the Ishiyama Honganji, the Ikkō-ikki's 'fortress cathedral' built on the site of present-day Osaka castle. The defenders had three thousand harquebuses, to which Nobunaga responded with guns of his own, so that 'the thunder of the guns of both friend and foe made heaven and earth shake by night and by day'.

In 1576 Nobunaga suffered a slight wound when he was hit in the leg by a bullet fired from Ishiyama Honganji, but by then it had already become clear to him that he was not able to defeat this mass movement by the application of firepower alone. With a ruthlessness driven by necessity and made palatable by his utter contempt for the 'rabble' that opposed him, the dark side of Nobunaga's military genius asserted itself against the Ikkō-ikki. Yet it was not the Ikkō-ikki who were the first to experience his wrath. That was to be the fate of the 'soft target' of the Enryakuji, the ancient monastic complex situated on Mount Hiei to the northeast of Kyōto, revered for centuries as the guardian of Japan's capital city and its major centre of monastic learning. In 1570 its monks had unwisely provided sanctuary to certain of Nobunaga's defeated enemies, so on the last day of September 1571 Nobunaga's troops surrounded the mountain and slowly advanced up it, burning and killing every living thing in their path. The horror of the attack was noted by the Jesuit Luís Fróis, who fully appreciated the message that it sent out to Nobunaga's other better-armed Buddhist rivals.

In 1574 the indiscriminate weapon of fire was brought to bear upon the defenders of Nagashima, a major fortress of the Ikkō-ikki located among a maze of muddy islands in a river delta. Nobunaga had failed to take Nagashima in both 1571 and 1573, but in 1574 the application of superior force enabled him gradually to drive the defenders into an area of the delta that was sufficiently small to allow him to erect wooden palisades around the complex and then burn to death at least twenty thousand people.

But his most notorious act of ruthlessness was to be reserved for 1575, the year of his triumph at Nagashino. In a well-organized operation involving the coordination of three armies, Nobunaga moved into Echizen province, which the local Ikkō-ikki army had captured from him the previous year. The province was retaken within a few days, but then the retribution began. The former magnanimity with which Nobunaga had incorporated defeated enemies into his own army was not extended to the twelve thousand five hundred prisoners taken from the lower-class 'rabble' of the Ikkō-ikki. Instead words such as 'eradicate' and 'wipe out' were used. In Echizen, Nobunaga's *koshō* (pages) were given the grisly task of either executing the prisoners or overseeing their removal as slaves. Nobunaga described his triumph in a letter to his *shoshidai* (representative) in Kyōto, Murai Nagato-no-kami: 'Within the town of Fuchū dead bodies lie everywhere with no empty space between them. I would like you to see it. Today, hunting mountain by mountain, valley by valley, I have to complete the task of seeking out and exterminating them.'

The death toll in Echizen may well have reached forty thousand men, women and children, but this undisputed stain on Nobunaga's character has to be seen in the context of the times. By eliminating the Ikkō-ikki from the equation, Nobunaga spared his successors Toyotomi Hideyoshi (1536–98) and Tokugawa Ieyasu (1542–1616) from having to engage in dishonourable warfare. Their opponents were, by and large, of similar stock, for whom magnanimity in victory was regarded as appropriate, and it can be argued that their concern over the threat posed by Christianity in

Japan was based on a fear that Japanese Christians might become a second Ikkō-ikki. As it was, Nobunaga had done their dirty work for them.

In conclusion, Oda Nobunaga deserves to rank with the greatest generals of all time. His willingness to embrace new military technology with thoughtful application, his ability to think strategically and respond appropriately, having created and maintained a loyal and cohesive army, sit well beside the ruthless pragmatism with which he discharged his role. If Nobunaga, like his fortunate successors, had needed only to fight fellow samurai then his calculated ruthlessness may well have been seen as an additional martial virtue.

FURTHER READING

THEODORIC

Thomas Burns. *A History of the Ostrogoths* (Indiana University Press, Bloomington, 1984).

Peter Heather, *The Goths* (Blackwell, Oxford, 1998).

Thomas Hodgkin, *Italy and her Invaders. Volume 3: The Ostrogothic Invasion* (second edition, Oxford, 1896). Or better, the Folio Society reprint of 2001 entitled *The Barbarian Invasions of the Roman Empire. Volume 3: The Ostrogoths* with an introduction by Peter Heather. Although old, this is detailed Victorian narrative history at its very best.

CLOVIS

Edward James, *The Franks* (Blackwell, Oxford, 1988).

Ian Wood, *The Merovingian Kingdoms* (Longman, London and New York, 1994).

BELISARIUS

John Julius Norwich, *Byzantium*, volume I (Penguin, London, 1990).

Procopius, *The Secret History of the Court of Justinian* (The Echo Library, Teddington, 2006).

Robert Graves, *Count Belisarius* (Penguin, Harmondsworth, 1955).

E. Gibbon, *The Decline and Fall of the Roman Empire*, abridged (Penguin, Harmondsworth, 2000).

Robert Browning, *Justinian and Theodora* (Thames & Hudson, London, 1987).

MUHAMMAD

Michael A. Cook, *Muhammad* (Oxford University Press, Oxford, 1983).

Efraim Karsh, *Islamic Imperialism: A History* (Yale University Press, New Haven and London, 2006).

Hugh Kennedy, *The Great Arab Conquests: How the Spread of Islam Changed the World We Live In* (Weidenfeld & Nicolson, London, 2007).

CHARLEMAGNE

Alessandro Barbero, *Charlemagne: Father of a Continent* (University of California Press, Berkeley, 2004).

P. D. King, *Charlemagne* (Methuen, London, 1986).

P. D. King, *Charlemagne: Translated Sources* (Lambrigg, 1987). This includes translations of the main contemporary sources relating to Charlemagne's campaigns.

ALFRED THE GREAT

Richard Abels, *Alfred the Great: War, Kingship and Culture in Anglo-Saxon England* (Addison, Wesley, Longman, Harmondsworth, 1998).

Justin Pollard, *Alfred the Great: The Man Who Made England* (John Murray, London, 2005).

Simon Keynes and Michael Lapidge (translator), *Alfred the Great: Asser's Life of King Alfred and Other Contemporary Sources* (Penguin, Harmondsworth, 1983).

John Peddie, *Alfred, Warrior King* (Sutton Publishing, Stroud, 2001).

HASTEIN

John Haywood, *The Penguin Historical Atlas of the Vikings* (Penguin, Harmondsworth, 1995).

Gwyn Jones, *A History of the Vikings* (Oxford University Press, Oxford, 1968).

WILLIAM THE CONQUEROR

Matthew Bennett, *Campaigns of the Norman Conquest* (Osprey, Oxford, 2001).

Stephen Morillo (ed.), *The Battle of Hastings: Sources and Interpretations* (Boydell, 1996). This includes John Gillingham's essay 'William the Bastard at War'.

David Bates, *William the Conqueror* (Sutton Publishing, Stroud, 2001).

M. K. Lawson, *The Battle of Hastings 1066* (Tempus Publishing, Stroud, 2002).

Jim Bradbury, *The Battle of Hastings* (Sutton Publishing, Stroud, 1998).

BOHEMOND I

Gesta Francorum et aliorum Hierosolimitanorum ('The Deeds of the Franks and the other Pilgrims to Jerusalem'), edited by R. M. T. Hill, translated by R. A. B. Mynors (Clarendon Press, Oxford, 1962).

J. France, *Victory in the East: A Military History of the First Crusade* (Cambridge University Press, Cambridge, 1994).

R. B. Yewdale, *Bohemond I, Prince of Antioch* (Princeton, 1924).

FREDERICK BARBAROSSA

Otto of Freising, *The Deeds of Frederick Barbarossa*, translated by C. C. Mierow (Columbia, 2004).

P. Munz, *Frederick Barbarossa: A Study in Medieval Politics* (Eyre & Spottiswoode, London, 1969).

R. Rogers, *Latin Siege Warfare in the Twelfth Century* (Oxford University Press, Oxford, 1992).

GENGHIS KHAN

Paul Ratchnevsky: *Genghis Khan: His Life and Legacy* (Blackwell, Oxford, 1991).

John Man: *Genghis Khan: Life, Death and Resurrection* (Bantam Press, London, 2004).

J. J. Saunders: *The History of the Mongol Conquests* (Penn, Philadelphia, 2001).

KUBLAI KHAN

Morris Rossabi, *Khubilai Khan: His Life and Times* (University of California Press, Berkeley, 1990).

John Man, *Kublai Khan: The Mongol King who Remade China* (Bantam, London, 2006).

David Morgan, *The Mongols* (Basil Blackwell, New York, 1987).

ALEXANDER NEVSKY

John Fennell, *The Crisis of Medieval Russia: 1200–1304* (Longman, London and New York, 1983).

Mari Isoaho, *The Image of Aleksandr Nevskiy, Warrior and Saint* (Brill, Leiden and Boston, 2006).

BAIBARS

Ibn 'Abd al-Zahir, edited and translated by F. Sadeque, *Baybars I of Egypt* (Oxford University Press, Dacca, 1956).

R. Amitai-Preiss, *Mongols and Mamluks: The Mamluk–Ilkhanid War, 1260–1281* (Cambridge University Press, Cambridge, 1995).

P. Thorau, *The Lion of Egypt: Sultan Baybars I and the Near East in the Thirteenth Century* (Longman, London, 1992).

TAMERLANE

Justin Marozzi, *Tamerlane: Sword of Islam, Conqueror of the World* (HarperCollins, London, 2004).

Beatrice Forbes Manz, *The Rise and Rule of Tamerlane* (Canto, Cambridge, 1999).

Harold Lamb, *Tamerlane the Earth Shaker* (Thornton Butterworth, London, 1929).

THE BLACK PRINCE

Richard Barber, *Edward Prince of Wales and Aquitaine: A Biography of the Black Prince* (Boydell Press, Woodbridge, 1978).

Jonathan Sumption, *The Hundred Years War*: i, *Trial by Battle* (Faber and Faber, London, 1990); ii, *Trial by Fire* (Faber and Faber, London, 1999).

HENRY V

J. H. Wylie and W. T. Waugh, *The Reign of Henry V* (Cambridge University Press, 1914–29), three volumes.

Christopher Allmand, *Henry V* (Methuen, London, 1992).

Robert Hardy, *Longbow: A Social and Military History* (Patrick Stephens/Haynes Publishing, Sparkford, 1976–2008).

Anne Curry, *Battle of Agincourt: Sources and Interpretations* (Woodbridge, 2000).

Juliet Barker, *Agincourt* (Little, Brown, London, 2005).

Matthew Strickland and Robert Hardy, *The Great Warbow: From Hastings to the Mary Rose* (The History Press, Stroud, 2005).

JOAN OF ARC

Kelly DeVries, *Joan of Arc: A Military Leader* (Sutton Publishing, Stroud, 1999).

Joan of Arc: La Pucelle, edited by Craig Taylor (Manchester University Press, Manchester, 2007).

Marina Warner, *Joan of Arc: The Image of Female Heroism* (Weidenfield & Nicholson, London, 1981).

SULTAN MEHMET II

Steven Runciman, *The Fall of Constantinople* (Cambridge University Press, Cambridge, 1969).

Patrick Balfour Kinross, *The Ottoman Centuries: The Rise and Fall of the Turkish Empire* (William Morrow, London, 1979).

John Julius Norwich, *History of Byzantium, Volume 3: The Decline and Fall* (Penguin, Harmondsworth, 1996).

HERNÁN CORTÉS

The Codex Mendoza, edited by Frances Berdan and Patricia Anawalt, four volumes (University of California Press, 1992).

Hernán Cortés: Letters from Mexico, translated and edited by Anthony Pagden (Yale University Press, New Haven and London, 1986).

Matthew Restall, *Seven Myths of the Spanish Conquest* (Oxford University Press, New York, 2003).

Bernardino de Sahagún, *Florentine Codex*, edited by A. J. Anderson and C. E. Dibble, thirteen volumes (University of Utah Press, 1975).

Hugh Thomas, *Conquest: Cortés, Montezuma, and the Fall of Old Mexico* (Pimlico, London, 2004).

SÜLEYMAN THE MAGNIFICENT

A. Clot, *Suleyman the Magnificent* (translated from the French) (Saqi Books, London, 1992).

Patrick Balfour Kinross, *The Ottoman Centuries: The Rise and Fall of the Turkish Empire* (William Morrow, London, 1979).

John Julius Norwich, *The Middle Sea: A History of the Mediterranean* (Chatto, London, 2006).

GONZALO DE CÓRDOBA

G. de Gaury, *The Grand Captain: Gonzalo de Córdoba* (Longmans, Green and Co., London, 1955).

A. L. Martín Gómez, *El Gran Capitán: Las Campañas del Duque de Terranova y Santángelo* (Almena, Madrid, 2000).

J. J. Primo Jurado (ed.), *El Gran Capitán, de Córdoba a Italia al Servicio del Rey* (Córdoba: Publicaciones Obra Social y Cultural Caja Sur, 2003).

M. J. Quintana, *Memoirs of Gonzalo Hernandez de Cordova, Styled the Great Captain*, translated by J. Russell (E. Churton, London, 1851).

P. Pieri, *Il Rinascimento e la crisi militare Italiana* (Einaudi, Torino, 1970).

M. Purcell, *The Great Captain* (Alvin Redman, London, 1963).

AKBAR THE GREAT

Abul Fazl, *The Akbar Nama*, translated by H. Beveridge, three volumes, reprint (Ess Ess Publications, Delhi, 1993).

John F. Richards, *The Mughal Empire: New Cambridge History of India* (Cambridge University Press, Cambridge, 1993).

ODA NOBUNAGA

Jeroen P. Lamers, *Japonius Tyrannus: The Japanese Warlord Oda Nobunaga Reconsidered* (Hotei, Leiden, 2000): the only biography of Oda Nobunaga in the English language.

Two articles in John Whitney Hall, Nagahara Keiji and Kozo Hamamura (eds) *Japan Before Tokugawa: Political Consolidation in Economic Growth, 1500 to 1650* (Princeton, 1981) give insight into Nobunaga's political role.

INDEX

INDEX

INDEX

China and Chinese
  caravan trade 319–20
  Mongol conquest 148–9, 154, 155–69
  and Tamerlane 202, 211
Chinon 246, 247, 248
Chippenham 78, 80
Chita peninsula 331
Chitor, siege of 315–17
Chlothar, king of the Franks 25
Chlothild, queen of the Franks 19, 20, 21
Cholula 277
Chosroes, king of Persia 39–40
Christianity 19–20, 23
  Charlemagne 61–2
  in Japan 337–8
  Russians 170, 174
  Vikings 73
Churchill, , Winston 237
Cilicia 124, 197
circuses 11
Clarence, duke of 233
Clovis, king of the Franks 13, 14, 15–28
Colchester 99
Coleridge, Samuel Taylor 156
Cologne 16, 19
Colonna, Fabrizio 306–8
Colonna, Prospero 306
Columbus, Christopher 271
Compiègne 243, 255
conquistadores 271–83, 310
Conrad III, king of Germany 128
conscription 147
Constantine the Great, emperor 37
Constantine XI, emperor 259–60, 263
Constantinople 2, 11, 35, 40, 41, 116–17
  see also Istanbul
  fall of 257, 261, 262–7, 269
  Nika riots 30–2
  and Orthodox Christianity 170, 174
Córdoba 298, 300
  see also Gonzalo de Córdoba
Corfu 115, 294
Corsica 41
Cortés, Hernán 270–83
Cotentin peninsula 218
Courtrai, battle of 214, 215
Crécy, battle of 215, 216–17, 234
Crema, siege of 131–4
Crete 288
Crimea 153, 185, 186
Croatia and Croatians 173, 291
crossbows 110, 132, 207, 215, 217, 240
crusades
  First Crusade 113–26
  Second Crusade 127, 128, 139, 140
  Third Crusade 127, 138–40
  Seventh Crusade 186, 187
Cuba 271

Cynocephali 272
Cyrenaica 191
Cyril, Metropolitan 175

daimyō 326–30, 335
  Asai and Asakura 329
Dali 159
Dalmatia 173
d'Alviano, Bartolomeo 308
Damascus 192, 193
  see also Vikings
  and crusades 128
  and Tamerlane 198, 200
Daniyal, prince 321
Danube, river 2, 12, 19, 67–8, 285
Dara 30
d'Aubigny, Robert Stewart 303
Day of Judgement 140
Deccan 312, 317, 321
Delhi 198, 204, 207–8
de l'Isle Adam, Philippe Villiers 286, 288
Denmark 62, 92, 111
Desiderius, king of Lombards 59–60, 64
Devon 84, 95
Diet of Roncaglia 131
Dijon 22
Din-i Ilahi cult 323
Dives-sur-Mer 106
Dnieper, river 170–1, 172
Domesday Book 111
Domfront 102–3
Domrémy 245, 248
Don Alfonso 299
Doña Marina 279–80
Doria, Andrea 293
Dorset 77
Dorylaeum 117–18
Dōsan, Saitō 330
Dover 70, 110
Drava, river 289
Dublin 91
Dudo of St Quentin 86, 91, 97
Dumat al-Jandal 55–6
Dunois, count of 248, 251
Durazzo, siege of 120, 125

East Anglia 72, 75, 81, 84, 94, 96
Eastern Roman Empire 6, 13, 21, 172
Ebro, river 224
Echizen 336–7
Eddington, battle of 80, 94
Edirne see Adrianople
Edmund, king of East Anglia 75
Edward, the Black Prince 213–26
Edward the Confessor, king of England 105
Edward, earl of March 234

INDEX

INDEX

INDEX